Robert Campbell
August 198+

UNEASY LIES THE HEAD

THE HEAD

The Truth About Canada's Crown Corporations

UNEASY LIES THE HEAD
The Truth About Canada's Crown Corporations

Walter Stewart

Collins
Toronto

First published 1987
by Collins Publishers
100 Lesmill Road, Don Mills, Ontario

Canadian Cataloguing in Publication Data

Stewart, Walter, 1931-
    Uneasy lies the head

Bibliography: p.
Includes index.
ISBN 0-00-217757-9

1. Corporations, Government – Canada.
2. Corporations, Government – Canada – Provinces.
I. Title.

HD4005.S74 1987   354.7109'2   C87-093375-2

Typeset in 12 pt. Baskerville by Q-Composition

Printed and bound in Canada

CONTENTS

For my wife, Joan

1
The Icebergs Cometh

"Crown corporations are like . . . enormous icebergs floating in the foggy Atlantic, silent, majestic, awesome."

Kenneth Dye, *Auditor-General*
May 22, 1984

John Smith (or, if you like, Joan Smith) groans, stirs, swims up through layers of sleep to wakefulness. His radio-alarm clock, using electricity provided by a municipal Crown corporation, which bought it from a provincial Crown corporation, has turned on automatically, to bring him the news, through the facilities of a federal Crown corporation. After absorbing twelve minutes of gloom and disaster, Smith arises and staggers into the bathroom and turns on the light—municipal/provincial Crowns again—and draws a bath with water supplied by a municipal Crown and heated by the municipal/provincial combination.

Cleansed, he descends to the kitchen. Here he cooks eggs, marketed through a federal Crown, and toast, the wheat for which was marketed through another federal Crown and moved to him via a federal railway Crown and a federal seaway Crown. These culinary delights are made more toothsome by butter churned out of the warehouses of yet another federal Crown. Free enterprise provides the jam and coffee.

Breakfast done, Smith strolls to the subway—a municipal Crown—and heads to work at the local office of a federal Crown. Why not? There are 263,000 federal Crown employees in Canada. That's more than all other federal bureaucrats combined, excluding the armed forces. Smith's paycheque used to go to a bank which unfortunately collapsed, but his savings were insured by a federal Crown, the Canadian Deposit Insurance Corporation, which is quite sore at another other federal Crown, the Bank of Canada, which seemed to be looking the other way when John's bank was sinking into the swamp. Now he deals with a provincial Crown savings bank. The Bank Rate, which indirectly determines the interest paid on his money, is manipulated by that aforementioned federal Crown, the Bank of Canada, which also determines where the Canadian dollar will stand among world currencies. Incidentally, when John turns his paycheque into cash, the money he receives will *not* have been printed by a Crown, but by a private corporation, the Canadian Bank Note Company, a subsidiary of Genstar Corporation; however, the coins in his pocket do come from a Crown, the Canadian Mint.

All day long, John keeps encountering the Crowns. His health is insured by a provincial Crown. (John's cousins in Manitoba and British Columbia have their cars insured by provincial Crowns, too.) Much of his food is funnelled through Crown corporations, who collect it, move it, store it, sometimes market it—and occasionally lose it. A Crown corporation brings him his mail, unless there happens to be a strike on or it unaccountably gets dropped in a sewer somewhere. That federal Crown uses other federal, provincial, and municipal Crowns to—ha!—speed his letters on their way.

Mr. Smith travels on Air Canada, a federal Crown, or on Via Rail, another of the same, unless he goes to Saskatchewan, where a provincial Crown provides a bus. If he moves to British Columbia, that bastion of free enterprise, he can drive his Crown-insured auto onto a Crown ferry, slip through Crown-run harbour facilities to a Crown-run airport to catch a Crown-run airline. Thank God, he'll tell himself, we've beaten back Socialism. He may telephone this thought to his cousin in Manitoba, who will receive it courtesy of a provincial Crown phone company.

John's house, originally built under a provincial Crown project and financed through a federal Crown, is heated by oil pumped by another federal Crown. Incidentally, this latter federal Crown is the same one that fuels his car. The furniture in the Smith house was purchased through an import arrangement worked out by a Crown financing firm and shipped via a Crown container facility and a Crown trucking line. His snappy suit and vest come from a new clothing manufacturer who went into business with a loan from a provincial Crown in a factory financed by a federal Crown. His skivvies come from the free market.

His economic well-being is under the constant scrutiny of federal and provincial Crowns, whose work is criticized by the journalists employed by the CBC, the same federal Crown that woke him this morning, with help from a provincial Crown, TV Ontario.

Like most of us, John is something of a dreamer, so once a week, he spills his wallet into the coffers of a provincial Crown lottery, which always gives the money to someone else. That makes him so damn mad that he takes to drink, which a provincial Crown is happy to provide for him. When he absorbs so much of this Crown's products that he begins to see giant purple spiders or imagine that he is a poached egg, he may find himself staring into the concerned eyes of a psychiatrist at the Clarke Institute, a provincial Crown. The psychiatrist will tell him to relax more. Why not get out to a concert, subsidized through a federal Crown in a theatre supported through a provincial Crown, with municipal help? Or take in a film, financed through Telefilm Canada, a federal Crown. Or he could take a stroll up the 2,570 steps to the top of the CN Tower. Not only is that a Crown, it also has a separate Crown on hand to operate the revolving restaurant where he may dine after his exhilarating climb.

John vaguely recognizes that there are a lot of Crown corporations in Canada, although he doesn't know much about them. Not even the one he works for, because, as he knows, Crown corporations are much more tight-lipped about their operations than either commercial firms or government departments. (He knows Via Rail and the CBC and the post office, and if he thinks about it, he realizes that electricity comes from provincial Crown corporations, and that Petro-Canada, the oil giant, is a Crown. Actually, he's kind of proud of the Canadian Crowns; we have a tradition, he thinks (quite wrongly), which is different from that in the United States, where everything (wrong again) is done by free enterprise. Anyway, he knows the Crowns are being privatized, because he keeps reading it in the newspapers. If anyone were to tell him that most of what he reads about the Crowns being sold off to private enterprise is codswallop, he would be astonished.

Like Mushrooms, They Grow in the Dark

Indeed, much of what Canadians think they know about the Crowns is wrong, or insufficient, or misdirected. We are led to believe—the fact is reinforced by our newspapers, almost daily—that the Crowns are now coming under control. Growth is being checked, we are told, and accountability re-established. Would that it were so, but the fact is that the Crowns are able to multiply faster than we are able to shed them, because we are so often ignorant of what they are up to. Like mushrooms, they grow in the dark. Although they are public institutions, they are adept at dodging public scrutiny. Moreover, the information they do give out is often studiously misleading. Many of them are created in secrecy, operate in obscurity, and spend in silence—until something goes wrong, and then, too late, we hear of them. There are corporations out there that have the right to spend your money and mine, to expropriate your house and mine, to raise your taxes and mine, to act in your name and mine all over the world and nobody, not the Prime Minister, the Auditor-General, not even Simon Reisman, knows who they all are, or what the rascals are all up to.

The current Auditor-General, Kenneth Dye, whom we pay to worry about these things, worries quite a lot about the federal Crowns (he doesn't concern himself with the provincial or municipal ones; he has enough on his plate); Auditor-General Dye thinks there are too many Crowns, and that they are too secret, and that they do not behave themselves as they should. In one of his annual reports Dye sounded an all-too-familiar warning when he stated, "The growing practice of using Crown-owned corporations to conduct a widening range of government activity has so strained the capability of the existing accountability framework that Parliament may not be able to exercise its fundamental responsibility for overseeing receipts and expenditures of funds,"

Auditors-General have to write in that potato-mouthed manner; what Dye meant was, "These guys are out of control." He also pointed out in his 1982 report, now cooling on the shelf, that he and others—the Public Accounts Committee, the Lambert Commission, the Privy Council Office—had been screaming about the Crowns for six years, but the central problem of accountability had not been solved. "We are disappointed that this has not been done," Dye wrote. I think that is called "meiosis"—vast understatement.

Compounding the problem is the fact that neither the Auditor-General, nor anyone else, knows exactly how many Crown corporations there are. Auditor-General Dye reported that in 1977 the Privy Council Office (PCO) had gone around counting the federal Crowns—sounds simple, eh?—and had come up with 366 of them. Then in 1981 the PCO made another count and came up with 306. Did this mean that 60 Crowns had gone to the great Treasury Board in the sky? Not on your Nellie. It meant that the boys had simply stopped counting "a number of mixed and associated corporations." When the government owns part of a corporation, the balance of which is owned by private enterprise, the entity is a mixed corporation. Thus, the Canada Development Corporation, Lower Churchill Development Corporation, and Telesat Canada, are "mixed." So are corporations whose shares are jointly owned by the federal government and other governments or organizations, such as the African Development Fund and the International Development Association. Associated corporations include all the ragtag and bobtail of other bodies owned, partly owned, controlled, or partly controlled by the government and its fleet of Crowns. By and large, "associated" means the government owns less than 50 per cent of a corporation.

The Auditor-General thought we ought to be told about all these mixed and associated corporations; who they were and how many of them we have, and what they spend. Unfortunately, he didn't seem to think there was much hope of us finding out any of those details. After considering the legislation then under contemplation by the federal government he noted, "We are alarmed by the extent to which Parliament's role in the control, direction and accountability of Crown corporations has been overlooked."

Well, listen, we all have other things to worry about; the mortgage, the kids' schooling, and that funny noise the car made just now as we rolled into the driveway. Still, we ought to recognize that what the Auditor-General was saying, and has been saying for some time, is that a major portion of the power, policy, and money that flows into and through the federal government passes through Crown corporations which have succeeded in escaping from parliamentary control. In the fiscal year ended March 31, 1983, the federal Crowns that came under the Auditor-General's purview (and that isn't all of them; he was only able to look at Crowns where government control exceeded 50 per cent) took in $40 billion and spent $44.2 billion. The Public Accounts, which are supposed to tell us what is going on in government, only show the difference between these two figures, $4.2 billion, as "financial assistance, Crown corporations," but in fact we are talking about a sum almost equal to the entire federal budget. In the same year, on a Public Accounts basis, the federal government spent $55.1 billion.

What we have here is a parallel budget, that is close to the size of the parliamentary budget; but with no noisome, time-consuming accountability process attached to it. This budget is arrived at without anyone's even knowing how many of these Crowns there are, what they're for, and how much of our tax money they scatter on the wind.

We ought to be interested in the Crowns for more than their sheer bloody size. Just in the money they lose they cost us more than most government departments spend in total. Yet every time we want to know what one of them is up to, the minister responsible rises in the House of Commons to say that he (or she) cannot comment, because while he is responsible for the Crown in question, in policy matters—as the honourable members opposite will appreciate—the government will not interfere with the corporation. We know what the honourable minister himself makes because that is on the public record, and we know what the head of a similar private corporation makes, if it sells shares, because that is also on the public record; but we don't know

what Petro-Canada Chairman Wilbert Hopper makes because that would be telling. When a federal Crown drops
a billion dollars and change over the side of the ship of
state, as Canadair did, we don't learn about it until we hear
the splash. And then there isn't much even Parliament can
do except to hold a public inquiry to say, Isn't that the
darndest thing?, wipe out the debt, and try to flog the
remains to somebody. You can't drop a billion into a government department's rathole without somebody getting at
least a little curious, and even if you could get away with it
once, you can't keep it up for years; but things are different
with a Crown. The system was not designed to make Crowns
directly responsible—that's why they're so popular with
governments—and, by golly, the end result is that they are
sometimes completely irresponsible.

Crowns Can Overwhelm Governments

Crown corporations can do more than lose money on the
sly. They can direct policy. By their sheer size, their long-
windedness, and the complexity of their operations they
can, and do, overwhelm governments (we will come to examples later). They can pervert, reverse, and nullify the
will of parliaments, and they can, by the exercise of independent spending powers, foreclose options and redirect
spending priorities. In short, Crowns can get away with
fiscal murder. They can take enormous powers unto themselves to expropriate land and to hold themselves beyond
the reach of the people they displace. It's difficult—although not impossible—to get a Crown into court. They
can represent (and sometimes even misrepresent) Canada
abroad and, as has happened more than once, pay kickbacks
to foreign nationals in defiance of Canadian law and policy.
A Crown can join in a price-rigging conspiracy and then
block attempts to get at it on the grounds that it is, after
all, a servant of the Crown! Crowns hold power without
responsibility, spend money without sufficient accountability, and set policy without consultation—all anathemas
to the democratic process, besides costing a hell of a lot of
money.

Send me no Taxes

Crowns are often said to be created for purposes of efficiency or convenience, but no one says *whose* efficiency or convenience. The federal Income Tax Act specifically exempts from tax "a corporation, commission or association not less than 90 per cent of the shares of capital of which was owned by Her Majesty in right of Canada . . . or a wholly owned subsidiary to such a corporation." Some Crowns, such as Air Canada, do not have this tax immunity, but most do.

Another bothersome aspect of modern society that Crowns are able to foreswear is that they don't have to comply with the Freedom of Information Act, which expressly exempts them. What this means is that if you are about to commit some form of skulduggery and don't want the peasants to find out about it, you ought to do it through a Crown because then the needle-nosers of the media can't get onto it the way they will if you operate through a department. Heaven knows the Freedom of Information Act is weak-kneed enough, but to drop out a major sector of government activity from this kind of outside scrutiny is simply asking for trouble.

Because the Crowns burst into the system without adequate planning or legislation, we have no way to bring them to heel except the oft-heard cry of "Sell the buggers!" It won't work and it doesn't make sense, for reasons we will come to later. For the moment just ask yourself, if we're going to sell the Crowns, will we be able to sell the ones that are efficient, socially useful, and make money, or the turkeys that are bleeding us to death? If the former, why should we do so? If the latter, who—except for the people who create them—would be dumb enough to pay good money for them?

No, if we are to come to grips with the Crowns, we have to employ more thought than that expended on writing a bumper-sticker. We have to know something about them, and what they are, and where they came from. And, just for starters, it would be nice to have an idea of how many of them there are.

What is a Crown?

In the 1977 Privy Council Office study impressively titled, "Crown Corporations: Direction, Control, Accountability," there is no definition of a Crown corporation, just definitions of various *types* of Crowns. Very wise of the PCO, since any definition of just what a Crown is runs into problems. The Auditor-General, in his wisdom, concurs. A little more foolhardy is the C.D. Howe Institute, which states in a study sponsored by the Institute, "A Crown corporation is . . . normally associated with wholly-owned state undertakings organized along corporate lines." Tell that to the CBC, which looks about as much like an ordinary corporation as Brian Mulroney looks like Kermit the Frog.

The truth is that a Crown is a Crown because somebody chose to call it so, or because of the mechanics of the way in which it was formed. Most federal Crowns are incorporated either under Part VIII of the Financial Administration Act or under the Canada Business Corporations Act. Or Parliament can rear up and create a Crown, as it did the CN. Or a Crown can create a subsidiary. Or an order-in-council may be passed. Or the thing just grows, like bindweed. Via Rail was created by government decree, and went on merrily losing millions for a decade before the legislation that told it what to do—besides losing money—was hammered into place.

The Financial Administration Act says a Crown is "a corporation that is ultimately accountable, through a minister, to Parliament for the conduct of its affairs and includes the corporations named in Schedule B, Schedule C, and Schedule D." The schedules referred to are appendices to the Financial Administration Act. Schedule A is reserved for government departments. The other schedules are meant to distinguish between corporations that are "departmental," such as the Agricultural Stabilization Board; "agency" (quasi-commercial), such as Canada Post, and "proprietary" (commercial), such as Air Canada.

Don't worry about these definitions, nobody else does. In theory, the difference is that departmental corporations are like government departments in their organization and direct relationship to the government; agency corporations have greater autonomy than the departmentals, but still have to submit operating budgets and long-term capital budgets to the appropriate minister; and proprietary corporations, while they submit capital budgets for approval, are not supposed to come to Parliament for money. They are commercial, see, so they raise the money on their own. Unless, of course, they lose money, in which case Parliament has to pick up the tab anyway.

The definitions are hopelessly out of date. Atomic Energy of Canada, which has become virtually a commercial venture, is listed as an "agency," for example, and the CBC is "proprietary," which means it is "ordinarily required to conduct its operations without appropriations," although if it were to attempt to do so, all we would get on the CBC would be "Hymns Ancient and Modern," and tips on how to decorate your den.

Then There are the Others

Then there is that great uncatalogued category, "others," which includes such giants as the Bank of Canada, Petro-Canada, Via Rail, and the Canadian Wheat Board and which, for a time, included Canadair and de Havilland Aircraft. Whenever you have a definition that doesn't include the biggest, most influential, and most expensive items in the basket, you know you are in trouble.

A large and increasing number of Crowns doesn't fit any of the preceding categories because they are the "mixed Crowns." Diluted Crowns, if you like. Corporations in which the public and private sectors join hands in a combination which may, or may not, make sense. The Canada Development Corporation (CDC), which former Finance Minister Walter Gordon wanted to make into a vehicle to "Buy Canada Back" has instead side-slipped into a mixed enterprise with such various bits as an energy company, a petrochemical industry, data-processing firms, and biological laboratories. CDC's public relations director, J. Patrick Howe, gets very cranky if you refer to his company as a Crown—it has 35,000 individual Canadian shareholders and it is only about 12 per cent owned by the government—but it is fair to say that Ottawa launched it, owned most of it, and controlled it. I reminded Mr. Howe of the legal dictum that if something looks like a horse, smells like a horse, runs like a horse, and eats like a horse, chances are it's a horse. He said that that may be, but CDC was not a Crown.

Do you begin to see what Kenneth Dye—to say nothing of such ignoramuses as you and me—was up against? The highest estimate of the number of Canadian Crowns I have seen put the number at "more than 4,000." This figure, which appears in a study undertaken by a Halifax legal researcher, includes corporations at the federal, provincial, and municipal level. It's also mostly just a guess.

In the Appendices you will find my own attempt to count the Crowns. At the federal level, I used the Auditor-General's list, the Comptroller-General of Canada's list, a 1984 study done for the Privy Council Office, the annual reports of Crowns that issue them, other studies, such as the C.D. Howe Institute's excellent report *Government in Business*, and the Statscan document called *Inter-Corporate Ownership*, which shows who owns whom in the corporate world, and which turned up many of the subsidiaries of Crowns not listed elsewhere. One of the many difficulties of this business is that Crowns can be created in any of a number of ways, besides the normal one of going through Parliament, and subsidiaries frequently don't turn up on the public record. Sigh. Anyway, I came up with 403 federal Crowns (which is more than the Auditor-General found), mostly because I included corporations in which the government has less than 50 per cent ownership. (And why not? It's rare for a large private corporation to be more than 50 per cent owned by one body. If we are striving to find out which corporations are likely to carry direct government influence, the "50 per cent" rule makes no sense.)

I know my list isn't right because the numbers keep changing all the time, After I patted the thing into shape, I spotted an ad in the *Globe and Mail* for a Director of Information and four Program Officers for something called the "International Centre for Ocean Development," an outfit I had never heard of in all my born days. According to the ad the International Centre for Ocean Development is a "recently created Canadian Crown Corporation headquartered in Halifax whose objective is to assist developing coastal countries in the management and development of their ocean resources." The ad didn't say why we need another Crown to do this—we already have a number of departments, agencies and, yes, subsidiaries of Crowns charged with the same thing—but that isn't my point here. My point is that the ICOD (presumably pronounced "I Cod," as in "I Cod, you smelt") suddenly popped up out of nowhere, and I knew nothing of it. I'll bet the Auditor-General doesn't know much about ICOD either.

Let's put it this way. At the federal level, we have somewhere between 300 and 450 Crown corporations, depending on whether we count all the subsidiaries. These corporations control assets in excess of $77 billion, and take in and spend annually an amount of money close to the entire federal budget. Over all, they lose money, somewhere over $4 billion in a good year, accounting for upwards of 15 per cent of the federal deficit. Federal Crowns employ more people than all the rest of the civilian federal bureaucracy, and they touch our daily lives at almost every turn.

Provincial and Municipal Crowns

Remember, we are still just talking about the federal Crowns. The provincial Crowns are something else again. In the Appendices you'll see that I have tracked down 483 provincial Crowns, ranging from a meagre 9 in Prince Edward Island to 121 in Quebec. Again, exact numbers are impossible to determine because some provinces define Crowns one way and others another way. Ontario treats some of its farm price support bodies as Crowns while others are "Agencies." Newfoundland sets up separate companies to fund a number of hospitals, which no other province does. Ontario and Alberta both have Crown banks (or near banks); when British Columbia tried that, the federal Senate killed the project. There is absolutely no consistency in the way the provinces deal with these things. What else is new?

It will be easier to get a handle on the provincial Crowns, which is where much of the growth has taken place over the past few decades, by comparing them to the federal Crowns and to private industry. You will see in Appendix II, that the three largest non-financial corporations in Canada, measured in terms of assets, are provincial Crown corporations. You will also see that eight of this nation's fifteen largest firms are Crowns, and that four of the eight belong to the provinces. Our biggest corporation by far, Ontario Hydro, is almost three times the size of any federal Crown, as well as being almost one-and-a-half times the size of our largest private firm. Even more staggering, to me at least, is that our third-largest Crown, Quebec's Caisse de Dépôt et Placement, owns shares in all but one of the private firms that make the Big Fifteen list. The only one of our really giant firms that the Caisse does not own any part of is Dome Petroleum, although it does own shares in Dome Canada Ltd. and Dome Mines. Dome Mines owns 22.8 per cent of Dome Petroleum, and Dome Petroleum owns 48 per cent of Dome Canada Ltd., so they aren't exactly strangers. To put it another way, every single one of the fifteen largest companies in this nation is either a Crown or connected to a Crown. Nor are the shareholdings of the Caisse—the company that invests Quebec's major pension funds—incidental. The Caisse holds 11 million shares in Bell Canada Enterprises, 29 million in Canadian Pacific, 8 million in Alcan and 3.5 million in Seagram. In all, the Caisse has shares in 130 corporations, and the number grows every year as it reinvests its $2 billion annual profits. It has major investments in everything from the Alberta Energy Company Ltd. to George Weston Ltd., and even owns chunks of such foreign companies as Volkswagen.

The provincial Crowns are the real comers of the corporate world. Some of them even make money, for example, the Caisse and the provincial lottery corporations, your friendly Crown numbers game.

As for the municipalities, no one gathers statistics on the corporations they own, but virtually every one of Canada's 325 urban centres of 5,000 people or more—and hundreds of rural municipalities owns a water and sewer system, which usually run through a corporation. Most power utilities are delivered through a combination of a municipal corporation and a provincial one.

What is interesting—or alarming, depending on your point of view—is the way these things have mushroomed. In 1958, according to the figures carried in Statscan's surveys of federal and provincial government finance, Canada boasted a total of 86 Crowns, 28 of which were federal, and 58 provincial. The federal Crowns controlled assets of $6.5 billion and the provincial ones, $5.1 billion. Twenty years later, by the end of 1978, the numbers had not quite doubled. There were 50 federal and 106 provincial Crowns, for a total of 156. However, the federal assets had jumped almost sixfold to $35.1 billion while the provincial ones had jumped more than tenfold to $55.6 billion. Now we have, if you accept my figures, somewhere over 800 Crowns controlling assets of well over $150 billion.

Good intentions, even determination, have not been enough to control this mushroom growth. A 1985 study into how Ontario had fared in the five years since its 1980 declaration of war on proliferating provincial agencies and Crowns, disclosed that the province had actually created a new Crown subsidiary once every two months. And that was while they were trying to cut back on the things! You think you can take a Crown or leave it alone; one more won't hurt, especially if it's just a little one, but first thing you know, you're hooked.

Some Tail, Some Dog

Contrary to Canadian mythology, most of the Crowns are new to us. Most of their clout is new, too. While the Crowns' growth merely parallels the growth in the government sector over the past few decades—a growth much deplored and much enjoyed by most Canadians—it has an aspect to it quite different from the general ballooning of government expenditure. That is the element of unaccountability, of secrecy. Then there is the addition of all these "mixed" Crowns at both the federal and provincial levels. We have no idea what the total assets of these companies are, except that they are huge. We don't know what control governments exert inside these companies. What we do know is the companies form a large and increasing segment of the economy. We also know that the activities of all these companies, Crown and mixed, affect political and economic policy beyond the limits of our control. Crowns are becoming the tail that wags the dog. Some tail, some dog.

It may be some comfort to know that the concept of

Crowns is not uniquely Canadian. Crown corporations, under various names, exist all over the world, and their growth is the subject of increasing concern everywhere. The Soviet Union has them as a matter of course, and so does China and every other nation that wishes to hang its hat in the parlours of socialism, state socialism, or communism. But as you will see in Chapter 4, government enterprises, state enterprises, national enterprises—call them what you will—form an important and increasing part of the public economy of almost every modern nation. Airlines from Air France to Air India, auto makers from Volkswagen to Volvo, chemical firms, oil giants, and state trading companies are thick on the ground across the globe.

The explanation for this universal phenomenon—that there are strong, worthy, intelligent reasons for using the vehicle of a state-owned corporation in a mixed economy—should be borne in mind as you read this book. In my view, it is a vehicle which is badly in need of a major overhaul, not a mere tuneup; however, it would be a mistake to think that we can solve this growing problem merely by dumping the Crowns onto the public market. Where would the money come from to buy them, supposing we could find takers? What would happen to the public purpose—and usually there was a public purpose—for which the Crown was created in the first place?

Why the Crowns Came Into Being

There are a number of solid reasons to set up a Crown corporation. There may exist a natural monopoly, for example. Hydro electricity can be provided more effectively through a single corporation than in competition, whether that corporation is public or private. In the United States they have gone, with some notable exceptions like the Tennessee Valley Authority, to private monopolies, regulated by the state; in Canada we have gone to public corporations. There are dangers in both routes, but until recently, we did well out of this arrangement.

A second powerful impetus to create a Crown is to serve a national or provincial interest, which may be economic or merely a matter of pride. The Bank of Canada and the

CBC fall under the first category; Quebec's steel corporation, Sidbec, falls mainly under the second. (In fact, Sidbec was created in part for a third legitimate purpose: to provide local employment and to ensure that the major corporation about to be launched would buy its supplies at home.)

Or we may be confronted with a need to develop regional economies. In these instances Crowns may seem the natural and obvious instrument to reach for. So we create a Sidney Steel Corporation or a Cape Breton Development Corporation. Should we wish to dismantle these at some point we ought to know what we are about.

A Crown may be created to buy a nation's, or a province's, way into a closed market system: that is one of the reasons Canada created Petro-Can, to find out what the Seven Sisters of the oil industry were going to do to us next.

Canada Post was turned from a government department into a Crown mostly in an attempt to break the deadlock between entrenched unions and an enraged management, to start over and try again. It's a perfectly legitimate reason to create a Crown, even if it didn't work.

A Crown may be created as a solution of last resort, and indeed, that is the most common, and in my view, the most dubious reason. Is an aircraft company a sawmill a packing plant about to go under? Buy it out and keep it going. It may not make market sense, but sometimes it makes political and social sense.

The *Encyclopedia Canadiana* says a main reason for forming a Crown corporation is "to avoid compliance with the somewhat cumbersome civil service methods of appointment and tenure, which are less appropriate to a business undertaking than to the civil service." I always giggle when I read that because it implies that Crowns are lean machines, when they are often the opposite, and intended to be the opposite. That is, they come into being to create jobs and they keep going for the same reason.

Then, of course, there is patronage. There is a notion, which may be believed somewhere, just as it is still believed by some, that babies are born under cabbages, that Crown corporations are free of influence peddling. In fact, they often exist in large measure to provide niches for all those party favourites who can't be fitted into the Senate. When an election comes, the directors of many of the major federal Crowns immediately fit themselves with parachutes because they know that if the election goes the wrong way, they are headed for the pavement. They got their Crown appointment through the political system and they will lose it the same way. This may not be a noble purpose for the Crowns, but it is a real one.

Then, there are Crowns formed to perform specific tasks, which are usually the preserve of the private sector, but which it seems unwise or inefficient to leave to free enterprise. The first thing the folks in Ontario did when they finally decided to give Toronto its own domed stadium was to form a Crown corporation to put it together. British Columbia's Expo 86 was run, successfully, by a Crown. When I say "successfully," I don't mean that it made money; it was scheduled to lose $300 million, and when all the bills are in, will probably lose about $400 million. What could be more Crown-like?

Finally, Crowns are created to do all sorts of jobs that the private sector either can't or won't take on, such as stabilizing prices in the wheat industry or running harbours and airports.

Some of the reasons for forming Crowns may be shaky, but many of them are legitimate and worthwhile, and that is why these bothersome creatures are here to stay. But because they are so powerful, so large, so intrusive in the economy and in our daily lives, it has become absolutely vital to Canadians to learn more about them. We need to discover what's good about Crowns and what's not so good, to learn how they can be fixed and made responsible, and how they can be trimmed.

Although it is one of the myths of long duration that the Crowns are monumentally inefficient, that is not necessarily the case. Your friendly department store can lumber you just as offensively as a Crown. A number of studies have indicated that, person for person and dollar for dollar, we do as well out of some of our Crowns as out of private companies in the same business. For example, when *Government in Business* looked at electric utilities, telephone companies, airlines, and steel companies operated privately in competition with Crowns, it found that there was not much to choose between them in terms of efficiency. CP Air made a better return on investment than Air Canada, but then it didn't have to service remote areas. In return, Air Canada did far better in terms of passengers boarded per employee. Provincial telephone companies are just as efficient as investor-owned ones, and the CN, which lagged for years behind CP, is "closing the gap."

So it is not the argument of this book that the Crowns are wrong and dumb and crooked and ought to be disposed of; but that they are powerful and important, and running out of control. First, we have to understand them, and where they came from, and what they do.

Then we can set about bringing the buggers to heel.

2

Screwups

"We have no interest in Canadair, de Havilland or anything else the Canadian Government has managed to screw up, and you can quote me on that."
Douglas Reekie, *President, CAE Industries Ltd.*
November 26, 1984

The impetus to write this book came to me on Monday, April 30, 1984. It is not often that an author can be so exact, but in this case I still carry the searing memory of the incident that propelled me to begin making those irritable notes on a bit of paper that turned, three years later, into a book. On Monday, April 30, 1984, Pierre Bussières, then Minister of National Revenue, was confronted by Flora MacDonald, then a Tory MP, later a cabinet minister, with the fact that "the day after Parliament recessed for the Easter break, we learned that substantive bonuses, totalling $155,000 had been paid to twelve senior executives of the Crown corporation, de Havilland. Just a few days before that, it had been announced that hundred of workers were going to be laid off by de Havilland and that others would be asked to take a cutback of one kind or another.

"The Canadian people want to know how the Government can justify these bonuses."

Mr. Bussières replied that the bonuses were paid for the year ending May, 1983, "to ensure that this aircraft manufacturing company will be viable and solid."

Miss MacDonald was outraged. "Mr. Speaker," she said, "that is absolutely incredible. Any other corporation that had the kind of record that de Havilland had last year would have fired its senior executives rather than paying them bonuses."

De Havilland had recently announced that it had lost $236 million for the period ending December 31, 1983. Over the previous eighteen months, the government had pumped $500 million into the Crown corporation to keep it from foundering, and it was anticipated that another $200 million would fly from the public coffers to de Havilland over the next decade. The executives who were being rewarded made an average of $119,333 annually. Michael Wilson, the Conservative industry critic of the time, later the Finance Minister, didn't think much of the bonuses. He claimed to have a document— although he refused to produce it for reporters—that outlined plans to force de Havilland workers to accept wage cuts on the grounds that the company was in financial trouble. In addition, the Canada Development Investment Corporation, the government holding company into which de Havilland had been folded, had already indicated that de Havilland was going to lay workers off to save money. And it did, too. Mr. Wilson was exercised by what was going on: "The government has the attitude that management should be rewarded for losing $230 million [Well, he was close] while the workers are punished."

Mr. Bussières, in his reply to Miss MacDonald, seemed to be saying that bonuses were not for the year in which de Havilland had lost $236 million; they were for the year ending May, 1983. I decided to check the records for de Havilland, but couldn't find any statement with a year end of May, 1983. What I did find in the Public Accounts was a period ending March 31, 1983, during which de Havilland lost $265,159,000. I also found a note saying the year-end was being changed from March 31 to December 31. The company had not lost $236 million in a single year at all; it had lost $265 million in *seven months*. Even more impressive.

As a Crown corporation de Havilland continued to flounder. No matter. Money kept gushing forth from the great public teat. Jobs were to be preserved, for some, rewards increased, for some, while others were to meet the test of the market-place, and take their places on the breadline. It seemed fundamentally wrong. I knew as everyone does that private corporations behave in bizarre ways; but this was a public corporation, our corporation. If it was going to be a market corporation, dammit, let it stand on its own two feet: in de Havilland's case, this would have meant disappearing faster than you can say "bankruptcy." If de Havilland was going to be a government corporation, then it ought to meet another series of tests including complete and open disclosure of all its workings, and fair employment policies applied across the board.

It couldn't have it both ways. And yet it did, along with the vast majority of Crown corporations. We had succeeded in creating the worst of corporate entities, a corporation funded by the taxpayer but not responsible to the disciplines of Parliament or of the market; a corporation without social or political responsibility; an entity with neither heart nor head in proper working order. There are sound reasons for creating companies within the shelter of government care, even though they lose money. There are reasons for creating government companies that will, in the course of nature, make some money. There is no reason, however, to create and maintain at public expense corporations operating in the private sector that neither respond to a public goal nor make money. Just pouring taxpayers' funds down a rathole did not seem an adequate reason for going to all the trouble of setting up a vast array of Crown corporations. That's what we have a Treasury Board for. So it seemed to me that if the whole confusing, irritating, mind-boggling array of Crowns in Canada could be looked at in light of two questions—what we want the Crowns to do, and what, in fact, they are doing—we might reduce the problem to dimensions that are within the reach of ordinary men and women.

Simply to rail against the apparent stupidity of de Havilland was not enough; the de Havilland incident had come on the heels of a whole series of such mind-boggling events, which were creating a perception in the public mind that there was something inherently wrong, wicked, and wasteful about the Crowns. This perception promoted the notion that we ought to dump the whole boiling of them overboard. Since this didn't make any sense, either historically or economically, I thought we might gain something by looking at recent disasters in the ranks of the Crowns and go from there. Accordingly, this chapter is devoted to some of the blunders, outrages, and ineptitudes affecting Crowns that have come to my attention in recent years. You would call it the abridged version of a Domesday Book of Dumbness. I hope it will also prove instructive and help us—at least me—to get rid of some of our rage so we can deal more calmly in the ensuing chapters with the questions of how we got to where we are and how we may be able to proceed from here.

Canadair, the Champ

In some future time, when our descendants—if we have any—are sitting of an evening around the campfire spitting and telling stories of old, unhappy, far-off things and battles long ago, someone may want to know about the greatest government screwup of them all. The wisest story-teller of the land will adjust his robe, hand around the money-bowl, pluck his lute, and sing the saga of Canadair. If he is a fairminded minstrel, he will give due credit to Eric Malling and the CBC-TV programme, "fifth estate," because it is one of the ironies of this saga that when the whistle was finally blown, it was due in some measure to the extensive research one Crown corporation—the CBC—did on another. I would like to believe that even had the "fifth estate" shows not lit the lamp of outrage under Parliament, the Canadair mess would have come to light anyway. I'd like to believe a lot of things. It is hard to escape the suspicion, though, that without the reporting job done by Malling—all confirmed by later parliamentary investigation—we would still be in ignorance of what happened to our money once it vanished behind the doors of Canadair.

Canadair was a company with a mixed-up background. It was created as a Crown corporation during World War II to make airplanes to smite the foe. When we ran out of foes to smite, it began to produce water bombers and air surveillance drones. But its heart wasn't in it, and in 1947 the company was sold for $4 million to the Electric Boat Company, a firm that eventually became General Dynamics Corp., of St. Louis, Missouri. The event caused a bit of a rumpus at the time, as these things always do. George Drew, then leader of the Conservative opposition, thought the sale, pushed through without any public bidding, was something of a steal. The real price should have been $22 million, he claimed. He said a Canadian firm had been turned over to a "sinister group of arms manufacturers," and that we would all come to regret it. However, the din died, and Canadair remained an American company until 1976. For a time it made money; then it began to lose money. Enter the Canadian government with grants and tax concessions to preserve the jobs Canadair represented, some 1,500 of them in Montreal. But the handwriting, in red ink, was on the wall. In the early 1970s, after a long boom period, the market for aircraft began to shrink. General Dynamics, following the pattern of most foreign manufacturing concerns, begin to shift orders back to its plants in the United States and away from the Canadian branch-plant. It became clear that General Dynamics wanted to dump the Canadian firm, and with it all those politically essential jobs.

To prevent such a debacle, the Canadian government bought Canadair for $38 million, or $25,333 per job saved. Not a bad deal, as these things go. Eric Malling later calculated that, in dollar terms, it would have been cheaper to pay every Canadair employee $60,000 a year for life; but of course that was not the way it was seen at the time. Canadair would not only provide jobs and preserve Canada's place in the world aircraft industry—it would make money. That was because it had on its drawing-boards a new jet aircraft, the CL-600 Challenger, which was going to wow the world. Actually, although the Challenger was given a prominent place in the lexicon of Canadian goodies, it was the brainchild of Bill Lear of Reno, Nevada, the man who designed the Lear jet. Most of Canadair's top employees also came from the United States. The really Canadian thing about it was its debtload. Never mind, the Challenger was to be bigger, better, faster, and have a longer range than the Lear jet. And executives need jets, right? So a prospectus was drawn up showing that Canadair could produce and sell 235 aircraft in three years and net $335 million in profit. A nice return for our $38 million investment.

The cabinet minister who originally bought the Canadair dream was Jean Chrétien, then Industry Minister, who became converted to the Challenger jet in the course of a telephone call from Bill Lear in Reno. Chrétien has many accomplishments to his credit; the Challenger jet is not one of the ones he emphasizes. Anyway, the government wallet was pried open and funds began to pour out for the development of this surefire money-maker. Alas, there were problems. By the time the aircraft had been made bigger and fatter, it couldn't fly very far; instead of being an intercontinental jet, which was one of its major selling points, it became another transcontinental hopper. Fuel costs rocketed, which made it very expensive to jet around the country. Truth to tell, there were times when pessimists wondered if the damn thing would ever fly. There were problems with the engines, and some unexplained crashes on test flights, and a delay getting the proper licensing from the regulatory authorities.

While the money poured out, the orders (surprisingly) poured in. Although the Challenger made its first flight on November 8, 1978, and would only travel half as far as first advertised, and had a number of question marks hanging over it, by 1981, there were 125 advance orders for the aircraft. This spate of orders, it turned out, was not entirely due to the qualities of the Challenger; Canadair had some unusual sales methods, methods which could not, with profit, be used in the private world.

For example, Malling unearthed a deal through which Federal Express, the American delivery company, put in an order for twenty-five Challengers, although in the end, it only took one. First the contract was amended so that Federal Express would buy the planes, but Canadair would resell twenty of them on its behalf. Canadair would get $22 million for the five sold. Then there was another change; Canadair agreed to sell four of the five still consigned to Federal and give Federal a profit of $2.1 million on each. When Federal finally took delivery of one aircraft in March, 1983, it paid $4.4 million for it. Then Canadair gave Federal a cheque for $8.4 million—its profit on the four planes sold through Canadair. When the Federal boys went back home, chuckling, I imagine, they had received one $4.4 million jet free and another $4 million as a bonus, courtesy of the Canadian taxpayer.

Federal wasn't the only lucky winner. Continental Can Corporation, another American company, ordered two Challengers in 1977, but they weren't delivered until 1981.

By this time, the company decided it didn't want them, so it sold them back to Canadair, Malling reported, for $4 million more than it had paid in the first place. It seemed that the way to riches lay in *not* buying Challengers.

These goings-on, needless to say, were not featured in the annual report of Canadair. The company drew the veil of decent silence over many of its activities. Indeed, Jean-Pierre Goyer, a former Liberal cabinet minister who was placed on the board of Canadair, later claimed that his attempts to draw the attention of the government to what was going on received scant attention. In June, 1981, Goyer wrote a memorandum to Michael Pitfield, then Clerk of the Privy Council, in which he claimed that everything had changed when Canadair moved from private enterprise to the public sector. Under General Dynamics, Goyer wrote, the company had been lean and tightly controlled; when the federal government took over, it became "arrogant, over-generous, super-optimistic, and eager for success at any price." As a result of the Goyer memo, the government *did* set up a Task Force to look into the workings of Canadair. While the Task Force report remained secret, and still remains secret—under the general Canadian rubric that in matters involving the expenditure of public funds, it is better not to let the public know anything that will make it uneasy—a suspicion began to percolate through government and industry circles that the company was in serious trouble. (By the way, nobody knew about Goyer's memo until more than four years later, when in September, 1985, Goyer unloosened to the press.)

Canadair was financed, in the main, by loan guarantees from the federal government. Most of these were not given by way of formal arrangements passed through and debated by Parliament. They were authorized by orders-in-council and signed by a minister, in documents called "Letters of Comfort." The Auditor-General doesn't like Letters of Comfort. "They amount," he says, "to guarantees issued without parliamentary approval. The use of Letters of Comfort effectively forces Parliament to approve all *de facto* loan guarantees by Canada."

With these silent and potent weapons at its command, Canadair ran up a debt of $1.35 billion by 1982, and, the Task Force report suggested, it would need another half billion, perhaps as much as a billion, in additional funds to keep going.

But the Task Force report was nothing for the taxpayer to bother his pretty head about; it was simply a rustle behind the curtain. As far as the public record was concerned, everything was coming up roses. In November, 1982, the House of Commons Finance Committee had occasion to examine Canadair in one of those symbolically reassuring gestures we go through to show that everything is being looked after. This became necessary because Canadair wanted another $200 million for walking-around money, just, you understand, in the interval before profits began to pour in. This committee was assured that everything was hunky-dory. Canadair President Fred Kearns was asked about the Challenger's engine, the subject of some disquieting rumours. He replied, "We have had relatively few problems. . . . We are very happy with the Lycoming engine."

I guess it all depends on what makes you happy. There were delays in getting the engines into the aircraft. At one point Canadair was taking engines out of planes that it had sold, but not delivered, switching them into new planes, and flying with those until it could get delivery on other engines. Which cost, incidentally, $1 million each. U.S. customers were reporting the loss of engines in flight, and so were Canadian buyers, among them the Ministry of Transport. On May 16, 1982, when External Affairs Minister Mark MacGuigan was in Cork, Ireland, the engine on his departmental Challenger disintegrated on take-off, and the flight was aborted. On July 20, a Challenger carrying Immigration Minister Lloyd Axworthy was forced to make an emergency landing when the engine shut down. On July 28, Pierre Bussières was aboard a Challenger taking off from Ottawa when an engine blew, requiring another emergency landing. It was after these incidents that Mr. Kearns made his statement to the House of Commons Finance Committee. And how were they to challenge him? It was the CBC's Eric Malling who dug out the information about the Challenger's malfunctioning engine. Malling also unearthed a report which revealed that the U.S. Federal Aviation Administration had ordered inspections on the Challenger engines in response to complaints. And all this eight days after Kearn's upbeat (and successful, the $200 million was forthcoming) appearance before the Commons Committee.

Perhaps the most embarrassing engine failure came in January, 1983, when Trade Minister Gerald Regan was grounded in Saudi Arabia, while on a trade mission, because the Challenger he was flying in wouldn't take off. A new engine was ferried over to the stranded Challenger and installed; on the way home it failed, at 40,000 feet, near Shannon, Ireland. The plane limped back to the airport.

Never mind, as far as the public record was concerned, the Challenger was a success. Kearns told the Commons committee that in 1982 alone, his company had 31 orders, three times as many as its nearest rival, Gulfstream (only ten of these orders were firm, though). Canadair, he was able to report, expected to sell 900 of the aircraft over 22 years. A gold mine.

So the money kept pouring out. In December, 1982, $200 million; in June, 1983, $240 million; in March, 1984, $310 million. That was $750 million on top of the $1.350 billion, a round total of $2,100,000,000. Canadair was not likely to get all that money back if its sales methods included paying people for not buying its aircraft. And so, in the words of the 1983 Public Accounts Report, "Management determined as at December 31, 1982, that there was no longer reasonable assurance that the inventoried costs . . . would be recovered from future sales and accordingly, those costs incurred prior to 1982 were written off in 1982 as Unusual Items."

I love accounting talk. "Unusual Items" is good. What that meant was that the government, at your expense and mine, wiped out $1,054,300,000. Removed it from the books. Forget it. All is forgiven. In 1983, another $95 million in "Unusual Items" disappeared down the public maw, but by that time Canadair had a new president—Kearns had been disinvited—and a new corporate set up. Two Canadairs were cloned from the same set of books. One, Canadair Financial Corporation, owned all the debt and the continuing interest payments; the other, Canadair Limited, owned all the assets, except the technology behind the Challenger. Both companies were owned, in turn, by Canadian Development Investment Corporation, along with that other aircraft manufacturer, de Havilland Aircraft of Canada,

Limited. To learn how that came about we must tiptoe away from Canadair for a few pages, to follow the saga of its sister aircraft firm.

Meanwhile, Back at de Havilland

The Canadair problem dropped into a pond already crowded with the debts of de Havilland. This was another formerly foreign company, the Canadian offshoot of a British firm, Hawker Siddeley. De Havilland was taken over in 1974, when the parent company seemed likely to close it down (this time, most of the jobs lost would be in Toronto). The price, again, was $38 million. De Havilland had an excellent reputation, earned over fifty-six years, as an aircraft manufacturer. Included in its claim to fame were such successes as the Otter, the Twin Otter, and the Beaver. Besides, the government was already pouring money into the company by way of subsidy, and as then de Havilland President John Sandford, said, "If you're going to share the risks, it seems reasonable that you should share in the benefits."

Once under the government wing de Havilland, like Canadair, set out with great energy and even greater infusions of money to carve out a new niche for itself as the manufacturer of commuter aircraft—the fifty-seat Dash 7 and the thirty-six-seat Dash 8. True, the startup costs would be high, but the Dash 7 would break even if 122 of them could be sold. For the Dash 8 the magic sales number was 400. Not impossible. Hawker Siddeley, which knew all about the Dash aircraft, was not willing to finance them because it had a commuter aircraft of its own to sell; but that didn't mean they weren't a good idea.

Like the Challenger, the Dash aircraft were important not only because they could, in theory, make money, but because they were on the leading edge of technology. Worth taking a chance on. In fact, de Havilland was described, in another of those terms I love, as a "technologically advanced money-loser." The Dashes are Short Take-off and Landing or STOL aircraft, with admirable reputations and they do live up to them. De Havilland did not create the same record of weird sales techniques that marked the Canadair trail, but it was a company trying to sell commuter aircraft at a time of slow growth in the passenger aircraft industry. And it was trying to sell against severe and competent competition.

Company projections suggested the sale of 250 Dash 7s by 1982, which would indeed have made de Havilland a gold mine; instead, by mid-1984 it had sold fewer than 100. Glossy company brochures showed the plane lifting off from floating runways in the sea and settling into downtown STOLports. Alas the floating airports have yet to enter the water, and local political opposition delayed or killed most of the dreamed-of downtown STOLports. By the time the smaller Dash 8 came into production in 1984, in competition with four other aircraft aimed at the same market, the government had pumped $500 million into de Havilland. In November, 1984, another $150 million was pried out of the federal wallet.

But there was rescue in the offing. On May 26, 1982, under the Canada Business Corporations Act, the federal government created the Canada Development Investment Corporation (CDIC). You can tell how smart the boys were by the name; the initials "CDIC" are the same as those for the Canada Deposit Insurance Corporation, leading to quite unnecessary confusion. The CDIC—this one, not the other one—was born of the magic in the air evoked by the word "privatization." It was on everyone's lips. Well, maybe not everyone's. It started on Prime Minister Margaret Thatcher's lips, which are pursed, and spread from there. The notion was that if you had a government corporation that was giving you a hard time, you could unload the thing on a gullible public, pocket the proceeds, and be long gone before the purchaser had discovered that what he thought was a peacock was actually a turkey.

The CDIC was created—this is from the legislation— "To enhance the commercial mnagement of publicly owned assets and to facilitate privatization." It was to be a holding company, with a mandate to let go. Its holdings were Canadair, de Havilland, Eldorado Nuclear Limited, Teleglobe Canada, and the government shares in Massey-Ferguson (a deal it got into when the giant farm implement company was foundering) and in the Canada Development Corporation. Teleglobe is a consistent money-maker, as Canada's international telecommunications carrier (a monoply worth $679 million in 1985, from which the company made a profit of $53 million). The CDC and Eldorado are in-and-out runners, Massey-Ferguson changed its name in 1986, but still loses money, and the two aircraft companies shed money, year in, year out, with relentless regularity.

To make a long story short, CDIC finally managed to sell de Havilland in late 1985 to Boeing Corporation of Seattle, Washington. Boeing, the world's largest aircraft manufacturer with an annual sales of $13 billion, paid $155 million for de Havilland. By purchasing materials in Canada, it can earn forgiveness of a further $65 million, which would bring the eventual price down to $90 million. You and I will swallow the $750 million the government finally funnelled into the company. But that's not all. We will also be on tap for $40 million to support export sales, $30 million for the federal share of "producibility insurance," that is, our word that the airplanes will perform as specified, and $400 million in tax losses that Boeing can apply against future profits, if any.

The opposition parties were not happy—are they ever?—with the de Havilland sale. NDP leader Ed Broadbent called it, sarcastically, "business genius." The government replied that the aircraft company would go on losing money in government hands, and there would go all those jobs. Robert de Cotret, Minister of State for Finance, put the 1986 loss at $200 million, a figure that was later adjusted to $75 million. A private study suggested the 1986 loss would have been more like $14 million; the rest would be more development investment for the Dash 8. To protect the 4,850 de Havilland jobs, the government either had to go on shovelling out money or turn the task over to Boeing.

The taxpayer who foots the bill can't possibly know whether the government got a good price for de Havilland. The major reason for lashing out all this money was always "to protect jobs," but a secret cabinet memorandum written in April, 1984, indicated that as matters stood, de Havilland would have to shed 603 jobs in any event—313 of them that year. What is more, the company would lose $313 million between 1984 and 1988, and three-quarters of all the aircraft sold during that time would require some form of federal subsidy. We were going to pay more for fewer jobs, if this document had it right, so it might be better to cut our losses and leave the business to someone who knew how to do it.

The deal aroused the ire of some folks who wanted to know why our governments seem to be such lousy negotiators when they get into these messes. Theirs not to reason why, theirs but to get the shaft. The answer has nothing to do with shrewdness, or the lack thereof, but motivation. Government negotiators have the comfortable knowledge that it is not their own money they are dealing with, and that if they make a mistake, it will never be brought home to them as individuals. The government may be chastised; individual bureaucrats seldom are. The conditions on the other side of the table are quite different; reputations and careers may be at stake, sharp spurs both. Then there is the political pressure to get on with it, to have it over, so the cabinet minister responsible can make an announcement which everyone knows is coming anyway. On the company side, there is not the same pressure; a better deal later is preferable to a worse deal now, whereas on the political front, where everything is timing, the exact reverse may be the case.

On the surface, it seemed lunacy to walk away just when the debts had been swallowed and the basic excellence of the de Havilland aircraft seemed to be paying off. Most industry experts were agreed that the Dashes would both make money in the long run, although whether that would be the case if the company was in government hands remains a moot point. Boeing certainly knows how to sell and service aircraft, and things began to move and shake soon after the sale went through. In a single week in June, 1986, the company secured three sales worth a total of $410 million, and we can assume that none of these were giveaways. If it had been left in government hands, it may well be that de Havilland would have continued to be a bottomless pit.

The same reasoning was applied to Canadair, which we last saw being stripped of its debts in 1983. When someone else takes on all the development costs, it's easier to make money. By 1985 "new" Canadair (Canadair Ltd.) was showing a handsome profit of $27.6 million. The debt charges covering the old notes came to $143,864,000 that year, according the company's annual report, but who cared? The CDIC salesmen went out to hawk the "new" firm. Have

I got a company for you, they told the corporate bosses, during a campaign in which they approached 135 potential purchasers. Only six put in bids, and they were not generous ones. It was not until August, 1986, that the government was able to announce a blessed event: Canadair had been unloaded to Bombardier, Inc., of Montreal, for $120 million. This was not a great deal for the taxpayer. At the time, "new" Canadair showed assets of $478 million, with a book value of $224 million. Moreover, in a pattern that was to become familiar, the government was left with some of the flotsam and jetsam. Since "old" Canadair (Canadair Financial Corp.) owns the Challenger technology, "new" Canadair will have to pay royalties for that, on which the government may be able to claim about $5 million a year over the next two decades. This will not cover one-twentieth of the interest on the development money originally invested, money that we are now to forget about.

In addition, if no insurance company can be persuaded to take out liability coverage for "new" Canadair, in the event that the technology turns out not to be as advertised and somebody sues, the government will be on the hook for up to 90 per cent of costs of such coverage, with no guess as to how much that could be. Oh, yes, and the tab for three investment firms to give the government advice on how to sell the company came to $2.6 million, in addition to all the legal and other costs. The government reckoned the Bombardier deal as being worth between $205 million and $209 million. This financial spread includes a sum the government hopes to collect, someday, from a lawsuit against Avco Corporation of Greenwich, Connecticut, over the engines Avco provided for early Challengers. On the other hand, Avco is also suing Canadair, and the company has also been hit with an anti-trust action in the United States, for which damages of $52.5 million are being asked. The unloading of Canadair was a sale, like many we will meet later, driven by ideology, not business; the government's attitude was clearly one of "Lemme outa here." Considering Canadair's history, perhaps that was a shrewd attitude to take.

Time for a box score on the government's aircraft Crowns: In the past decade, the government has, in one way or another, poured $3 billion into Canadair and $760 million into de Havilland. Out of this, we have received, so far, $150 million for de Havilland, which may be more than offset by future commitments to that corporation, and $209 million, if we accept the government's reckoning, for Canadair. Then there is all the interest still owing on the original investments. The money side is not good; but then there is the policy side. Having created an ungodly mess under the aegis of Crown corporations, we got it into our nuts that Crown corporations don't work very well. So what did we do? Created another Crown corporation, the CDIC, and told it to get rid of the bums. And this new one, CDIC, well, it's going to need money, too, right? The justification for all this has been the preservation of about 6,500 jobs between the 2 companies. The cost is $578,462 per job. However, there is no guarantee that any of the jobs so preserved will remain.

I don't believe any government anywhere could justify spending more than half a million dollars per job against the hope of retaining said jobs—invested at 10 per cent, this sum would keep all these workers in clover forever.

If this was mostly a matter of jobs, why didn't the government sell these companies to their own employees? Although the details surrounding the bids are kept confidential, it is my understanding that among the 135 bids originally received on Canadair, at least one came from a group of employees. The government position is that in the complex aircraft industry, what counts is long-term experience, not enthusiasm. If an employee group took over, and failed, the government would be handed the company back, with all the weary work to do again. Well, it's an argument. But on numerous occasions private industries have been taken over by their own employees when the owners wanted out, and gone on to great success. The most spectacular case that springs to the questing mind is that of the *Toronto Sun*. When John Bassett, proprietor of the *Telegram*, folded his newspaper in 1971, a group of his employees started their own, and it blossomed into a highly profitable chain. No federal Crown has ever gone down this route and that, it seems to me, is a great pity.

One of the lessons we might get out of the de Havilland and Canadair imbroglios is to look to this solution. Another—the key lesson—ought to be the realization that it was precisely because these were Crown corporations that a situation evolved in which, under the cover of secrecy and silence, actions were taken which could never have withstood the scrutiny of an attentive Parliament.

The Great Uranium Cartel

It is this aspect that, it seems to me, sets the peccadillos of the Crowns off from those of either the government departments or private corporations. God knows, both these bodies have their scandals, but we are able to punish the authors of the former with our votes, and the latter are at least misbehaving with their own money more often than with ours. But with the Crowns, we have situations like the Great Uranium Cartel. This was a complex arrangement through which a cartel was constructed to support the price of uranium on world markets. Earle Grey's unravelling of the scheme in *The Great Uranium Cartel*, suggests that the cartel was born at a series of meetings in France in early 1972. The major Canadian players were Uranium Canada Limited, a Crown corporation created to hold the government's $100 million stockpile of uranium, and Eldorado Nuclear Limited, another Crown created to mine the stuff. From such information as has emerged, it's clear that the Canadian government itself promoted the project, and simply used the Crowns to do its dirty work. It was, in fact, a pretty lousy cartel, and did not prevent uranium prices from dropping. It did succeed in exciting the Americans considerably, after 200 pages of confidential files stolen from the Australian member of the group came to light in the United States. Lawsuits sprang up like noxious weeds. In an almost reflex reaction, the Canadian government passed regulations which made it illegal for any Canadian to talk about the cartel. Even though American newspapers by this time were publishing every scrap of information they could lay their hands on. No kidding. One judge, interpreting the Uranium Information Security Regulations, held that while it would be legal for Members of Parliament to talk about the cartel in Parliament and release information to reporters, if the reporters published that information, they could be chucked in the hoosegow for up to five years.

The Tories, who were in opposition when this bit of nonsense was passed—by way of an order-in-council—did absolutely nothing to change the regulations when they came to power.

The government's argument was that the wicked Yankees were trying to apply their combines law to our citizens, because the Canadian firms named in the lawsuits had been hauled into court and charged for their sins in the United States. So it was necessary to make it impossible for the Americans to get the information they needed to prosecute the case. Thus the gag law. Having passed that, the Canadian government—in response to a complaint by the Director of Investigations under Canada's Combines Investigation Act, that the cartel had led to violations of Canadian law—launched a prosecution against the companies it had pushed into the cartel. You couldn't put this stuff in a musical comedy; no one would believe it.

And then—this is the best part—Eldorado Nuclear and Uranium Canada went to court to argue that they could not be charged because they were Crown corporations. And on December 15, 1983, the Supreme Court of Canada ruled that, yes, they were immune, and the charges of violating the Combines Act were quashed. Five days later, Justice Minister Mark MacGuigan announced that charges against the private companies would be dropped because the Crown companies were beyond the reach of the law.

Let's make sure we have the sequence right:

1. The government pushes a number of companies, including two Crowns, into a cartel.
2. When the cartel comes to light, and the Americans move to prosecute, the government makes it illegal to provide the evidence on which such a prosecution could succeed.
3. Then the government launches its own prosecution against cartel members.
4. The two Crowns involved take the position that, as agents of the Crown, they are immune from prosecution, and the Supreme Court of Canada says, You're darn tootin'.
5. Then all charges are dropped.

Right. What could be more straightforward than that? In dropping the charges against private firms, the Minister of Justice acted properly; they were not the ones to blame. But surely this sequence of events ought to make every

Canadian wonder about the role of the Crowns, their apparent immunity from prosecution in many circumstances, and the fact that we like to use these corporations not for greater convenience and efficiency, but precisely because they can be more easily cloaked in secrecy than other government bodies.

Kickbacks and Other Skulduggery

This was the case, too, with Polysar, the Sarnia-based Crown corporation whose subsidiary, Polysar International, S.A., was discovered in 1972 to be paying kickbacks, illegal under Canadian law, to overseas customers. Maxwell Henderson, then Canada's Auditor-General, who was the joint auditor, with a private firm, of Polysar, refused to accept Polysar's explanation that the payments were "normal business practice" in Europe. But Henderson was retiring soon after the matter came to his attention, so he wrote a letter directly to Prime Minister Pierre Trudeau to lay his case before the head of government. Not long after this, Henderson reveals in his memoirs, the Auditor-General was removed from his position as a joint auditor of Polysar and "the questionable practices were continuing unchanged."

It was not until 1976 that the Polysar case came to public attention, and the Public Accounts Committee in due course confirmed that the corporation had been engaging in improper business practices. These ceased, forthwith. It had taken four years to bring under control a Crown whose activities had been held to be dubious by the government's chief auditor. In fact, the kickbacks hit their peak in 1973, the year *after* the Auditor-General brought them to the attention of the corporation's directors. That year, Polysar paid $1,600,000 into numbered Swiss bank accounts as "rebates" to customers; the rebates were the difference between the real price and an inflated price charged the Crown corporation. And, in fact, the Polysar case only came to light because Henderson's successor, James Macdonell, had caught another Crown, Atomic Energy of Canada Ltd. (AECL), paying bribes to help the sales of its CANDU nuclear reactors.

AECL paid $15 million, including $8 million in "expenses," to a company called United Development Incorporated (UDI) to act as "exclusive agent" for the sale of a CANDU reactor to South Korea, and $2.5 million to a mysterious agent acting for Italimplanti, an Italian construction company involved with AECL in selling a CANDU to Argentina. There was no indication as to what United Development Incorporated did to run up such an expense tab, and no receipts to account for it. Nor was there any mention of the unnamed Argentinian agent in either the joint venture agreement in Argentina, or in the AECL minutes.

In fact, we still don't know what happened to all this money. An investigation by the Public Accounts Committee—which most of the foreign witnesses, the ones with the money, declined to attend—traced the $2.5 million paid out in the Argentinian deal to two Swiss bank accounts. It also developed that UDI did do something for its expense millions; it set aside one room for one month in an office in Seoul, South Korea, for the use of AECL personnel. This set a mark for all future expense-account writers to aim at.

The Polysar and AECL cases finally convinced the government that financial management and control in the Crown corporations were totally inadequate, and led to a series of proposed reforms in 1977. Ten years later, these reforms are still being discussed and debated, but have yet to be implemented.

Is a pattern beginning to form in your mind? Hold that thought while we look at the creative works of some other Crowns.

That Petrofina Deal

In 1981, Petro-Canada, a Crown corporation, bought out Petrofina Canada Limited. Parliament authorized a sale price of $1.7 billion. Alfredo Campo, Petrofina's founder, said the price paid was "so far beyond what any company would pay for it, or what the market was indicating, that I wonder how it makes any sense." Petrofina's current stock price was about $90 a share; Petro-Canada paid $120. Pierre Nadeau, the Canadian president of Petrofina, said, "As a Canadian taxpayer, I am convinced the Government acted irrationally."

Not surprisingly, Canada's new Auditor-General, Kenneth Dye, wanted a look at the Petrofina deal, but the Liberal cabinet denied him access to the documents he required. The Tory opposition screamed bloody murder. Opposition Leader Brian Mulroney demanded that "The Prime Minister tonight open the books to the Auditor-General of Canada and to the people of Canada." But when Mulroney became Prime Minister in 1984, all the enthusiasm for book-opening went out of him, and his government, too, refused Dye the access he required. Dye took his own government to court to force it to allow him to do his job. He finally won, and I'm dying to read what he eventually makes of it all. But it may already be too late. The accounting firm of Ernst & Whinney, which was asked to do a study on the sale for the government, reported that because of "missing or destroyed documents," it could not properly estimate the exact value of Petrofina shares before the takeover. Nonetheless, it found that the money paid was probably "within the range" of "a fair price." When Kenneth Dye was told about the missing documents, he commented, "Something smells, doesn't it?" But exactly what, we may never know.

More Skulduggery

The beat goes on. Between 1979 and 1981, Canadian National Railways paid $610,000 to Cast Containers, S.A., in the form of secret rebates for moving freight along its lines from Montreal to Chicago. The rebates are illegal under Canadian law. The payments remained a secret until November, 1982, when the province of Nova Scotia laid a complaint before the Canadian Transport Commission (CTC), charging that the practice was diverting traffic from the Port of Halifax. The CTC held that the deal was illegal, all right, but no action could be taken because too much time had passed between the time the arrangement ceased in 1981, and the laying of the complaint. It warned the companies not to do it again.

There's no Deal Like Home

Again and again Crowns are used to perform functions on
the sly which, if done in the open and reported to Parliament, would send shrieks of outrage winging across the
land. Most of these goings-on we never hear about; some
we learn of only years later. There has just come into my
possession a cabinet document from 1971 setting out how
the Liberal government of the day proposed to take over
Home Oil Limited. Home's owner, a colourful and tough-
minded gent named Bobby Brown, wanted to sell his company, then one of the major Canadian firms, to an American Corporation, Ashland Oil. The Canadian government
didn't want that done, so it decided to buy Brown out. One
of the difficulties was that Brown owed the banks more
than his company appeared to be worth, and he wasn't
anxious to part with the assets and be stuck with the debt.
That is a form of financing reserved for governments. So
the Cabinet decided to pay him about twice what his stock
appeared to be worth. I am quoting now from the Cabinet
document: "In summary, it should be pointed out that the
purchase price of $14.00 per share as an average price per
share for 1.6 million shares exceeds the average market
price which is approximately $6⅞ per share."

Pretty tricky, giving a guy $22,400,000 for shares that
would apparently fetch $9,625,000 on a stock exchange.
Sooner or later, somebody was bound to raise hell. What
to do? Do it through a Crown. Accordingly, Eldorado Nuclear Limited was to be told off to buy the shares. The
effect—I don't know what the motive was, it may have been
high-minded as hell—would be to shield the questionable
terms of the Home deal from prying eyes. Eldorado wasn't
in the oil business, but a little detail like that didn't matter.

The deal blew up. At the very last moment, when Bobby
Brown was in Ottawa for the public announcement that
Ottawa had bought an oil company of its own, he had a
change of heart. According to Peter Foster, in *The Sorcerer's
Apprentices*, Brown suddenly thrust the sale documents to
one side and asked for the weekend to reconsider his position. In the end, he decided he just couldn't bear to sell
to the government. Eventually, Consumers Gas of Canada,
Limited, bought the company, keeping it in Canadian hands.

What interests me about the incident is the way a government will turn towards a Crown, like a sunflower turning to the sun, when it wants to do something that might be hard to explain to the folks back home.

Taking a Chance in Come by Chance

There is something about the Crowns, too, that makes rascals reach for their pens, and our wallets. Remember Come by Chance? The late John Shaheen constructed an oil refining deal which would bring instant prosperity to the flanks of Newfoundland, in the tiny village of Come By Chance. The deal he carved himself was a lulu. To put it briefly, the Canadian and Newfoundland taxpayers would take the bulk of the risks and Shaheen would take all the gravy. It was done through a provincial Crown corporation, naturally. The way it worked was that, if the project succeeded, Shaheen could buy the Crown corporation for $2,000, and have an asset that cost $165 million to finance. If it didn't work, he simply wouldn't exercise his option to purchase. Well, it didn't work, and went bankrupt in 1976. Today Come By Chance is a pretty dreary place. However— and this is the kind of dénouement I like—when no one in the wide world showed any inclination to buy the dismal remains after Shaheen walked away, it was unloaded onto Petro-Canada, our very own oil Crown, for $15 million, in 1981.

At that time, the Come by Chance refinery had run up debts of $700 million. To keep the refinery in trim, Petro-Canada spent $20 million on upkeep. Then, in July, 1986, the place was sold to an Israeli company, Dor Chemicals, which paid $2. That's right, two bucks—one dollar to Petro-Canada for the refinery and another to Newfoundland for the land. However, before this deal could be finalized, the Israeli company, which obviously knew how these things were done, let it be known that it would be nice if the province, or somebody, would put up $70 million to get the refinery going again. No dice; so, once more, Come by Chance was on the market. It was finally sold for $1—the price was cut in half, what could be fairer?—to Cumberland Farms of Canton, Mass., a chain of convenience stores and gas stations. Its plans to refurbish the refinery and re-open it. Hey, a refinery in Newfoundland, what a novel idea!

Trimming the Trees, and Taxpayers, in Manitoba

Remember Churchill Forest Industries? That was the deal that would bring blushes to the cheeks and prosperity to the pockets of Manitobans. The central figure in the scandal—which cost the province $150 million—was an Austrian, Dr. Alexander Kasser, who has not been seen on these shores since a judicial commission investigation in 1974 described the deal as "a massive fraud, planned and executed by Dr. Kasser." The enabling vehicle—need I say?—was a Crown corporation, the Manitoba Development Fund, which was supposed to develop a pulp and paper empire in northern Manitoba, but which seemed to spend much of its energy shovelling money into Swiss bank accounts for Dr. Kasser. He cleared $33 million, and didn't pay a penny in income tax. What made the whole thing work, the investigating commission said, was "anonymity and secretiveness. These elements include non-disclosure and excessive confidentiality. They thus made possible misrepresentations and deceptions without detection."

The pulp mill was eventually built, and turned out to be worth about $70 million; the other $80 million of government investment had all been siphoned off. Churchill Forest Industries went into receivership in 1971, but the government applied mouth-to-mouth resuscitation, creating a new Crown, Manitoba Forestry Resources (Manfor), to prove that it is possible to lose money without being crooked. Another $50 million went out to modernize the plant, which has just gone on dumping dollars. Manfor has lost $34 million in the past three years, but hopes to break even some day. Hope is a precious thing.

Hello, Central, Give me Saudi Arabia

Manitoba has had a rough time with another Crown corporation in much more recent times. The Manitoba Telephone System, a Crown, created another Crown called MTX

Telecom Services Limited, for the purpose of doing business abroad. MTX set up a joint subsidiary in Saudi Arabia called Saudi Arabian Datacom Ltd. (SADL) in 1981. The other owner was an Arab sheik. The contract under which SADL worked expressly prohibited the hiring of Jews or women. This meant that a Canadian province was getting into a business that deliberately discriminated on the basis of sex and religion.

When I asked Alvin Mackling, the NDP provincial cabinet minister responsible for MTX, if he knew about SADL's discriminatory hiring practices, he said that a lot of nations have different work rules. When I asked him if he would let a Manitoba Crown trade in South Africa, he said "No," because a United Nations resolution had condemned apartheid in South Africa. I guess you have to wait until the UN passes a resolution to know whether it is okay to discriminate against Jews and women.

MTX had a bad time in Saudi Arabia. Its own officers admitted to a legislative committee in August, 1986, that they had found a kickback in the company books of 43,421 riyals (about $15,000) along with a loan of $1.5 million to the Arab sheik that had never been properly authorized. But in the incident that had them buzzing along Winnipeg's Wellington Crescent, the committee heard that in 1983, eleven SADL employees were flogged by the Saudi religious police for the sins of working with a woman (the general manager's wife) and working during the Moslem prayer hours. One of the floggees, Ian Ferguson, later quit the company, complaining that his bosses wouldn't take action on his complaints about poor management and fraud. The Manitoba government declined the invitation of Conservative opposition members to set up an open judicial inquiry, and turned the whole mess over to the RCMP. Where it will end, time alone will tell. Certainly not in profit; at last report, the company had $17 million "at risk" in Saudi Arabia.

Well, enough; it is possible to keep on compiling these instances until we run out of paper and ink—and I haven't even mentioned some other provincial adventures, such as the Chairman of B.C. Hydro, Robert Bonner, resigning after two banks launched lawsuits against him for repayment of more than $1.8 million in personal loans; or the fraud charges levelled against three top executives of A.E. McKenzie Co., a Manitoba Crown that sells seeds; or the fact that an Ontario Crown, the Junior Farmer Establishment Loan Corporation, set up in 1952 to lend money to young farmers, hasn't made any loans since 1969, but still exists, and still owes the Ontario government $45.5 million.

It isn't the number, or the weirdness, of the Crown peccadillos that I want to bring to your attention, but their nature. Generally, that nature consists of erecting a facade of respectability and secrecy around some very dodgy operations. This has been going on for a long time, as we will see in the next chapter, when we look at the history of Crown corporations in this country.

3
Blue Blood and Red Ink

*"In Canada you are reminded of the government
every day. It parades itself before you. It is not
content to be the servant, but will be the master; and
every day it goes out to the Plains of Abraham or
the Champ de Mars and exhibits itself and its tools."*
Henry David Thoreau, *A Yankee in Canada*
1866

There is a notion, bred in the bone of most Canadians, that
one of the things that sets us apart from the Americans is
the degree to which government ownership has, like it or
not, been the making of us. Marsha Gordon, in *Government
in Business*, writes, "Government has traditionally played a
vital role in Canada's development. Public sector enterprises date back to pre-Confederation days, when the state
financed, built and operated" the canal system upon which
the commercial empire of the St. Lawrence was founded.
Sounds logical.

Herschel Hardin explained why we went the public route
in *A Nation Unaware*: "The given is the sparsely settled Canadian community next to the growing American giant.
The only way it can keep within hailing distance economically is by large public investment, and . . . the natural form
for this investment to take is public enterprise."

Hardin thought he was pushing this argument uphill,
and that his finding would come as rare and refreshing
fruit to Canadians (thus, a nation unaware), but my guess
is that most people just nodded. Yeah, yeah, we know that.
In fact, though, if we look at Canadian history carefully, it
is not until quite recently that public enterprise came to

loom so large in our economy. In the past—and in this we are more like the Americans than we realize—the pattern has been for governments to foot the bill for major undertakings which were to be performed by, and the profits therefrom skimmed by, private entrepreneurs. When the private entrepreneurs fell on their faces, or, as has happened a regrettable number of times, disappeared over the horizon with government funds tucked into their bulging wallets, then, and only then, did we have "public enterprise." Also known as trying to salvage something from the wreck.

Take the Welland Canal, since Marsha Gordon brings up the subject of canals. She says the "Lachine, Cornwall and Welland Canals were largely built with public funds," which is true enough, but misses all the fun. The Welland was actually the brainchild of William Hamilton Merritt, who was born in Bedford, New York in 1793, but came to Upper Canada five years later, and fought on our side during the War of 1812. He was taken prisoner during the battle of Lundy's Lane. After the war, he got hold of a piece of property on the ridge between Lakes Ontario and Erie. The notion popped into Merritt's mind that if someone were to carve a canal between the two lakes, two things would happen; one was that it would be immensely easier to move the produce of western Ontario, and the western United States, through to the St. Lawrence; the other was that his land would be worth a lot more than it then was. So one day in 1818, he went out with a spirit level and measured the height of the land. He worked it out to be about half what it actually is—it's actually 326 feet—and there is some doubt that he ever would have begun the job of building a canal except for the blunder that made the task seem only half as difficult as it really was.

Merritt was an industrialist, although not a wholly successful one. In fact he was bankrupt, and not in a position to finance his scheme himself; his idea was that the government of Upper Canada would take on the building of the canal. The government of Upper Canada modestly declined. However, Merritt's family chimed in to get him out of bankruptcy, and that cleared the way for him to form the Welland Canal Company, which would be financed by the sale of public shares. Merritt hoped to sell many of these to British speculators, normal practice in his day, and—which was also normal—he hired an incompetent member of the Family Compact as the company's agent in England. Merritt used the company seal to assign the commission, and signed a bank draft for the agent's expenses, although neither action had been approved by the directors. That was illegal, but hell, nobody's perfect.

The agent took off for London, and, except for spending his expenses, didn't do anything much. Because of his inaction, about half the capital supposed to be raised was never forthcoming, and the company was in deep trouble before construction began in 1824. As a result, it became necessary to scamp on construction; locks were poorly built and dams and banks were never properly protected against erosion. As a result, they developed a regrettable tendency to cave in. No proper books were ever kept, although it was clear the company was not doing well; William Lyon Mackenzie wrote that, "Economy and the Welland Canal are as far apart as earth and heaven."

Merritt applied for government help to keep the project going, and it was, reluctantly, given. The government was moved to contribute mostly by the fact that the Americans had completed the Erie Canal in 1825—incidentally, it was almost entirely financed by the State of New York—and if we were to get any business out of the West, we had to do something. In 1828, when the work was mostly done, the Deep Cut collapsed, necessitating a further infusion of funds. The canal opened in 1829, and immediately began to leak money. The locks and dams required continual, expensive maintenance, far above anything that could be covered by the tolls charged to freighters. The government had to come to the rescue again, by buying stock in the company. By 1836 the major shareholders in the Welland Canal Company were the governments of Upper and Lower Canada. Merritt's ownership was down to 38 shares—out of 20,024. Soon after, the government of Canada (the provinces were joined in 1841) became the sole owner, and the Welland our first Crown corporation on record. But nobody could accuse us of planning it that way.

The Grand Trunk's Grand Scam

When railways succeeded canals as the major transportation medium, the pattern was repeated. The Grand Trunk Railway was first proposed as a government enterprise. The legislation passed in 1850 provided for its construction as a public work, jointly owned by Canada and the municipalities through which it was to pass. Sir Francis Hincks, that foxy scalawag, and Finance Minister at the time, was sent to England to arrange a construction contract. He got into the hands of an English contracting firm, Peto, Brassey, Betts and Jackson, and first thing you know, there was a private company, the Grand Trunk Railway Company. Second thing you know, this company had given Peto, Brassey, Betts and Jackson the contract to build the railway. Third thing you know, £50,000 of paid up stock in the new company had been assigned to Sir Francis. He didn't get to keep it, though, because somebody ratted, and the Legislative Council was told to conduct an investigation into how the Finance Minister happened to get all this stock, which, it was finally established, had been paid for by Peto and the boys.

Sir Francis said he didn't even know about the stock, cross my heart and spit, and the Legislative Council said it believed him. The Speaker of the Legislative Council, by one of those happy coincidences that mark political life, was John Ross, who also happened to be president of the Grand Trunk Railway. What the Legislative Council's report actually said was that Sir Francis had no personal interest in the stock—although he owned it—that it was put in his name without his knowledge, and that, if cabinet ministers were speculating in the railway, well, "everyone else who could do so was doing likewise." Sir Francis repudiated the stock; Peto, etc., retained the contract to build the railway, and it remained a private corporation. I think we could call this Canada's first case of privatization, except that it was a kind of preventive privatization; the company was denationalized before it had been nationalized.

The Grand Trunk ran between Toronto and Montreal and then to the Atlantic, and was to get Canadian products to the ocean for overseas shipment. It was capitalized at £9.5 million, of which about one-third was guaranteed by the government. Stocks were sold to a gullible public on the basis of a prospectus written by three company stock-holders: Sir Francis (although he repudiated the £50,000, he held other stock), John Ross, and Alexander Galt, all of whom also happened to be cabinet ministers. The pro-spectus was more notable for its imagination than its ac-curacy, and promised annual dividends of 11.5 per cent, which were never forthcoming.

Alexander Galt and a group of friends controlled a rail-road called the St. Lawrence and Atlantic, which ran between Montreal and Portland, Maine, and which they proposed to dump into the Grand Trunk. They did, too, on the understanding that their railway was complete. But it wasn't, and after the amalgamation, Grand Trunk had to spend about a million dollars—real money in those days—to com-plete it. However, before the amalgamation, Sir Francis, tipped off about the forthcoming deal, bought stock in the St. Lawrence and Atlantic, and cleaned up. Whatever hap-pened, Sir Francis cleaned up.

The Grand Trunk and its sister, the Great Western, run-ning west to Sarnia from Toronto, made a lot of money, but only for a handful of inside investors and a number of sub-contractors, who made their killings either by system-atically cheating and underpaying their workforce, or more crudely, simply decamping with the funds. There was never enough in the coffers actually to build the roads properly. It was the Guarantee Act of 1849, which promised to repay railway debts, that allowed construction to continue when the company treasury was found to be bare. Even so, work was scamped so that both lines made for perilous travel. There were nineteen serious accidents on the Great West-ern in the year 1854 alone, in one of which sixty people died when a train went through a trestle that had been built of pine instead of the oak specified in the construction contract. (The company directors later explained that the trestle collapse was due to "an Act of God," rather than faulty construction.)

So much was siphoned out of the companies—bribes paid to members of Parliament to obtain the necessary rights-of-way did not come cheap—and so little left in that they were in constant financial difficulty. The Grand Trunk was incorporated in 1853, tottering by 1855, virtually bankrupt in 1860, and a ward of the state from that time on, through grants, subsidies, and loans. When Edward Watkin took over as supervisor of the company in 1861, he described it as "a sink of iniquity." Alexander Galt, one of those who prospered from the scams worked around the Grand Trunk, said that in financing the railway, the Canadian government was "in the position of the man who had the good luck to win the elephant."

The Intercolonial Railway: Crowned by Default

However, the Grand Trunk remained a private company. The only government railway for the first fifty-two years of Canada's existence was the Intercolonial, which was completed in 1874 to link Halifax to Quebec. Actually, the Intercolonial started out as a private line, too, although there had never been enough funding to complete the route from the Maritimes to the rest of Canada. A number of attempts by private interests to build the line failed, and eventually the Maritime delegates to the 1864 Confederation Conference insisted that the railway be written into the resolutions that became the British North America Act in 1867. So, far from being the child of federal policy, the Intercolonial was a regional orphan foisted on the central government. It was also a steady money-loser from the time the first train rolled in 1874 until it was folded into the Canadian National, in 1923.

Long before that, we had our first transcontinental railway, our National Dream, privately owned, the Canadian Pacific Railway.

The CPR was built in the usual way; that is, government put up the money, and private enterprise made off with it. Canadian historian J. Bartlet Brebner asserts that "the most casual review of the first six years of its financial history refutes any claim that it was a private corporation." The company was given subsidies of $25 million and 25 million acres of land along its right of way, together with a temporary monopoly. Even so, it twice received new infusions of funding from Ottawa, one of which was clearly illegal under the terms of the enabling legislation. The CPR, too, was marked by bribery and corruption, which eventually became so rampant that they led to the Pacific Scandal, and the temporary removal of Sir John A. Macdonald as Prime Minister. His sin, you will recall, was getting caught sending a telegram to a CPR official to demand $10,000 in election funds.

But at least Canadian Pacific got the job done, by 1885, and began to make money carting immigrants west and their produce east. This set off stirrings of envy in the breasts of the Grant Trunk and the Canadian Northern, a line that ran through northern Ontario and Manitoba. The CPR was "the Tory line," while the others had Liberal connections, and the Prime Minister, by this time, was a Liberal, Sir Wilfrid Laurier. He approved of the other two firms— in the name of competitive free enterprise—building parallel lines to the Pacific. Indeed, Laurier's government would help the process along, by building a railroad itself from Moncton to Winnipeg via Quebec City—called the National Continental—and then leasing the line to the Grand Trunk Pacific, the subsidiary the Grand Trunk was using to reach west. In addition, the government would subsidize the Great Northern's construction from Winnipeg east to Montreal and west to Vancouver.

Laurier's railway minister, A.G. Blair, argued that if the government was going to invest $100 million in another railroad, it should own the line itself. This position was rejected on ideological grounds, and Blair resigned while the enabling legislation went forward, and the railroads were built, more or less; there wasn't enough money to finish them completely, just enough to get them up and running. The result was a foreseeable disaster; there wasn't enough traffic to support three transcontinental lines, and the Grand Trunk repudiated its promise to lease the National Transcontinental. The government might want to give the thing away, but the Grand Trunk didn't have to take it.

Sir Robert Borden, who succeeded Laurier as Prime Minister, found himself lumbered with a railway he didn't want. And two other railroads about to go belly-up. Then a royal commission suggested that the proper course was for Ottawa to nationalize the Great Northern, the Grand Trunk Pacific, and the Grand Trunk, but Sir Robert Borden held that it was bad enough for the government to own one railroad; more would be just too much.

The CN is Born—Out of Wedlock

Circumstances, however, forced Borden's hand. The Canadian Northern had to have more money, but, railway scandals having become an almost annual occurrence by this time, it was clear that Parliament would not sanction any more loans. In the alternative, as the lawyers say, Canadian Northern would crash and take with it the Canadian Bank of Commerce, its principal banker. History has always shown that defunct banks make for unhappy politicians. So the government, muttering dark oaths to itself, nationalized the Great Northern in August, 1917. It now had two railways it didn't want, and was about to get more.

The Grand Trunk ordered its subsidiary, the Grand Trunk Pacific, which carried more debts than passengers, to cease operations. Not only would jobs be lost, so would all the money the government had ponied up, and so in 1919, the government took over the Grand Trunk Pacific, too. It did this under the authority of the War Measures Act, invoked during World War I and never withdrawn. Finally, the Grand Trunk itself was taken over because its lines in central Canada were necessary to make sense of Grand Trunk Pacific and the Great Northern. There was a fight about that—the Grand Trunk shareholders wanted some money for their shares, although an arbitration board ruled that they were worthless—which wound up in the courts. The Canadian National Railway Company was formed under the Canadian National Railway Act in 1919; however, CN didn't really get rolling until after the court cases were settled in 1923, when all the bits and pieces were cobbled together with the Intercolonial to form a transcontinental railway Crown. (In Appendix III you will see that the Grand Trunk still lives, as a subsidiary of Canadian National Railways, and indeed has sprouted a whole bunch of subsidiaries of its own which operate in the United States. One of them won the "Golden Freight Car Award" in 1985; another owns a piece of Conrail, the American railway company. Grand Trunk Corporation made a $13.6 million profit in 1985; the founders would be pleased. And astounded.) CN began life with long-term interest-bearing debts of $2 billion and $283 in current deficits. Never mind, debt loads were something it would get used to.

In short, the Canadian National was not brought into being as part of a history of Canadian government enterprise, but as an act of desperation. It was formed, a contemporary journalist wrote, "not as a noble experiment, but as a compromise with disaster"; it was the result, not of conscious planning, but of "the heaped up follies of the years."

The Wheat Sheaves of Wrath

Another of the classic Canadian Crowns, the Canadian Wheat Board, was born of the desperation of Canadian farmers. Lured out onto the Prairies to grow wheat and make babies, these farmers were then left to the mercy of the grain exchanges, the railroad, the banks, and the private elevator companies.

The grain was taken to an elevator, where the local operator pronounced as to its weight and grade, and then offered a price for it. The farmer could either accept the elevator's offer—which often didn't cover the cost of growing the stuff—or decline it and take his wheat back home again. The CPR enforced the elevator company's monopoly on storage by refusing to let farmers ship their own wheat.

The wheat was sold through grain merchants in Winnipeg, who set the prices daily. When the crop came in each fall, prices fell, because the market became glutted. Again, the farmers could refuse to sell, and take the crop home, hoping for better prices in the future. But if they did so, they would have to pay storage costs as well, against the hope that things might get better later. The banks added their own twist, by refusing to advance money to the farmers for more than three months, and making the notes come due at harvest-time. If the farmer didn't sell, he could lose everything; if he did, he had to take whatever price was offered.

The farmers complained, but it didn't do much good. A Board of Grain Commissioners was formed in 1912 to set uniform standards for various grades of wheat, but the pricing policy remained erratic and, as far as the farmers were concerned, disastrous. The CPR President Sir William Van Horne told them to "raise less hell and more wheat," while the farmers themselves prayed for "a good harvest and a bloody war in Europe." When the bloody war came, in 1914, there was, indeed, temporary relief. To ensure a steady supply of food to allied governments, the Board of Grain Commissioners was authorized to sell wheat at fixed prices in government-to-government contracts. The Grain Exchange was closed for two years, and the farmers found themselves getting prices that averaged seventy cents a bushel higher than they had been getting under the old system.

After the war, the old system returned, but not for long; now inflation was the fear, and the federal government established a separate corporation, the Canadian Wheat Board, to take over marketing. The Wheat Board was not to help farmers, mind, but to ensure stable prices; still, it ended up helping the farmers inadvertently. The Wheat Board would advance the farmer $2.15 per bushel on delivery of wheat to a country elevator, then pool the returns from the final sales, and distribute the proceeds. In 1919, farmers got an average $2.63 a bushel. (In 1986, they didn't get much more, in dollars that weren't worth 10 per cent of the 1919 variety.) They loved it, but it went against, you should excuse the expression, the grain of the day, and the Wheat Board was disbanded after one year.

Wheat politics dominated Western Canada for decades, and the farmers' unhappiness—made manifest through Grain Growers' movements, the Farmers Union of Canada, and the return of twenty-one Progressive MPs to the 1921 House of Commons—suggested that things could not long go on as they were. Still, no one was talking about Crown corporations. In each of the three Prairie provinces, co-operative wheat pools were organized between 1924 and 1926. These wheat pools sought to confound the grain dealers by bypassing the Winnipeg Exchange and selling the pooled wheat directly to overseas customers, as the Wheat Board had done. The concept came unstuck as the Great Depression took hold. The pools found they couldn't get as much on the world market as they had already paid the farmers in advance. As a result, the pools lost $25 million in two years, and were threatened with collapse.

The farm organizations began to demand, with increasing anger, the return of the Wheat Board. That didn't happen until 1935, and even then, it was as a temporary and voluntary pooling agency to help the pools meet their accumulated debts. Although the Wheat Board was incorporated in 1935, it wasn't until 1943—in the midst of another war and in the teeth of rocketing prices—that it became the sole purchaser of Prairie wheat, and again, the object was to hold prices down, not up.

Today, the Wheat Board is a $4 billion enterprise. It's as firmly fixed in the Canadian psyche as it is on the Canadian landscape, but it was born, not of planning, or instinct, or intuition, but as the result of a long series of forward and backward steps. Necessity is the mother of invention; and also, from time to time, of Crown corporations.

The Depression Lends a Hand

The Great Depression, which sponsored the return of the Wheat Board, also saw the birth of the Bank of Canada, in 1935; the CBC, in 1936; and Air Canada, born as Trans-Canada Air Lines, in 1937.

The Bank of Canada was formed in large part because the Canadian government couldn't get the private banks to behave. In a time of economic stagnation, the government wanted the banks to circulate money, instead of which they kept contracting, making things worse. There had been some earlier agitation—by farmers, not surprisingly—for the establishment of a central bank in Canada, and, in 1933, a royal commission recommended that the government set up an institution which alone would have the right to issue bills and control the money supply. So the Bank of Canada was formed. However, when it opened its doors on March 11, 1935, it was not a Crown corporation but a private institution, supported by a public share-offering (which was instantly over-subscribed) of $5 million. Because the private banks owned most of the shares, the new bank was used to reinforce their restrictive policies. The government, in some exasperation, bought up all the shares in 1938, and ran its own bank. That was how it became a Crown.

The CBC Takes to the Air

The CBC was brought into being for a higher (or lower, depending on your point of view) motive. It represented a genuine—and rare—example of a Crown created to meet a national emotional need, and was consciously conceived as a nation-building institution.

The CBC grew out of the Canadian Radio Broadcasting Commission, a body established as the result of the Aird Commission, in 1932. At that time, it was clear that if Canada did not do something drastic about the airwaves, they would be owned by Americans. Graham Spry, one of the founders of the Canadian Radio League, a lobby formed for the specific purpose of promoting a Canadian broadcasting system, put the issue in six potent words: "The State or the United States?" Everyone, even Conservative Prime Minister R.B. Bennett, replied, "The State." Actually, what Bennett said was "Canadians have the right to a system of broadcasting from Canadian sources equal in all respects to that of any other country."

Although there were three American private networks, no Canadian proposed a similar solution in Canada's smaller market. Indeed, about all the Canadian Manufacturers' Association could suggest was large government subsidies for a private entrepreneur. That might have worked, except that the memory of the railroads was still fresh in the national mind. Charles Bowman, editor of the Ottawa *Citizen* and a member of the Aird Commission, wrote, "It would be far more difficult to re-establish a national service of radio broadcasting after private extravagance had led to insolvency." He might have put it more simply: Once bitten, twice shy.

So a broadcasting commission was established, and when that proved an awkward thing to manage the government made an honest woman of it by forming it into a government corporation, the Canadian Broadcasting Corporation, on November 2, 1936.

For most Canadians, although we love to curse the CBC, that was a wise move.

The Absent-Minded Airline

An historian of the airline industry says that "Canada seems to have established a publicly owned monopoly of scheduled inter-urban air services in a fit of absence of mind," and indeed, that is what the record shows concerning the birth of Trans-Canada Air Lines (the name was changed to Air Canada in 1965). In the early 1930s there was a Depression on, and while everyone agreed we ought to have an airline, no one wanted to put up the money. Government became the fall guy, *faute de mieux*. The post office—not a Crown, then, but a government department—wanted to cash in on the money to be made in airmail. An airline would promote economic activity and jobs. Besides, the Americans were blossoming with airlines, and if we didn't want all the routes running north and south, we had to do something. So we did.

It was Clarence Decatur Howe, the American-born entrepreneur and Prime Minister Mackenzie King's man-of-all-work, who pushed through the legislation to establish the Canadian airline, but he certainly didn't think of it as a Crown. He always referred to it as "a private corporation." In *Public Corporations and Public Policy in Canada*, John W. Langford notes, irritably, that "the major actors involved in the decisions to create both the National Harbours Board and TCA seemed blissfully unaware of the political differences between a public and private corporation and, therefore, did not in any literal sense rationally choose the public over the private corporate instrument."

You want an airline, dammit, there's an airline. The first proposal was for a joint venture, with the publicly owned Canadian National Railways, acting for Ottawa, joined to the private CPR and Canadian Airways of Winnipeg, and the government subsidizing the inevitable losses. However, the CPR refused to play. CPR Chairman Sir Edward Beatty said that the CNR (his rival) and the government were indivisible, and he couldn't ask his shareholders to cuddle up to the CNR. (Wonder what Sir Edward's ghost makes of CNCP Telecommunications?) The final bill, presented to the House of Commons in March, 1937, allowed private interests to purchase up to 49.8 per cent of the 50,000 shares. The government would maintain a majority, but others could play. They didn't though; no shares were privately purchased, and as John Langford concludes, "However inadvertently, the Liberal government under Howe's strong influence created a thoroughly public airline."

The C.D. Howe Corporations

When World War II burst upon us, Canada had a number of Crown corporations, but no more than, say, the United States. There were fourteen of them in all, in rail, ship, and air transport; banking; harbour administration; and commodity marketing. You will find them listed, along with the dates of their establishment, in Appendix VI. With the opening of hostilities, C.D. Howe, impatient, brusque, and energetic, couldn't be bothered with trying to persuade private companies to do what he saw needed to be done, so he invoked the War Measures Act and began to create corporations to do the work. These corporations were not so much government enterprises as extensions of Howe's considerable ego, and were generally known as the "C.D. Howe corporations." They did not report to Parliament. In all, thirty-two Crown firms were formed, from Aero Timber Products Limited to Wartime Salvage Limited; however, they were never meant to represent a change in policy, only a wartime strategy. Most of them were abandoned once the war ended. In fact only two, Eldorado Mining and Refining (now Eldorado Nuclear Limited) and Polymer Corporation (now Polysar) still exist. The wartime Crowns are listed in Appendix VII.

However, other corporations were created to help with post-war reconstruction, and to dispose of wartime assets, such as Crown Assets Disposal and Defence Construction (1951). Government, and in particular the bureaucracy, was getting used to the idea of working through Crowns. By 1951, there were thirty-three federal Crowns, and a new law, the Financial Administration Act, which defined them and tried to control them.

But it didn't. The difficulty was that senior bureaucrats soon began to see that creating a Crown to solve a problem—such as the imminent collapse of a private enterprise firm, with all those jobs—was a quick and easy fix. And the

Crowns, once established, could form subsidiaries, which in turn could go forth and multiply, and make fruitful the land.

And they did. The real growth of the Crowns began in about 1961; it was never planned, or supervised, it just happened. Gordon Robertson, President of the Institute for Research on Public Policy, wrote in 1981 that "seventy-two per cent of public corporations were created in the last two decades," although I must admit I have never found statistics that were as exact as that. But what anyone can find is that, once established, it is the inevitable tendency of a Crown not merely to grow but to multiply. When Petro-Canada was formed in 1976, for example, it began with three men in a Calgary hotel room and an expense account for cabs. Today, it has $9 billion in assets, two mammoth office towers and eighty-three subsidiaries. If it had been suggested, while the enabling legislation was being discussed, that one company would become eighty-four companies in less than a decade, no one would have believed it.

But that, in brief, is how the Crowns grew, from modest and accidental beginnings early in the century, through two spurts during the Depression and World War II to a mushrooming—dark, but fruitful—in the 1960s and 1970s. It is as if the Crowns reached what might be called lift-off speed about 1961, and they've been flying ever since.

Provincial Crowns

At the provincial level, much the same sort of thing happened. From dabblings in hydro and telephones, the provinces found themselves pushed, usually reluctantly (the exception was Saskatchewan), into taking over troubled firms until, quite suddenly, the Crowns took on a momentum of their own.

A 1982 study by Aidan R. Vining (*Public Corporations and Public Policy in Canada*) points out that only 3 per cent of Canada's provincial Crowns, as closely as Vining could trace them, were in existence by 1920. Another 9 per cent appeared between 1920 and 1940, 23 per cent between 1940 and 1950, and 16 per cent between 1960 and 1970. The other 49 per cent—virtually half—sprang up in the decade between 1970 and 1980. The Crowns have grown in lumps, and most of the lumps have come lately.

That is the reality of the Crowns in Canada. They did not grow out of the pre-Cambrian shield, they are not as Canadian as maple syrup and pea soup; they appeared by accident and survived by bureaucratic stealth. As for Crowns setting us off from the Americans . . . well, perhaps we can learn something by looking at government enterprise in the United States, in the next chapter.

4

It's The Same The 'Ole World Over

"The National Council of Corporations defines corporations as the instruments which, under the aegis of the State, carry out the complete organic and totalitarian regulation of production with a view to the expansion of the wealth, political power, and well-being of the Italian people."
Benito Mussolini, *The Corporate State*
Florence, 1938

The gentleman in the bookstore in downtown Knoxville, Tennessee, wanted to set me straight. He had noticed that I was buying a book on the Tennessee Valley Authority *TVA: Fifty Years of Grass-Roots Bureaucracy*, edited by Edwin C. Hargrove and Paul C. Conkin, and he wanted me to know that he didn't hold with that Socialistic Nonsense. I said I didn't realize TVA was Socialistic Nonsense. I told him that President Ronald Reagan was not ashamed to take the $450 million the TVA makes every year. Besides, I understood that the United States owned 24,000 government enterprises, and the TVA, whose twin office towers loomed over us from the headquarters on West Summit Hill Drive, was just another one of the boys. Twenty-four thousand? He couldn't believe it; I must be making it up. Nope, I said, read it in a book. Annmarie Hauck Walsh, in *The Public's Business*, said that as closely as she could figure it, there were more than 24,000 of these babies—mostly local authorities, mind—scattered all over the United States. I offered to show the gentleman my notes. He waved them away; this needed thinking about. He paid for his paperback and left the store, heading for home, no doubt, and a large snifter of bourbon and branchwater. He was shaken.

Americans like to believe that they have avoided the creeping socialism, or worse, which they have been able to detect north of the border. When writing of the travails of Canada's Crown corporations, American business columnists, especially during 1985 and 1986, liked to remind their readers that it couldn't happen to them. Why? Because the United States doesn't have Crown corporations. And it doesn't either, lacking a Crown; what it does have are government enterprises, and it has them by the thousand. They are usually called authorities, or agencies or even commissions, but by any name, they are mighty like our Crowns. New York State has 230 of them, including the Port Authority of New York and New Jersey, which owns the bridges, tunnels, and terminals in and around New York, along with the New York City airports and Newark International. The Port Authority was established in 1921, and makes money out of tolls and other charges; it refinanced the Holland Tunnel and built the George Washington Bridge, the Lincoln Tunnel, the Port Authority bus terminal in New York City, and marine terminals in New York and New Jersey. It also owns and runs its own railway, PATH—the Port Authority Trans-Hudson. Pennsylvania has 1,882 enterprises, in charge of everything from the Pennsylvania Turnpike to housing in Philadelphia. California has 110 airports, 21 power utilities, 127 public transit systems, 76 stadiums, 267 sewer systems, and 250 water supply utilities at the state level alone, and the Census figures admit that not all were counted. No exact count of all of America's public enterprises at every level has ever been made, although the 1982 Census of Governmental Organization turned up 12,536 at the county, municipal, and township level—that is, not counting the states or federal government—owning everything from 2,189 airports to 5,605 sewer systems, and not a socialist in the bunch.

In fact, the real difference in this matter between our two nations is that while both swarm with government enterprises, the Americans have comparatively few at the federal level (they are listed in Appendix VIII). Still, what they have is impressive, and includes the Post Office, Amtrak, the Communications Satellite Corporation, the Pennsylvania Avenue Development Corporation, which looks after

President Reagan's neighbourhood, and the Pension Benefit Guarantee Corporation, which steps in if private pension plans go belly up. And, of course, the TVA.

When the Americans do a thing, they do it big. If you want to see a really big federal corporation, the place to go is Knoxville, where the emphasis is on corn liquor, coonskin caps—and the Tennessee Valley Authority. The TVA, famed in song and story, with two movies, two big novels, and dozens of non-fiction books in its background, is a hell of a big corporation. It's much bigger than Air Canada, Ontario Hydro, or Hydro-Québec. Americans will never believe it when you tell them this, but the TVA is larger, in terms of assets, employment, and revenue, than any other government corporation on the continent except another U.S. government corporation—the Post Office.

The TVA sells over $4 billion in electric power annually, and another $4 billion in farm products—about double Ontario Hydro's annual revenue—and is also involved in regional development, forestry, agriculture, and the manufacture and sale of fertilizer. It has 34,000 employees and operates thirty-nine dams, twenty-nine coal-fired steam plants, five other turbine plants and, until recently, two nuclear plants. Its entire nuclear programme is now on hold because of concerns over safety. That caused the TVA to write off $800 million in nuclear assets in 1984, but it still manages to sell its power much cheaper than private power companies. The TVA is even into solar and biomass energy. It supplies power to seven states—Tennessee and parts of Mississippi, Alabama, Georgia, North Carolina, Virginia, and Kentucky, and it pays them annually upwards of $170 million "in lieu of taxes"—like many of our Crowns, it is tax exempt. The company serves 91,000 square miles with a population of 8 million people. Ontario Hydro, our largest Crown, has 31,116 employees, owns eighty-one power plants (six more than the TVA), and serves just over 3 million customers. Impressive, but not as big as its American cousin, which is owned lock, stock, and share certificates by the U.S. government. Ronald Reagan, God's own free enterpriser, has one of the world's largest government corporations on his books.

It All Began With Bird Poop

The TVA owes its existence to the need for something to replace bird poop. In 1916, when the Americans were hovering on the edges of World War I, it occurred to the thinkers in their defence department that German submarines could easily cut off their supply of South American guano, which was used as a source of nitrates for explosives. Fearing that Americans might find themselves in a war without a way to make bullets, they decided to make synthetic nitrates, a task requiring enormous amounts of power. The upshot was the construction of a mammoth hydro development at Muscle Shoals, Alabama, on the Tennessee River. However, by the time the development was finished, the war was over, and the question became, what the hell to do with it?

Henry Ford knew. He offered to buy it for $5 million, and put up factories around it. However, since the government had invested $130 million, this deal looked like it would be better for Henry than for the United States, and the offer was refused. A number of private power companies wanted to buy the hydro plant, because they judged correctly that it might someday provide competition; but they wouldn't offer enough either. Nor would the chemical companies who wanted to make fertilizer. A battle royal raged over the complete, but unused, plant for seventeen years. A number of people thought it ought to be used to provide cheap power for a poverty-stricken area, and thus encourage employment, and two bills actually passed Congress to that effect. President Herbert Hoover vetoed both of them; that was the way to socialism. Then the Depression struck, and Herbert Hoover was out of a job. In the end, President Franklin Delano Roosevelt, who was creating all kinds of government corporations (although he didn't think much of socialism, either), gave the Tennessee Valley Authority Act his blessing on May 18, 1933. The original legislation, after setting down the TVA's purpose as being "to improve the navigability and to provide for the flood control of the Tennessee River," told the company to look after national defence by "the operation of Government properties at and near Muscle Shoals in the State of Alabama," and finished off with one of those dandy catch-alls, "and . . .

other purposes." Lumped in along the way was a lot of stuff about reforestation and agriculture. The TVA was in business, and turned itself into a power company that quickly ran the private firms out of the valley. Served them right, too. They were milking the locals something dreadful.

The TVA made money three years after it started into business and has been making it ever since. More importantly, it has drawn hundreds of manufacturing concerns to the area to take advantage of its cheap power. For 1984 alone, the annual report claims 350 new industrial facilities, representing investment of $1.27 billion and 24,000 jobs, were lured into the area. Perhaps the TVA's most important achievement lies in the fact that the annual per capita income of the Valley in 1933 was $168, 45 per cent of the national average; by 1981, it was $8,078, 77 per cent of the national average. The TVA has been shaken by scandals, marred by waste, and damned by ideologues, but it keeps on getting bigger every year. And the federal politicians who come in to attack big government always work something nice into their talk about the good old TVA.

It is not so surprising that the Americans would have something like SuperHydro in their midst; much of the early development of our two countries followed the same lines. That is, the general rule was for the government to put up the money and the scalawags to run off with it.

The Aldermen were Known as "The Forty Thieves"

The government held 20 per cent of the stocks in the First and Second United States Banks, back when Alexander Hamilton was telling George Washington how to run things. Thomas Jefferson, watching helplessly as the first bank was launched, remarked that "the credit and fate of the nation seemed to hang on the desperate throws and plunges of gambling scoundrels." Early insurance and even manufacturing concerns were government-owned. As in Canada, the people who ran the country very quickly got onto the joys of milking the public purse. Charles Beard, the noted American historian, wrote in his study of the Constitution that "at least five-sixths of the delegates to the Constitutional Convention of 1787, were immediately, directly and personally interested in the outcome of their labours in Philadelphia and were to a greater or lesser extent economic beneficiaries from the adoption of the Constitution." One result was that, as Nathan Miller says in *The Founding Finaglers*, "Corruption is as American as cherry pie." In the first part of the nineteenth century, the Board of Aldermen of New York were christened "the Forty Thieves" in honour of their habit of selling ferry and transit leases to the highest bribers. City Hall, including all its fixtures, was sold at public auction to satisfy a court judgement—fraudulently obtained—for $196,000. Actually, the Forty Thieves were pikers compared to the larcenous geniuses who built the railroads.

The Central Pacific Moved Mountains

Reading the early history of the American railroad industry is like watching a re-run on TV; Pierre Berton could go down there, change a few names, and peddle copies of *The National Dream* with no questions asked.

There were two railways to cross the continent, the Union Pacific, built west from Omaha, and the Central Pacific, built east from Sacramento; they met on May 10, 1869, at Promontory Point, Utah, where a golden spike marked the completion of a transcontinental route. The Union Pacific, like the Canadian Pacific, was given a land-grant to sweeten the pot, along with subsidies. As the company's backers passed out nearly $450,000 in bribes, the subsidies rose and the land-grant stretched until it expanded to from twenty to forty miles in width in what one Congressman called "the greatest legislative crime in history." Like our railway pioneers, the Americans appreciated the notion of having a separate company to undertake construction and through which funds could be siphoned. In the case of Union Pacific, the enabling corporation was called Credit Mobilier, which happened to be the name of a famous French firm. The original chief engineer of Union Pacific estimated the costs of construction at $30,000 a mile, but was persuaded by his employers to ask the government for more. He upped the ante to $50,000 a mile. This generous sum was still not enough, so he was discharged and another engineer brought in. In the end, the government paid Credit Mobilier subsidies of $60,000 a mile, and a total of $94 million for a line that actually cost $50 million to build. Union Pacific teetered on the edge of bankruptcy, while Credit Mobilier paid dividends of more than 300 per cent a year. To take the edge off any Congressional appetite to inquire into the funding details of the railway as it worked its way west, Credit Mobilier shares were distributed to such luminaries as Schuyler Colfax, the Speaker of the House and later Vice-President, Senators Henry Wilson and J.W. Patterson, and Representatives James A. Garfield (later President) and James G. Blaine.

The Central Pacific, working eastwards, also used a separate construction company to receive the rich subsidies doled out by the state. This company was called the Contract & Finance Company. No one ever learned how much it got away with because when the haul had reached about $50 million, and an investigation loomed, the company books disappeared, much mourned by all. This firm was also forced to dispense with the services of its chief engineer, Theodore D. Judah, because he wouldn't go along with a scheme to triple the subsidies for a run of line just east of Sacramento. Seems the company wanted Judah to declare that the right of way was part of the Sierra Mountains, even though it was flat as a billiard-table. With Judah out of the way, a state geologist was brought in to proclaim the mountainous proclivities of this flatland, and President Abraham Lincoln accepted his report. This, reports Nathan Miller, caused one legislator who was in on the scheme to declare, "My pertinacity and Abraham's faith moved mountains." The take from that one bit of fraud was $800,000.

However, while these lines were mostly financed out of the public purse, they did not become public lines; Union Pacific went into receivership in 1893, was restructured by Edward Harriman, one of the early Robber Barons, and absorbed Central Pacific. (Union Pacific still operates, but as a highly diversified company with only minor interests in railroading.)

In the United States, as in Canada, the real plunge into government corporations did not come until two wars and the Great Depression called for such a plunge, and then they went in deeper than we did.

The Progressive Movement that swept across the United States in the first decade of this century was aimed not so much at getting government into business, as at curbing the excesses of giant corporations. The reformers attacked corruption in municipal governments, only to find themselves frustrated because the state legislatures were often controlled by the railroads and other large corporations, who were able to frustrate attempts to clean up the slums, or pass child-labour laws. So the reformers turned to state politics. The election of Robert La Follette as governor of Wisconsin in 1901, signalled the arrival of the Progressives as a political force to be reckoned with. However, despite occasional forays into the promise of public ownership—mayors in Detroit, Toledo, and San Francisco were all elected on platforms promising the municipal ownership of public utilities—the emphasis was on regulating private enterprise, not trying to compete with it. The secret ballot, direct primaries, the initiative, and such social legislation as minimum wage laws, widow's pensions, and workmen's compensation—these were the aims of the Progressives. Theodore Roosevelt, who ran on the Progressive ticket in 1912, would have reeled back in horror at the notion that government ought to get into business for itself.

Although it did just that, once the Americans joined World War I in 1917. Government corporations were created overnight to build ships, finance the war, move and market grain, refine and sell sugar, and even—horror or horrors—to build housing for war workers.

With peace, most of these corporations were dissolved. Government again came into bad odour, in part because of the collapse of government-backed bonds which helped to secure the real estate bubbles of the 1920s. Here's how that worked. Private developers would buy up blocks of land and then, as residents of the area, vote for special tax assessments to secure loans for the construction of water, sewer, and road facilities. The municipal authority would issue bonds backed by the special assessments, to be paid back over the years. Then home-buyers would be lured into the area only to discover, too late, that they had been loaded down with debt. In Florida, the centre of a spectacular real estate bubble, a number of defaults in the repayment of these assessment bonds during 1926 convinced a great many

Americans that government was not the partner they wanted in any business dealings—although their complaints might have been more fairly laid at the feet of the real estate swindlers.

This was the era of the Muckrakers, when American journalists took delight in digging up scandals and created a literature which, among other things, reinforced the basic distrust for authority that was a part of the American heritage. Add to that the apparent overwhelming success of laissez-faire private enterprise in the booming development of the 1920s, and it is hardly surprising that, as Annmarie Hauck Walsh notes, "the role of government in that development was discounted and its reputation tarnished."

Then came the dawn—the Great Crash of the stock markets in the autumn of 1929, and onset of the Great Depression. President Herbert Hoover, using the powers that flowed to his office in an emergency, created the Reconstruction Finance Corporation (RFC) to help the banks out of their difficulties. (When times are tough ideology counts for less than action.) Unfortunately, the RFC wasn't too successful. However, things changed when Roosevelt replaced Hoover. FDR turned the RFC into one of the centrepieces of his New Deal, thanks to the corporation's forceful director, Jesse Jones, who told the bankers, "Be smart for once. . . . Take the government into partnership with you." FDR established the Federal Deposit Insurance Corporation (which still exists) as a safety net, and used government funds to buy bank stocks. By 1935, Washington owned more than $1 billion in preferred shares, representing part-ownership of about half the banks in the country. Government corporations, many owned by the RFC, began to multiply, often in conjunction with new agencies created as part of the New Deal. The Commodity Credit Corporation was created to work with the Agricultural Adjustment Administration to support farm prices. The RFC Mortgage Company worked with the Federal Housing Administration. The Export-Import Bank worked with trading agencies to promote exports. The Electric Home and Farm Authority, supporting the Rural Electrification Administration, financed electrical purchases and, of course, the TVA provided the power. The RFC financed public works, drove down interest rates, refinanced drainage programmes, aided victims of flood and drought, financed school construction, and at one point advanced the money to keep American Airlines and El Paso Gas in business. As Arthur Schlesinger, Jr., the pre-eminent Roosevelt historian, wrote in *The Coming of the New Deal*, the RFC " . . . was by far the largest single investor in the American economy as well as the biggest bank in the country." In seven years, it gave away, or loaned out, $10 billion, and that was a time when a billion dollars was quite a lot of money.

Inevitably, the RFC got above itself; Jesse Jones treated the President with condescension. "Whenever we did anything of importance, that was on the border line of our authority, I would try at first opportunity to tell the President about it," he said, "but after the fact." Court challenges and business hostility eventually dimmed its powers, but it lasted until 1954. Besides its adventures in rural electrification, banking and farming, the RFC developed the lower Colorado River, and built a spa at Saratoga Springs, the Hayden Planetarium and a railway, along with scores of irrigation projects from coast to coast. While the Depression lasted, no one—except Herbert Hoover—saw anything much wrong with a government corporation owning things.

One of the inevitable outcroppings of the depressed economy was that as scandals and collapses involving the states and cities piled up, corporations, cities, and even state governments were forced to repudiate their debts. In many cases, investors had been persuaded to plunk down their dollars in the first place by the fact that a government was part-owner of the operation. Not surprisingly, the demise of many of these operations led to a certain amount of bitterness. The upshot was the gradual replacement of government equities by public authority revenue bonds. Interest from these bonds is normally tax exempt. The public authority uses these bonds to raise money to do what needs doing, and guarantees both principal and interest. By 1948, all but seven states had passed laws allowing public enterprises to sell these bonds. Mixed ownership of the kind common in Canada—where a private company and a Crown share equity in the same operation—is illegal in the United States.

It is this difference in financing, rather than any difference in ideology, that marked the divide between American and Canadian government enterprises in the 1940s and 1950s. In this period, housing, urban renewal, airports, hospitals, industrial development, utilities such as water, power, and sewer, and even investment banking all became government enterprises.

With the onset of World War II, the Americans created new corporations with which to finance and fight the war, just as we did, and the RFC sprouted subsidiaries in petroleum, metal, rubber, and other defence supplies. By war's end, there were 63 directly held federal corporations in the U.S., and 138 subsidiaries—far more than in Canada—with far greater prominence. The trend was to continue right up until the Red Scares of the early 1950s.

As Annmarie Hauck Walsh writes in *The Public's Business*, and in defiance of nearly everything conventional wisdom tells us about the American system, "By 1953, the federal government was the largest power producer in the country, the largest lender and the largest borrower, the largest landlord and the largest tenant, the largest holder of grazing land, the largest owner of grain, the largest warehouse operator, the largest shipowner and the largest flat truck operator."

In 1953, the year Walsh singles out, Dwight Eisenhower was President and Senator Joseph McCarthy was riding high; and government was not merely in bad odour, the presence of government in the market-place was just another manifestation of the worldwide Communist plot. The Chambers of Commerce and the American Manufacturers' Association, alerted by McCarthy to the dangers of state control, mounted a campaign on behalf of "the American way of life." Later, McCarthy was to become a sick joke, remembered with shame, but at that time, he was some punkins. William F. Buckley, Jr., a man who looks as if he would wipe his gloves after shaking hands with the Queen, wrote in 1954, "As long as McCarthyism fixes its goal with its present precision, it is a movement around which men of good will and stern morality can close ranks."

But there was no "present precision" about McCarthyism, it was a long howl of outrage against government, for which read "communism." For the time being, however, its dictates ran. In response to public pressure, President Eisenhower created a special commission to look into the extent

to which the American economy had already been su-
bourned. He put Herbert Hoover, the former President,
in charge of the commission. Hoover's reputation as an
economic wizard had apparently survived his handling of
the nation during the early part of the Depression. Hoover
turned in a report that was more notable for its clichés than
its originality, but which argued that the economy was in
danger of being taken over by the Lefties. Less hysterically,
the report also said that, as a matter of principle, government ought to do as little as possible in its own name, and
should instead contract out as much of its necessary work
as it could to private firms. This policy applied especially
to public water resource development, and especially to the
Tennessee Valley Authority.

Hoover's report hit Eisenhower's desk just at the time
when the TVA was asking for more money with which to
build bigger dams. The administration countered, under
the direction of Sherman Adams, an influential presidential
aide, with a proposal to dismantle the corporation. The
Bureau of the Budget then suggested that a private utility
company, Dixon-Yates, should build and operate any new
facilities required to produce power in the South. The lines
were clearly drawn, with the Eisenhower administration
portrayed as "reactionary" by the friends of TVA, and TVA
supporters dubbed "creeping Socialists" by Sherman Adams. The battle dragged on from 1954 to 1959, with neither
side able to win a clearcut victory. Then news stories broke
revealing that the major private consultant who had helped
the Bureau of the Budget with its proposal was in the pay
of Dixon-Yates. By this time, Sherman Adams was gone,
too, on his way to infamy for accepting a vicuna coat from
a contractor who had business with the government.

Cheese Down the Federal Rathole

While the TVA survived, most of the other government
corporations were either sold off, wound up, or allowed to
wither and quietly die. The sixty-three federal corporations
of post-war America dwindled to twenty-three in the 1970s.
But even these few were able to get into trouble. The Overseas Private Investment Corporation made it onto David

Lambro's list of "The Eight Least-Needed" public entities by lending $414,000 to a resort in Haiti for the "elegant, exotic, and erotic." Lambro, author of *The Federal Rathole*, couldn't understand why American taxpayers should be in the exotic and erotic game in Haiti. The man is obviously a spoilsport.

However, despite all the rhetoric flowing across the United States, and indeed the world, on behalf of curbing government enterprises, the numbers seem to be mounting again. You will see in Appendix VIII that in early 1987 I was able to identify fifty-one federal government enterprises from the U.S. Government Manual, along with six "quasi-official Agencies" and fifty-eight federal boards, centres, commissions, and advisory groups which serve many of the same functions as some of our Crowns (for example, the Mississippi River Commission and the California Debris Commission), but which have no shares for anyone to own.

The government railroad is Amtrak (officially, the National Railroad Passenger Corporation), formed in 1970, after one hundred individual railways announced to the Interstate Commerce Commission that they intended folding up operations. Amtrak was given $40 million, federal loan guarantees of $100 million, and told to go out and make a profit. It hasn't done that, but it does run 210 trains a day into 500 stations serving 24,000 route-miles. With a workforce of 18,500, and 4.2 billion passenger-miles per annum, it is larger than Via Rail. Its official literature proclaims, "Every train in the Amtrak system is operating with new or completely rebuilt, all-electric equipment" which, as you will see in Chapter 8, is enough to give our national railroad the megrims and an envy attack.

The U.S. Postal Service, which was also turned into a government corporation in 1970, has 661,325 employees—more than twice as many as all of Canada's Crowns. And there are more than 1.1 million Americans whom we would call, in Canada, Crown employees. Given the size of the United States, ten times our own, it is clear the proportion of people at work in these firms is smaller than in Canada. But it is hardly negligible; indeed, given the prevailing public myth that Americans eschew government enterprise, it is astonishing.

Still, even with all the public utilities, airport corporations, and public sewer companies that litter the American landscape, in recent years, the Americans have turned increasingly to contracting-out provisions and public authority bonds to perform many of the tasks which we perform through Crowns. It seems evident that the decision to go this way was inspired by ideology, not economics. The Hoover Commission asserted flatly that "free enterprise is the best way to organize economic resources for maximum production," but that is more a bumper-sticker than a proven economic fact. Free enterprise certainly does many things, even most things, more quickly and efficiently than does a government department, but there are a great many areas of our economic life, from the production and distribution of electricity to the provision of telephone service, where the most efficient system, economically, appears to be a monopoly. That infers either some form of government regulation or the payment of a very high monopoly rent to an unregulated entrepreneur. There is little difference in the efficiency of public and private telephone systems in this country, and the TVA is at least as efficient as any private enterprise rival in the United States.

As to contracting out, there have been cases in which it works wonderfully well—when, for instance, Canada bought much of its space hardware when we first developed our satellite programme in the 1960s. It seemed crazy to reinvent the wheel, or a space satellite, so we didn't, and concentrated our dollars on developing some of the most sophisticated satellite programmes in the world, all uniquely our own. There have also been occasions when contracting out has not worked so well. In purchasing spare parts for C5-A transport planes, the U.S. Air Force paid $74,165 each for aluminum ladders, $7,622 each for what were called "hot beverage units," and turned out to be ten-cup coffee brewers, and $171 each for "emergency lighting units"—in layman's language, flashlights. Then there was the time in 1985, when, under Congressional pressure, Boeing Military Aircraft Company agreed to trim the cost of duckbilled pliers, worth about $9 a pair, back from its original charge of $748 to a modest $80. To make up for the reduction, the company added a new item to its billing, a "support equipment management" charge of $143,000. About the same time, another contractor was discovered to

have billed the Defence Department $802,000 for the cost
of fighting allegations levelled by the Justice Department
that the corporation had padded its bills. This is known as
chutzpah. Major U.S. defence contracts have always been
marked by the kind of cost accounting that would make
the boys who ran the Union Pacific burst into envious
applause.

In short, the American experience, until the 1950s, roughly
paralleled our own, and only recently have we gone in quite
different directions—Canada towards government enterprises and the United States away from them. In western
Europe, government corporations rose to prominence, for
the most part, about the same time ours did, after World
War II. In Europe, this increase in government corporations was driven, in many cases, by the need to reconstruct
quickly in the aftermath of the war. Austria is an example
of this. In other cases—Sweden, for example—the combination of a series of socialist administrations, inherently
sympathetic to government activities, and the need to move
into export markets in a massive way resulted in the creation
of such industrial giants as Volvo.

In virtually every modern economy, except the American
one, government corporations occupy a central role. And
here's a funny thing; in many cases, these corporations find
themselves in business with American free enterprisers. They
get along just fine.

Private Firms in Public Wedlock

An item appeared in the back pages of a Toronto newspaper on July 31, 1986, announcing the wedding of ITT
Corporation of New York—big, aggressive, free enterprise,
multinational—to Compagnie Générale d'Eléctricité, a
French state-owned corporation. To the immortal question,
Your place or mine?, the happy couple replied, neither;
they were forming the world's second-largest communications company to operate in seventy-five countries, with
annual sales of $10 billion. They hope to involve "all the
main countries in Europe."

Here is a mixed corporation with a vengeance, and it is

being formed at a time when France, according to the press, is doing its best to dismantle its long line of state corporations. There are more than 4,000 of these, which control 30 per cent of the nation's industrial revenue, almost the entire finance sector, and much of energy, commerce, the media (TV, radio, magazines), insurance, and automobiles (Renault, the giant French state-owned auto maker, controls American Motors of Canada; there's another mixed blessing).

In 1982, the Mitterand government nationalized private firms worth 50 billion francs, to be paid over the next fifteen years. With the defeat of the Socialists, the new government of Jacques Chirac announced its determination to get rid of as many of these corporations as possible, but it won't be easy; not only because Mitterand is still around, as President, but simply because there isn't enough loose money available on the French stock exchange to re-purchase the companies. The situation doesn't become any clearer when the state electric company teams up with ITT. The tide of public opinion may be flowing against government firms in France, but there is no sign that they are about to disappear. Nor is France an exception; the European landscape is littered with state firms.

A Lot of the Household Names Don't Belong to Households

Volkswagen, the giant German car maker, started out as a gleam in Adolph Hitler's eye, and the West German state still owns about 20 per cent of the company. Volvo, the Swedish car maker is state-owned, and so is Saab.

National oil companies have become increasingly popular; France has two of them, Compagnie Française des Pétroles and Société Nationale Elf-Aquitaine, Germany has Veba, Italy has ENI, Britain has BP and Britoil, Norway has the giant Statoil, Austria has OMV, Finland has Neste, Sweden has Swedish Petroleum, Portugal has Petrogal, and Spain has four national petroleum firms.

Then we have the airlines: Lufthansa, KLM, Swissair, Air France, Alitalia, Japan Air Lines. Indeed, almost every modern nation, with the exception of the United States, has a national airline (the Americans have had to bail out airlines, but never owned one).

As with airlines, railways are, usually, state-owned in Europe, as they are in places like Burma, India, and Pakistan, as well as (naturally) Russia and China. Amtrak is in crowded company.

In Germany, government firms dominate energy, chemicals, aluminum, automobile manufacturing, airlines, ship repairing, oil and gas exploration, and banking. The state owns about 900 enterprises either outright or in conjunction with private partners.

In Norway, Statoil, which owns much of the North Sea development, and has dealt itself into every patch developed by other entrepreneurs, has become so rich and independent that the government has had to introduce a new law compelling it to turn over a portion of its wealth from each field to the government, instead of reinvesting it and becoming larger still.

The Italians do it with Pasta

The common factor abroad, as at home, is that government corporations have tended to be brought into being to accomplish worthy goals, and as in Canada, have developed the deplorable habit of becoming ever more independent and unaccountable.

Two of the world's largest state firms belong to Italy, and are the legacy of the Italian fascist dictator, Benito Mussolini. *Il Duce* created a series of state holding companies to carry out the government's policies prior to World War II; succeeding left-wing governments that hold his memory in contempt still use his tactics. One of his creations, IRI (Istituto per la Riconstruzione Industriale), Europe's largest non-oil enterprise, is a state-owned holding company financed by commercial borrowing, guaranteed loans, and endowment funds from the state. Since World War II its task has been to direct the strategic sectors of the Italian economy, especially steel. In form, it is not wholly a state corporation, but rather a joint enterprise, since many of its subsidiaries also have private shareholders. It is something like the Canada Development Corporation writ large, and with pizza on the side. IRI created Italy's integrated steel companies, installed its telephone system, and built most of the national expressways. Like most state enterprises, the giant firm also became the sinkhole for companies that were going broke and which politicians wanted to protect. It now consists of more than 1,000 firms, involved in banking, telecommunications, manufacturing, the steel industry, and state broadcasting. The Alfa Romeo car company is one of its holdings, along with Alitalia airlines, a number of food manufacturing firms, a railway, and even a state farm. It employs 550,000 people, and in 1984 sold $21.7 billion worth of goods and services, on which it lost almost $2.1 billion.

The company is a bit of a mess, especially its steel segment, which makes our own beleaguered steel Crowns, like Sidbec in Quebec and Sysco in Nova Scotia, look like models of thrift and decorum. Throughout its existence, IRI has been rocked by scandals, which are the norm for state firms, especially Italian state firms.

The other Italian giant is ENI (Ente Nazionale Idrocarburi), which provides more than half the nation's oil and gas supplies. It was founded in 1953 to reduce Italy's dependence on the multinational oil giants, and expanded until it owned 293 companies. With a 1985 revenue of $23.6 billion, ENI is about twice the size of Italy's largest privately owned firm, Fiat SpA. Like IRI, ENI has been burdened by a series of scandals, and pushed by politicians anxious to create jobs in their own bailiwicks (sound familiar?) into areas where it has neither skill nor experience. Franco Grassini, in *State-Owned Enterprises in the Western Economies*, says that while ENI is supposed to make money, and is designed to make money, and exhorted to make money, it never does because, "decisions . . . are made by managers for whom growth, power, salary, and personal security are often more important than profit."

I have picked out only a tiny handful from the rich selection of government enterprises available, to indicate how deeply entrenched they are in countries other than our own. The temptation to plug any hole in the economy with a government firm is well-nigh universal, especially as smaller nations see government enterprises as the only suitable alternative to having their economies overwhelmed by the multinational giants.

Vodka-Cola, and Other Wonders

While we have seen that the Americans are more modest in this regard, we ought also to be aware that their private firms are in partnership with state firms all over the world. They always have been. One of the more bizarre outgrowths of this trend was the famous Vodka-Cola deal, negotiated by Richard Nixon in 1972. Pepsi-Cola agreed to build a plant in the Soviet Union, with the Russians picking up the tab in vodka and wine because cash was in short supply. Through a new company, called Henri Wines, Pepsi was made the sole American agent for all Russian wines sold in America.

Nobody even blinked at this deal; there have been other and far more sinister ones in the past. ITT, now in a deal with France (and yes, this is the same ITT that was so notoriously active in the overthrow of the Allende regime in Chile in 1973), was heavily involved with the German government during World War II. As Anthony Sampson, in his scathing history of the company, pointed out: "While ITT Focke-Wulf planes were bombing Allied ships . . . ITT direction-finders were saving other ships from torpedoes." ITT even had the nerve to apply for, and collect, $5 million in war reparations for damages to its Focke-Wulf factory. General Motors and Ford also collected reparations from their own country for damage done to plants in Germany which were, in effect, state firms for the Reich. In 1983, a former *New York Times* reported, Charles Higham, published a book called *Trading with the Enemy* that details how such American giants as Ford, GM, ITT, RCA, Standard Oil of New Jersey, and the Chase National Bank became corporate partners with both Germany and Japan. Ideology, this time, gave way to practicality, or as Higham argues, a new ideology emerged, "the ideology of Business as Usual."

After the war, the inter-linking of public corporations with private firms became even more pronounced, until today it takes a real expert to work out who is doing what, with which, and to whom.

At this writing, Volkswagen is in the process of buying 51 per cent of Seat, which is owned by the government of Spain. At the same time, Volkswagen is working through a process of privatization at home, where government ownership of the company, once 100 per cent, will soon be down to about 10 per cent. I don't know what that makes Seat, a company famous for its Seat 600, which was designed by Fiat, the privately owned Italian firm.

Meanwhile, Volkswagen, the more-or-less German state firm has moved to China, through a subsidiary, Shanghai Volkswagen. This firm, in partnership with three Chinese state companies, is building Chinese Volkswagens in a converted tractor factory outside Shanghai. These Chinese VWs are intended to invade the Asian market in competition with the Japanese and Taiwanese. Serve them right, too.

The French state firm that owns the Paris Métro is busy expanding into Venezuela and Mexico, where it works with both government and private firms. Métro's engineering subsidiary, Société Française d'Études pour le Transport Urban (SOFRETU) has recently sold $325 million worth of equipment and engineering services in Caracas and Mexico City. It was SOFRETU that helped to construct Montreal's Métro, and it is also building subways in Rio de Janeiro, Santiago, and Cairo.

As we will see in Chapter 11, everybody is talking about privatization, but as fast as government firms are chopped off in one direction, they reappear in another. It's a little like the experience Perseus had with the Gorgon girls.

The phenomenon is universal. It occurs at home as well as in foreign countries, and indeed, nowhere in the world are there Crowns more aggressively expansive than the ones we will meet in the next chapter—the provincial hydro authorities.

5
The Light Fantastic

"I do not understand that any revelation has ever been made from Heaven to the effect that a democratic government commits an unpardonable sin when it assists in the establishment of a great and necessary public work for the well-being of the people of whose interests it is the trustee."
Sir Adam Beck, *creator of Ontario Hydro, 1911*

One of the difficulties of trying to come to grips with the provincial Crowns is that they are so sprawling, and they follow no discernible logic. You might expect that provinces with a history of left-wing governments would leak the things from every seam, while right-wing provinces would stick to private enterprise, but it isn't so. In forty-four years of Conservative rule, Ontario created 77 Crowns, including the biggest of them all, Ontario Hydro, with $29 billion in assets, 31,166 employees and $4.7 billion in annual sales. That is more than Saskatchewan (67), although the Prairie province, in three decades of socialist rule, set out consciously to enclose more and more of its economy within the government sector.

As you will see in the Appendices, the Crown champion among the provinces is Quebec, with 121, but most of these appear to have been created for nationalist reasons—to establish or maintain a distinctively Quebec approach—rather than from any inborn belief in the efficacy of government. Alberta, resolutely wedded to the doctrines of free enterprise since William Aberhart was a pup, has 45 Crowns, including its own banking system, Alberta Treasury Branches. That's one-and-a-half times the Manitoba total (30), although Manitoba has twice been ruled by socialist governments (still is, at this writing), and that province still has to bank with strangers.

Nova Scotia has almost twice as many Crowns as New Brunswick—37 to 21, but that's probably just because Nova Scotia is slightly larger. Newfoundland has an impressive 36 government corporations, presumably to make up for the fact that the private sector in that province is even less-developed than it is among its Maritime neighbours. Even tiny little Prince Edward Island, conservative to the core, has its own Crowns. Once you arrive on the island—via a Crown ferry, of course—you can stay in a Crown hotel and dine on meat prepared in a Crown packing-house, cooked in a Crown-made frying-pan, and served with a bottle of wine from the provincial Crown booze emporium. The Yukon with 2 provincial Crowns, stands as the last free enterprise bastion in the land—mostly because, like the Northwest Territories, where there are 4 Crowns—the federal government reaches in over the heads of the locals with its own batches of enterprise.

Ideology cannot explain the Crowns, but neither can hard-nosed pragmatism. If these things came to us because they made sense, why would we have provincial Crowns to run the telephone systems in Manitoba, Saskatchewan, and Alberta, but private corporations to run them everywhere else? (Well, almost everywhere else; there is a separate municipal Crown to run the phones in Thunder Bay, Ontario, and another in Edmonton, Alberta.) Ma Bell rules in Quebec and Ontario; British Columbia is serviced by a subsidiary of an American corporation; and investor-owned companies look after eastern Canada, with a little help from Canadian National Railways, which provides some of the service in Newfoundland. Then there is Quebec-Telephone, which is partly owned by the Quebec government, but mostly owned by General Telephone and Electronics, the same American firm that controls B.C. Tel. Quebec Telephone operates on the south shore of the St. Lawrence, but not in the Gaspé—that is left to another subsidiary of General, La Compagnie de Téléphone Bonaventure et Gaspé Ltée.

Telephones are what the economists call a "natural monopoly," viz., a service that can be delivered more efficiently by a single supplier than by a number of them in competition. But there is nothing that says that the single supplier has to be government-owned, or privately owned, and by most measures, there is not a hair's breadth of difference between the provincial Crowns, and say, Ma Bell, in terms of effective, cheap service. The telephone companies don't even fall under the same regulatory agencies, for pete's sake. Bell Canada and the British Columbia Telephone Company are regulated by the Canadian Radio-television and Telecommunications Commission (CRTC), a federal Crown, while the others come under the sway of provincial regulators. They all gang together for long distance through the TransCanada Telephone System. Satellite services are provided by Telesat Canada, which is partly a federal Crown and partly a private company, and overseas traffic is handled through Teleglobe Canada, which is, at this writing, a wholly owned federal Crown, which Ottawa, for reasons of its own, is dying to sell to somebody nice. And rich.

The sale of natural gas provides another "natural monopoly"; however, with two exceptions, Saskatchewan, where a left-wing government assigned the job to a provincial Crown in 1949, and British Columbia, where a right-wing government gave the Lower Fraser Valley—but not the Interior—to a Crown in 1961, gas remains in the private domain. Why should electrical energy be (mostly) public and gas and oil (mostly) private?

The Crowns of Sin

The only fields in which the provinces follow a consistent pattern have to do with sin. Every province runs its own liquor distribution system—not beer, mind you, only wine and the hard stuff. Why is this? Why should amber liquid in a 1 L bottle, with no fizz, require a provincial Crown to sell it, while amber liquid, fizzy, in a 341 mL bottle responds to the call of the free market? They will both make you drunk, and poor, but only one of them will make your government rich.

The Numbers Racket

Finally, every province, one way or another, is into a Crown lottery corporation. Sometimes they gang up, as in Atlantic Lottery, or the Western Canada Lottery Foundation, sometimes they are confined to a single province, as in the Ontario Lottery Corporation, but every one of them is into what used to be called the numbers racket. That used to earn you a quick trip to the deepest, darkest dungeon beneath the castle moat, before your government took over from the goons and got into gambling officially, instead of merely at budget time. The federal government had its own lottery corporation, too, Loto Canada, but the provinces screamed bloody murder, and got them to consent to going out of the business. (The corporation still exists, but is winding down.) The provinces' argument, although put in more high-minded terms, came down to the fact that it is better to have your pockets picked by a government close at hand than by those bums in Ottawa. Not only are the odds stacked against you in your friendly government lottery—the chances of winning one of the really big prizes are about the same as the chances of being hit, twice, by lightning—there isn't even as much of the bet available to the pool as there is at the racetrack. When you go to the track to bet the rent money on a horse that will probably sit down about half way through the home stretch to contemplate nature, you at least have the satisfaction of knowing that of every dollar wagered, about eighty-six cents is returned to the suckers— pardon, bettors. In the case of government lotteries, the return is between forty-five and fifty cents. Horse-players are smarter gamblers than lottery enthusiasts. There is no economic, pragmatic, political, or social reason why any government should be in the lottery racket, other than official greed, but every province is there, and they all use Crowns to do the dirty work. Go figure.

But if you find something to raise the eyebrows at in the way the provinces peddle booze and abet gambling, you should watch them at work operating the nation's largest corporations by far, the provincial power utilities. That's when they really get aggressive.

Shedding Light on Hydro

By far the most important, and largest, of the provincial Crowns are their power companies. Three provinces— Newfoundland, Prince Edward Island, and Alberta—use private companies to distribute electricity; everywhere else, generation, transmission, and sale are all in the hands of provincial Crowns. The largest of these, and the one that will help us to understand how these things work in practice, as opposed to the textbook theory that has them portrayed as the innocent handmaidens of government, is Ontario Hydro.

If you will cast your mind back to 1906—high collars, buggies on the street, King Edward on the throne, and Roald Amundsen has just made the first trip through the Northwest Passage, remember?—you may recall that there was a Grand March on April 11 through the streets of Toronto, from City Hall to Queen's Park. More than 1,500 people, a considerable crowd in those days, joined in the march, wearing badges, and carrying signs that said, "Cheap Power." They were pretty damn mad and they wanted Tory Premier James P. Whitney to know about it. They thought that, along with the rest of the province, they were about to be hornswoggled by one of two groups then wrestling for control of electric power from Niagara Falls. And they were right.

Electric power was the coming thing. J.P. Morgan's American Electric and Illuminating Company had been selling generators in Canada since 1878, and Thomas Edison had installed incandescent light in a factory on Craig Street in Toronto in 1879. But it was still coal that drove the engines of industry; indeed, electricity was known, for a time, as "white coal." However, you couldn't count on coal. In 1902 there had been a disastrous and bloody strike in the Pennsylvania coalfields (run by that same J.P. Morgan), and a "coal famine" that shot the price up from $2.50 a ton to $10 a ton. All over Ontario, factories closed, and people were thrown out of work because of events beyond the border. It wouldn't do, and if electric power could help the province out of that bind, Ontario was in favour.

The difficulty was that there were two syndicates vying for control of Niagara Falls' hydro. One, the Ontario Power

Company was, in fact, controlled by J.P. Morgan (the rascal was everywhere), while the other was Canadian, the Electric Development Company. Its backers were William Mackenzie (of the duo of Mackenzie and Mann; he was a failed railway baron from the days of the Canadian Northern), Frederick Nicholls, an electrical equipment manufacturer, and Henry M. Pellatt, the financier who built Casa Loma in Toronto.

Both groups made the general citizenry nervous; what would happen if either got a monopoly on electricity? Well, they knew the answer to that one; they would jack up prices and control Ontario's industrial development. A number of municipal leaders began to suggest that public ownership of the transmission lines would be one way out of this difficulty. No one suggested public ownership of the resource itself. At a meeting in Berlin, (now Kitchener) Ontario, Alderman F.S. Spence of Toronto spoke at great length and with some eloquence of the twin evils of monopoly power and alcoholic beverages. In the audience was Adam Beck, a cigar-box manufacturer from London, Ontario, who had parlayed an eloquent tongue and aggressive manner into the twin jobs of mayor of London and Conservative member of the provincial Parliament. Beck did not go along with Spence on the subject of booze, but he did agree with Spence's argument that there ought to be "a government Commission . . . preventing the power from falling into the hands of any monopoly and in this way securing to the industries of this province advantages of cheap electric energy."

Adam Beck was a Character

Adam Beck was an interesting character, one of those strong, noisy types, not unlike C.D. Howe, who blossom in private enterprise, and who upon somehow finding themselves in government, go on running things as if a government enterprise was a cigar-box factory. Beck threw himself into the battle for cheap power with characteristic energy, and launched a speaking campaign to promise new industry to the province, and new convenience for home and farm. There was another angle to the argument as well. If an

American monopoly controlled Ontario energy, that would
be bad, but would it be any better if a monopoly from
Toronto—hated Hogtown, even then—got its fingers around
the provincial throat?

The Liberal government of George Ross initially refused
to consider any government involvement with Niagara. Then
as the clamour rose, Ross decided to take the usual course
and appointed a commission of inquiry to look into the
subject. Before it could report, in 1906, the Ross government was out and a Conservative government under James
Whitney was in. Whitney made Beck a Minister Without
Portfolio, and set up another commission of inquiry into
hydro, with Beck as its chairman. Moving fast—he already
knew the answers, so there was no need to dawdle over the
collection of facts—Beck brought back his report at the
same time as the Ross-appointed commission, in March,
1906. The Ross bunch suggested a municipal co-operative
to build and own transmission lines; Beck suggested a provincial hydro-electric commission with the power not only
to build transmission lines, but to regulate private companies.

In case his own government hung modestly back from
taking the plunge, Beck helped to stage the Grand March
on April 11, 1906, which we joined above, and that outburst
of spontaneous zeal persuaded Premier Whitney to act on
his report. On May 7, 1906, the Hydro-Electric Power Commission of Ontario (the name was changed to Ontario Hydro in March, 1974) was formed as a provincial corporation,
with Adam Beck as its first chairman. It had a motto, *Dona
Naturae Pro Populo Sunt* ("The gifts of Nature are for the
people"), a mandate, to transmit and regulate electric power,
and a chairman who was, to put it mildly, hell on wheels.
It's my own view that if Beck had been on Henry Pellatt's
team, Ontario Hydro would be a private company today,
although I don't suppose they could run the thing out of
Casa Loma.

Under Beck's prodding, Ontario Hydro grew by leaps
and bounds from a small distribution company delivering
2,000 kilowatts of power to ten municipalities in 1910 to
one of the world's largest hydro-electric empires, delivering
250,000 kilowatts a mere seven years later. From the beginning, the chairman ran the commission as his personal
fiefdom. "In Beck's view," writes H.V. Nelles, in *The Politics*

of Development, "the functions of government would be limited to empowering the commission, supplying it with unlimited credit, and providing it with the weight of its legal sovereignty when the occasion demanded."

To promote Hydro, Beck established the Hydro Circus, which visited rural communities and county fairs in the summer of 1912, and spent $30,000 that no one seemed to have approved. Between 1911 and 1915, Hydro spent over $4 million more than the legislature authorized—and annual audits thereafter failed to bring the spending under control. By 1919, one generating project, budgetted for $20 million, had consumed $50 million on the way to a final price-tag of $80 million.

It was the Crown corporation form of organization that allowed—and still allows—Ontario Hydro to do pretty much what it pleases. That form was adopted for reasons which have now become rote: to allow the industry to be run on a businesslike basis; to keep Hydro at arm's length from "meddlesome politicians," as Beck said; and "to keep Hydro out of politics," to quote Beck again. In fact, the most meddlesome politician attached to Hydro was Beck, and Hydro never kept out of politics. Beck organized marches on the legislature to promote his schemes, secretly subsidized two pro-Hydro pressure groups, and actively supported the Whitney government in the election of 1914. He was rewarded for this support with a knighthood. The ultimate tribute to his political stature was paid when the United Farmers of Ontario came into office and offered Beck the premiership. He refused. Why should he give up control?

Beck conceived the notion of block buying of electricity, rewarding large customers with lower rates. The business thus generated justified ever-expanding expenditures. By 1923, Hydro accounted for half the provincial debt (as it does today), had become the largest utility in the world, and its construction projects alone were having a major impact on the provincial economy.

Nothing was too big for Beck

Beck wanted more; he wanted a "Greater Hydro" to control not only power, but telephones, gas, and water services, and a network of radial railways powered by electricity. "Nothing is too big for us," he said, "Nothing is too expensive to imagine. Nothing is visionary."

One of the daffier of Beck's schemes was the notion of a network of electric railways for the province. He got pushed into the idea because Hydro was now the proud possessor of more power than it could sell. Beck unleashed another lobby on the legislature, which dutifully passed legislation under which Ontario Hydro would build and operate the trains on behalf of municipalities. There were those who jibbed at the cost—first estimated at $30 million—and wondered about the need, what with cars coming on so fast, to say nothing of the fact that other, non-electrical railways were already sprouting up like weeds. But what Adam wanted, Adam got; a monopoly on the "radials," as they were called, and the promise of subsidies of $3,500 a mile for construction. The real opposition came from the city of Toronto, which balked at giving up control of its streets to Beck's trains. He attempted to get around this by offering to buy out the Toronto Street Railway Company, but the city refused to sell.

The intervention of World War I slowed down the construction of the radials, and a change of government killed them. A United Farmers government, now in power in the province, appointed a royal commission to look into the scheme. The commission reported that the final cost would be $45 million, not $25 million, and that, because of the growing popularity of the automobile, the radials would run empty. Using Hydro funds, Beck promptly brought out a forty-two page booklet rejecting the commission's findings and attacking the commissioners' competence. The government, for once, refused to bend the knee; funding dried up and the radials died. Still, the feeling remained that, as Lawrence Solomon wrote in *Energy Shock*, "Ontario Hydro had gone out of control, expanding on all fronts at an incredible rate, acting like a sovereign state, running roughshod over other institutions and over local communities. Yet the organization, a juggernaut oblivious to all around it, had too much momentum to be easily slowed down."

It wasn't even slowed down by the death of its remarkable founding chairman in 1925. On his deathbed, Beck said,

"I had hoped to live to forge a band of iron around the Hydro to prevent its destruction by politicians." He builded better than he knew; politicians haven't been able to do much with it, for good or ill, from that day to this. Within months of Beck's death, his successor, Charles McGrath, convinced the new Conservative government that Ontario faced an imminent power shortage, and ruin. (The theme recurs.) So the cabinet authorized the signing of a series of contracts to purchase power from private Quebec companies, and from Abitibi, a private paper company then building a hydro site in northern Ontario. These deals were hammered into place just about in time for the Depression, which knocked Hydro's projections out of whack and left the province with an enormous power surplus. And with the bills.

Hepburn to the Rescue

Then there were the scandals. A Conservative party fund-raiser was discovered to have taken a bribe in return for steering a power contract to one of the Quebec firms, and both the Ontario premier and a leading Hydro commissioner were discovered to own stock in Abitibi. That became all the worse when the Abitibi subsidiary that was building the northern project collapsed, and Hydro was stuck with it, at $18 million. The Liberals, under Mitch Hepburn, promised a "clean up" of Hydro in the 1934 election, to which Hydro replied with a series of pamphlets that attacked the Liberals and attempted to show that they were in the pocket of "private power interests." If they were, Hydro couldn't prove it, not even when it hired a private detective to tail Liberal leaders, including Hepburn.

The Liberals won the 1934 election, fired the Hydro commissioners, and set up a royal commission which exposed the active role Hydro had played in the election—and in spying. Hepburn then cancelled the Quebec power contracts. The government was going to run things, by golly. No, it wasn't. By 1937, Hydro had discovered a new impending shortage of electricity, and the Quebec contracts were hastily restored. That was in the fall of 1937; by winter, there was another glut, and by spring, Ontario was promoting electricity exports to the United States to absorb the surplus that had been created because Hydro was sure there was going to be a shortage.

Sound familiar? It ought to. The cycle has repeated itself endlessly ever since. Ontario Hydro is in the business of selling electricity, and it has promoted that business with unrelenting ferocity from the beginning. First, Hydro announces an impending shortage, and with that established, goes out and builds more power-plants; then, before the plants can be completed, we discover that there will be a surplus. Hydro then makes a deal to sell the surplus abroad, thereby creating another paper shortage, which in turn is used to justify the building of more power-plants.

But there is nothing new in this. Adam Beck would recognize the technique at once, and so would all his descendants. Between 1922 and 1951, Ontario's electrical grid grew at the rate of 7 per cent per annum—a doubling every ten years. By 1951, it was clear that hydro power alone could not provide the needed energy, so first coal, and then oil, and then nuclear sources were tapped to feed demand— a demand that was certainly real, but which, whenever it showed signs of flagging, Hydro stimulated with programmes like its "Live Better Electrically" campaign.

Sisters of the Skillet Flogged Electricity

This was set off by the arrival of natural gas via pipeline from the West, which threatened to take over the water-heating and electric-cooking segment of the market. Hydro's sales department responded with a "National Electric Week" and a display at the National Home Show in 1958, featuring a Gold Medallion Home crammed with a "galaxy of appliances." We had a "Sisters of the Skillet" cherry-pie contest, and the "Academy of Lighting Arts," which taught the theory, application, and sales of residential lighting.

In co-operation with the electrical manufacturers and the public utilities commissions of Ontario cities, Hydro pushed the electric way of life as the only true-blue Canadian way. School home economics classrooms were festooned with free "appliance packages" and thousands of new jobs were created to build and sell the appliances. By 1961, four out of every five Ontario homes had electric lighting, refrigerators, stoves, washing-machines, and televisions. Then Hydro really got rolling, with a campaign to persuade Ontarians to eschew gas water-heaters—which would heat water five times as fast as an equivalent electrical unit—by dropping the electricity rates, even though these were not enough as it was to cover the cost of building the plants that were required to meet the demand that had just been created.

I'm not making any of this up.

Electric heating became the "completely modern" way to go; only louts allowed themselves to be warmed by what one Hydro press release described as "some form of fire contained in a stove or furnace." By 1970, electric heating was being installed in one out of every four new houses built in the province. Hydro went into a frenzy of salesmanship, all paid for by the captive consumer, and launched a massive public relations campaign designed to "assist the Hydro Family to build a reservoir of good will, develop a defence against attacks, and expand the sale of electricity."

Nobody asked, Do we want to expand the sale of electricity? Or should we be promoting electricity to heat water and homes when natural gas is more efficient? These are the kinds of questions governments ought to ask. But Hydro was not a government—it was a corporation, and behaved as such.

It was not until the energy crises of 1973 and 1979 that Hydro began to push conservation and to urge people to cut back on use of the electricity it had been pushing at them for decades. By that time it was too late; the corporation had held costs down to encourage consumption, and now it was stuck with the costs. No matter, they were passed along to the consumers as rate increases while Hydro flexes its muscles to build newer, bigger, and more expensive facilities.

If you think about it, it is a perfectly natural thing for any corporation to try to increase its market, and a Crown corporation reacts just as any other corporation would. The difficulty is that it is not just any other corporation; it has a bottomless pit of funds to draw on in the form of provincial guarantees for its loans. It also has the ability to pass on increased costs to consumers in a captive market. Money borrowed by Hydro dries up the funds for other pur-

poses—or threatens the province's credit line—and fore-
closes other options.

Looking at Hydro's performance during the 1950s and
1960s, decades which were devoted to relentless expansion,
"the electric home," rebates for massive use of power, and
other wonders, it seems little short of insanity; but from a
corporate point of view—more jobs, promotions, bigger
expense accounts—it makes perfect sense. We are left to
wonder what is the purpose of a corporate philosophy di-
recting a provincial economy, and the answer to that is,
none at all. It's just the way it is.

As I write this, the Ontario government has decided to
proceed with the completion of an $11 billion nuclear fa-
cility at Darlington. And this is despite the fact that the
legislative committee which made the recommendation to
go ahead also noted, along the way, that Ontario Hydro
had overestimated the peak demand for electricity by almost three times, and may not even require the power from
Darlington, which will be completed in 1992, until well into
the twenty-first century. Then, what the hell will they do
with the extra power? Sell it, silly, to the Americans. Hydro
peddled $2.06 billion worth of power to the Americans in
the period 1981–85. You get the neatness of this? First,
there is the mistaken projection, which creates the need for
a giant new plant; then the sale of power, which takes off
at least some of the surplus, and creates another new demand.

The Liberals, who now form the government, opposed
Darlington when they were in opposition, on the sound
grounds that it wasn't required. Nuts to that, said the Liberals, we've been this road before. However, once in power,
they discovered that the province "couldn't afford" to moth-
ball the project because so much money had already been
spent. Between the time the Liberals took power in 1985,
determined to can Darlington, and the time they made a
final decision on the project in mid-1986, more than $2
billion had been spent, on top of the $7 million previously
committed. Wouldn't want to waste that, would we? So Darlington is to go ahead after all. This is known as creating
policy to fit the hardware a Crown corporation has contracted to purchase, and hoping for the best. Adam Beck
would approve.

And yet—this is the part I like best—the Lennox Generating Station near Kingston, Ontario, which was built in the 1970s for $500 million, *was* mothballed by Hydro because there is no demand for its output. Hydro estimates the 2,000 megawatt station will not be required until 1990 at the earliest, and then for only about 5 per cent of the time. Not that Lennox is the only plant in mothballs; there are three other fossil fuel generating stations described in the corporation's annual report as "non-operating reserve facilities," along with a heavy water plant which cost $237 million to build, and which has been benched until further notice. In all, Hydro has $1.03 billion in assets sitting idle and, at the end of 1985, had already written these down by $611 million in depreciation. So you can see why the boys need a few more billions with which to put up new plants.

These expenditures are bound to affect all public policy in the province. Hydro's annual report for fiscal 1985 shows long-term debt of $22.5 billion (up from $13.6 billion four years earlier; a jump of 65 per cent), and interest payments of $2.5 billion a year ate up more than half its total revenues of $4.6 billion. It lost another $176 million in foreign exchange—to pay interest on money borrowed abroad—and capitalized another $1.16 billion in interest. In all, more than three-quarters of its annual revenues were swallowed up by interest charges. But that isn't the only impact of its spending spree. The province has guaranteed $10.1 billion in debt, most of it on behalf of Hydro, and the combination caused Standard and Poor to put both the province and Hydro on a "credit watch with negative implications" in 1986. Hydro officials said at the time that "there's no evidence that Hydro's borrowing has affected the province's credit rating," although how it could *not* affect the province's credit rating, since the province would certainly have to pony up if Hydro got into trouble, is one of those impenetrable mysteries, like why does the Sphinx smile?

To put this in perspective, consider that Ontario's total budgetary expenditures in 1985 came to $26.4 billion, and its net debt was $22.8 billion at the end of that year. A single Crown corporation owes almost as much as the entire province, and the province, in addition to guaranteeing

Hydro's bonds, owns $7.19 billion of them in its own right. How can the province escape the financial implications of the actions of its creation?

Because so much of Hydro's borrowing constitutes foreign debt—American, in large part—it has to be paid back in currencies rising against our own. All of these costs will have to be met either by raising rates rapidly, or passing the debt on to a future generation. This means that the decisions Hydro made when it was pushing happy housewives into electric homes will not only affect government policy today, but for years to come.

Is Hydro worried? You bet. It's afraid it may not be building fast enough; the 1985 annual report begins with one of those neat coloured charts that depicts "Planned Generation vs. Most Probable Load Growth," and, sure enough, it shows that in the year 2005, Ontario will need 40,000 megawatts of power, but only have the capacity to produce 34,000. Great scott! Call in the bulldozers, shut down the hospitals, and convert the funds to more hydro stations before it's too late! With any luck, the entire Ontario budget can be consumed in power projects and the interest thereon.

The Quebec Case

Outsiders seldom get a chance to see how decisions made by a Crown corporation can determine the entire budgetary policy of a government, but economist Eric Kierans, who was Minister of Revenue in the Province of Quebec, tells a revealing story. Hydro-Québec was formed in 1963, as part of the Quiet Revolution. Montreal Heat, Light and Power and Beauharnois, Heat, Light and Power, the major suppliers of electricity to Montreal, had been nationalized in 1944, but the rest of the province was served by private companies. There was some resentment against "les grands trusts"—English-owned—which were suspected of making large profits at the expense of French consumers, but that wasn't the key point in the takeover. It was the fact that, as we know, Crown corporations don't have to pay taxes; in 1961, Quebeckers paid $20 million into Ottawa's coffers as a tax on the power sold through private power companies. There was no such levy in Ontario. The result was that nationalization of the power companies became a central plank in the Quebec Liberal election platform of 1962. René Lévesque, then a Liberal, and then Minister of Natural Resources, pushed through the nationalization bill, and Hydro-Québec was born. In 1965, when Kierans was drawing up provincial requirements for the next year, he decided that the most the province could afford to borrow was $500 million, of which about half would be required for Hydro-Québec and the other half for all other purposes. Anything more than that, he feared, would strain the province's credit rating. Premier Jean Lesage accepted this, and the decision was made and communicated to Hydro-Québec. Hydro-Québec replied that, well, you see, it planned to borrow $500 million itself. It was told to change its plans; $250 million was the maximum. Certainly, said Hydro-Québec, what could be fairer than that? After all, the government was boss. There was just one little thing; in these circumstances, it would not be possible to begin the construction of a mammoth dam in northern Quebec, which had already been announced, and the jobs for which might prove to have some political importance. Um, ah, said Kierans and Lesage. Hydro-Québec got its way and the provincial budget was redrawn accordingly.

We will see this tail-wags-the-dog phenomenon come to full fruition when we look at Ontario Hydro's joint venture with another Crown corporation, Atomic Energy of Canada Ltd. in the next chapter.

6
Power, Inc.

"The reactors aren't the easiest things to market. One Atomic Energy salesman has made nineteen trips to Turkey in an attempt to sell a CANDU to that country and he still hasn't come close to a deal."
Toronto Star, *April 28, 1984*

On the morning of May 16, 1930, prospector Gilbert LaBine was checking outcroppings on the shore of Great Slave Lake in the Northwest Territories, when, "I noticed a great wall there that was stained with cobalt bloom and copper green. . . . Following along, I found a tiny piece of dark ore, probably the size of a large plum. Looking more closely, I found the vein. I chipped it off with my hammer, and there it was—pitchblende."

It kind of wrecks the story to point out that LaBine wasn't looking for pitchblende; he was looking for gold, or silver, or anything to keep going Eldorado Gold Mines, the company he and his brother Charles had started in 1925. They had poured half a million dollars of borrowed money into a gold claim in Manitoba, but failed to develop anything worth exploiting, so Gilbert's trip to Great Slave Lake was a last roll of the dice. But if he wasn't looking for pitchblende, the ore in which radium and uranium are bound together with silver, he certainly knew what he had found. Uranium wasn't all that exciting. In those days it was used, in pigments, ceramic glazes, and fluorescent glass; but radium had been used in medicine since its isolation by Marie Curie in 1898. It was worth far more than gold. And silver is always nice.

The LaBines set up a new company, Eldorado Mining and Refining (El Dorado was the legendary city of gold the Spaniards kept murdering South American Indians for), built a mine and mill on the shores of Great Bear Lake, in the new town of Port Radium, and shipped the concentrates 4,400 miles to Port Hope, Ontario. Here they were refined into lumps of radium, uranium, and silver. Not that it did the LaBines a whole lot of good; there was only one ounce of pure radium produced by 1936, along with tons of uranium oxide, which was going for about $1.50 a pound on the market—when it could be sold. The uranium was stockpiled at Port Hope, and in 1940, the mine was closed down and allowed to fill with water. Not to worry, the LaBines, unwittingly—history is like that—were going to show Ontario Hydro (whom we left in the last chapter building power-plants fit to bust) how to really spend money.

When World War II began, scientists all over the world were working on nuclear fission, which could, in theory, produce an atomic bomb. You bombarded uranium atoms with fast neutrons, and that split more atoms, which split more, until you had a chain reaction and, first thing you know, a hell of a bang. The Americans, with a group of international scientists, were working on the Manhattan Project in Chicago, while a group of British scientists had set themselves up in Montreal to work with specialists from McGill on the atom.

The major known supplies of uranium were in the Belgian Congo and at Eldorado, so pretty soon things were humming at Radium City again. (The first shipment of sixty tons to the Manhattan Project in Chicago didn't have to be dug out of the ground; it was already sitting in the Port Hope stockpile.) Eldorado made a deal to sell all its output to the U.S. Army Corps of Engineers, and that made the British, and many Canadians, furious. Even before an atomic bomb had been exploded, it was clear that fission could be used to produce peaceful energy. All you had to do was to slow the atomic reaction down so that it wouldn't produce a bang, merely a huge amount of heat. If the Americans hogged it all, they would control the major source of postwar energy.

After much pushing and shoving, a deal was struck through which research and information would be shared among the Allies. But how was Canada to keep control over the uranium? The sensible thing seemed to be to take over Eldorado. The federal government's minister-of-all-things, C.D. Howe, did just that, paying the shareholders $5 million, which was slightly more than the market value for the shares. Howe then established a Crown corporation, Eldorado Nuclear Limited. When he made the announcement to the House of Commons on January 28, 1944, Howe said, "In the interest of military secrecy I hope that no questions about this matter will be asked." The last eleven words were to become the watchword of the nuclear industry.

Enter the "Friendly Atom"

Canada's nuclear research programme was originally operated by Defence Research Limited. Acting for the National Research Council, the company ran two reactors at Chalk River, Ontario, on the Ottawa River. These reactors, NRX and NRU, used heavy water not only to moderate the reaction, but also as a coolant; they were Canadian Deuterium-Uranium reactors or, in an acronym that would become famous in song and story, CANDUs.

At war's end, the government established the Atomic Energy Control Board (AECB) to regulate the nuclear industry, and the board took charge of the Chalk River projects. Although the AECB was a Crown corporation, it was essentially a regulator. When it became clear that the nuclear industry was going to be a huge commercial one— sprouting uranium mines and rich ore contracts with the United States—the decision was taken to form another Crown to conduct research, acquire production facilities, and "sell or otherwise dispose of" atomic discoveries, inventions, and processes. We were going into business for ourselves. We had already begun to sell the Americans plutonium, which is one of the end-products of the reactions inside a CANDU, and which provides the core material for atomic bombs.

The new company, Atomic Energy of Canada Ltd., (AECL), was formed under the Companies Act on February 14, 1952. It was a Schedule C Crown, which is to say, "quasi commercial," while the AECB is Schedule B, a "departmental corporation," reporting through the Energy Department. In law, AECL was supposed to report through the AECB, but it never did. The company was always far more dominant than the board, and in 1954, the law was changed to allow it to report directly to the minister.

What happened to AECL was that it shifted its emphasis from research and development—although it still has such a division—and went into the selling game. Mostly, it sells reactors, and heavy water to go with the reactors, and technology to sort it all out. But you couldn't call it a really successful salesman. Since 1952, AECL has gobbled up more than $3 billion in subsidies. However, since these subsidies show as income in parliamentary appropriations, a casual glance at the company's annual reports could lead you to think the company makes money. It doesn't; oh, my, no.

Throughout most of its early existence, AECL's only customer for reactors was Ontario Hydro. Thanks to its aggressive sales tactics, Hydo had run out of rivers to dam, yet still couldn't provide the electricity for which it had created-a market, unless—a roll of drums, please—it could harness what was then called "the friendly atom." At the time, this route seemed the intelligent and responsible way to go, although when all is said and done, a CANDU reactor is nothing more than an elaborate, expensive, and potentially dangerous way to boil water.

It works like this. The reactor core, contained within a large cylinder called the calandria, is set on its side and filled with heavy water (deuterium), which serves as a moderator in enhancing the atom-smashing process. Pressurized tubes containing uranium fuel bundles run through the core, and when the reactor is operating, more heavy water is pumped through the tubes. The uranium fuel consists of a high concentration of U235 atoms, which are unstable and tend to fly apart, as opposed to the more tranquil U238 atoms, which are not readily fissionable. Inside the uranium tubes, the radioactive material gives off tremendous heat from the disintegration of its atoms, and this heat is absorbed by the water being pumped through. This water is then circulated through boilers, where its heat is transferred to ordinary water, which boils, thereby producing steam. The steam is used to drive turbines, which produce electricity. There are many ways to drive turbines; falling water will do it, as at Niagara Falls, or you can produce steam by burning oil, or gas, or coal. The big advantage of the nuclear reactor is that it is—when it is working right—enormously efficient, and can produce more steam, and thus more electricity, for less money than any other method yet known.

It has a slight disadvantage, however, which J.W. Beare of the Atomic Energy Control Board once captured in a rivetting quote in an AECB booklet called "Nuclear Safety and All That":

The worst possible accident at a site like Pickering might result in several thousand deaths, tens of thousands of injuries, and billions of dollars in property damage. In short, a disaster.

Why should we court a disaster in order to boil water? Well, no one thought of it in those terms when nuclear energy was making its bold beginning, any more than anyone ever thought of what we would do with the deadly radioactive waste. ("Somebody will think of something," is what they said forty years ago; they're still saying it.)

In the glorious springtime of AECL, what mattered was that a CANDU, although costly to build and even more costly to supply with uranium and heavy water, would pay for itself, and more, in electricity. The Ontario Hydro reactors at Pickering produce 4,000 megawatts of power, more than twice the capacity of the Saunders-Moses complex at Niagara Falls. Consequently, AECL officials contend that the $3 billion invested in CANDUs should be offset against what they reckon to be $5 billion that Ontario might otherwise have spent importing coal to produce the same power.

To move Canada into the nuclear age, Ontario Hydro and AECL combined in 1954 in a study team to plan construction of a 20-megawatt Nuclear Power Demonstration (NPD) reactor at Rolphton, Ont., to prove the feasibility of the process. This reactor was not expected to produce electricity on a competitive basis, merely to find out whether the trick could be done. However, the pressure from Ontario Hydro to get something going before the lights went out, or imported coal priced the province into the poorhouse, led to what was called "leapfrogging technology." That is, before we knew that the NPD would work, another reactor, first slated at 100 megawatts, then doubled to 200 megawatts, was approved. It would be built at Douglas Point, Ontario, and feed directly into the Ontario Hydro network. At the time, no one of importance wondered what sense it made to undertake a four-year project to check out the process and, while it was still in the early stages of construction, start building another project, ten times the size, on the assumption that the first one would pass muster.

The Costs—Sound Familiar?—Soared

It was a time of great faith in technicians; besides, there was a slowdown at new uranium mines, such as the one at Elliot Lake, and one of the objects of the exercise, as Trade Minister Gordon Churchill told the House of Commons, was "to expand the civil market, both domestic and foreign, for Canadian uranium."

Douglas Point was supposed to cost $13.5 million, last thirty to forty years, and make money. It cost $81.5 million, was mothballed after seventeen years, and lost money. But that was all in the future. At the time, all we got was the good news, as Hydro and AECL pushed ahead with reactors which were, we were assured—and still are assured—safe, cheap, and reliable. The taped propaganda film at Hydro's Pickering Visitors' Centre chimes, "Nuclear power is a marvellous new boon to mankind . . . an energy source that is clean, cheap, reliable, and safe." Three Mile Island and Chernobyl are not mentioned. It was not until an Ontario legislative committee got its hands on background documents in 1980 that Canadians discovered that none of Ontario's nuclear stations, at Rolphton, Douglas Point, Pickering, or Bruce,* have met the safety system standards under

---

* As of early 1987, Hydro has reactors in four Ontario locations. It has a small pilot plant at Rolphton, on the Ottawa river, built in 1962; a mothballed facility at Douglas Point, on Lake Huron; two facilities, Bruce A and B, which will eventually have eight CANDUs in operation, also on Lake Huron, just north of Douglas Point, and two facilities, Pickering A and B, at Pickering, on Lake Ontario, just east of Toronto. There are eight units between the two facilities. A four-unit plant is scheduled for Darlington, east of Pickering and again on Lake Ontario; its first units are scheduled for completion in 1988 and 1989.

which their licences were granted. It was not until 1985, when secret minutes of AECB meetings became available, that Canadians learned that the four reactors in the Bruce system—the world's largest—had been operating for eight years with a safety system the regulatory board described as "inadequate." The board recommended that Bruce be run at only 65 per cent of capacity—which would, incidentally, make a hash of its finances—until an adequate system could be installed, and then turned around and allowed capacities of first 88 per cent and then 92 per cent.

CANDU Goes Calling

Long before safety issues came along to bedevil the nuclear industry, AECL and Ontario Hydro had committed themselves to the programme. They were given a job to do—in Hydro's case, to market power, in AECL's case, to market nuclear facilities—and they kept on doing it as aggressively, as persistently and as single-mindedly as any private corporation might push computers or Cabbage-Patch dolls. In 1966, Hydro produced projections—long since abandoned—requiring a new Pickering-size reactor to be built every year between 1970 and 1980. In 1974, the ante had been raised; now, within twenty years, the province would require twenty-four "energy centres" each generating six times the electricity of Niagara Falls. Otherwise, the lights would dim across Ontario.

To fuel the nuclear wonders, Hydro signed contracts with two private companies to buy almost 200 million pounds of uranium. The contracts would cost between $6 and $7 billion, depending on the world price, and would guarantee the two firms a minimum of $1 billion in profits. It's hard to imagine any private firm signing a deal whereby a supplier would be guaranteed an optimum price and a fixed profit no matter what happened. For a Crown, such a deal presented no problem; the taxpayer's pocket has no bottom.

When nuclear growth skidded to a halt and uranium became a drug on the market, it suddenly appeared that Ontario Hydro, in moving to assure long-term supplies of uranium based on its own growth projections, had made a little boo-boo. By 1985, Hydro was paying $90 a pound for uranium, when the world price was $20. Moreover, Hydro was projecting a surplus of uranium on hand, under existing delivery contracts, worth $2.8 billion by the end of this century. Not to worry, consumers will pay it. They have no choice. Or maybe the stuff can be sold to somebody else.

(Incidentally, the innocent who goes looking for this overhanging debt in Hydro's annual report is in for a tough time. There is a note in the financial summary referring to "contingencies," but it has no dollar figure attached to it. The footnotes contain an item that says, "Commencing in 1994 through 2012, contracted deliveries exceed requirements of the nuclear generating facilities currently in service and under construction by approximately 900 megagrams per year." Translation: We blew it. The accountants attach no dollar figure to this oversight, because as their report notes, "the financial implications . . . are not determinable.")

But if Hydro was pushing power, AECL was pushing CANDUs, not only at home—a limited market, after all, even with Hydro's boyish enthusiasm to account for—but abroad. The CANDU had an enormous advantage over the American reactors that were its chief competitors in the early days; that is, it used heavy water and ordinary uranium. The American system didn't require heavy water, which made it cheaper to install in the first place, but it required enriched uranium (i.e., uranium with a higher percentage of fissionable U235 among the ordinary U238 atoms) to operate. The trouble was that while ordinary uranium is found in many places around the world, enriched uranium must be manufactured. To get it, you could either build your own plants, at $2 billion a pop, or buy it from the Americans. Most foreign nations did not want to bind themselves to an American supplier, so it looked for a time as though Canada was going to lead the pack in nuclear sales.

Heavy Water, Heavy Bills

Then there were the heavy water plants. If we were going to go the CANDU way, we had to have deuterium, not only for our own needs, but for all those lovely units we would sell abroad. So AECL entered into an arrangement to buy heavy water from a factory that was to be built in Nova Scotia, with a little help from Industrial Estates Limited, a provincial Crown. This plant, at Glace Bay, would explore a new technique invented by an American, Jerome Spevack, that used sea water. It was, not to put too fine a point on it, a disaster, and Industrial Estates Limited had to take the whole thing over and run it as a Crown corporation. Losing, I need hardly add, money with every barrel produced. Still, there were all those CANDUs coming, so another plant was built, at Port Hawkesbury, and AECL undertook to buy all its output, too.

When it began to dawn on the world that the friendly atom was not so friendly after all, and nuclear sales went into a tailspin, there were still those contracts to buy heavy water. The sensible course—and the course that would have certainly been followed by any private firm—would have been to cut the losses and close the plants. But the plants represented jobs in a province desperate for work; not insignificantly, they represented jobs in the fiefdom of Allan MacEachen, the Nova Scotian clan chief and cabinet minister. So the heavy water kept piling up, $100 million worth of it every year. (We will hear more of this in Chapter 11.) It was not until 1985, after the Conservatives took over in Ottawa, that the decision was taken to stop storing the stuff. Word was beginning to seep out that we were not, after all, going to get rich selling CANDUs to the world.

How We Gave India the Bomb

Heaven knows we went at the business greedily enough, and that is how we came to give India the bomb. It all began quite innocently, when we donated a CANDU to India for research purposes—and to show off our system—in 1956. No safeguards were attached to that reactor, called CIR, for Canada-India Reactor, because no one realized its potential. Then, in 1964, India built a plant that would allow it to extract the plutonium from the spent fuel in the CIR, and make a bomb. That set off a jangle of alarms, but no action, not even when India announced solemnly that it would not sign the Nuclear Non-Proliferation Treaty.

Now it was clear to even the dimmest intellect that India was going to build a bomb, and Pakistan, which had been at war with its neighbour three times in seventeen years, made forceful complaints to Canada. We brushed them off and sold—no gift this time—two more CANDUs to India, called RAPPI and RAPPII, for the site at Rana Pratrap Sagar.

During the RAPP negotiations, a quarrel erupted among the Canadians who wanted more safeguards and those who wanted to see the CANDU sold, and to hell with safeguards. The salesmen won. The RAPP deal called for safeguards to be overseen by the International Atomic Energy Agency. So far, so good, except that the agreement contained no enforcement provisions, and no punishment for violations.

In 1971, when Prime Minister Pierre Trudeau stopped off in Pakistan en route to a Commonwealth Conference, President Yahya Khan told him that India was making a bomb with Canadian technology. Trudeau told him not to worry; however, when Trudeau returned to Ottawa, he fired off a letter to Prime Minister Indira Gandhi, expressing his "concern" on the subject. She told him politely but firmly to buzz off.

Finally, on May 18, 1974, India set off an atomic explosion and, yup, it turned out that the material for it came out of good old CANDU. External Affairs Minister Mitchell Sharp called it "most regrettable." It came as something of a shock to Canadians, because all of this stuff was done under wraps, but that didn't stop AECL from trying to sell more CANDUs. Our next customer was Pakistan, then, and now, in the throes of upheaval. Then came South Korea, whose leader was a paranoid dictator, followed by Argentina, then in the midst of its war with Great Britain over the Falkland Islands. Argentina was interested in our CANDUs because it was working on a uranium separation plant, a necessary step for bomb making.

When you raise the issue of CANDU sales with AECL officials, they get quite huffy. A senior sales official told me, "The Canadian taxpayer has spent all this money and if he can get it back, he deserves it. . . . If we don't sell these reactors, you can be damn sure somebody else will, and maybe even under worse conditions."

I told him I could hear the same argument from the gun

dealer who sells Saturday night specials to bank robbers, but at least the gun dealer is in private enterprise, and doesn't need government funding.

The gotta-make-a-buck argument would have a sharper point if we did, in fact, make money on our CANDU sales, but as far as I can tell, they're all loss-leaders. As we have already seen in Chapter 2, we had to use bribes to unload CANDUs in South Korea and Argentina. In addition, when the details came to light on the Argentinian deal, it was so structured that AECL projected a loss of $130 million on it. That led to the "retirement" of the then president of AECL, John Foster, and some renegotiation. It is now expected that we'll only lose $40 million on that one.

We also sold two CANDUs to Romania, for $2 billion, which sounded nice until it turned out that Romania won't pay in cash, only in goods. This sale, like all the others, was defended on the grounds of protecting jobs in Canada, although the influx of $2 billion in goods will obviously displace Canadian workers.

Finally, we nearly concluded a deal which Southam News has called "the oddest proposition ever to emerge from the nuclear industry." We were to build a reactor which would cost $2 billion, in Turkey, on the edge of the Mediterranean Sea. We would pay for the reactor and sell electricity to the Turks for fifteen years, after which time they would own it. If we could make money out of it in fifteen years, it would have been a world first. Never mind, it would provide 8,000 jobs for five years according to AECL's figures. Incidentally, this reactor was to be outside the jurisdiction of the Atomic Energy Control Board, but when a Southam reporter asked an AECL public affairs officer how the plant would be regulated, he said he didn't know and *wouldn't find out*. AECL has not been boasting about the Turkish deal, and the details were actually let loose by a bemused executive from Westinghouse Electric, whose firm had dropped out of the bidding when it saw what the Turks had in mind. "It just didn't make any sense from a private enterprise perspective," is how James Moore of Westinghouse put it to Southam's Margaret Munro. However, the Canadian Export Development Corporation refused to finance the contract AECL won, and the deal died. So, in

January 1987, a new deal was announced in which AECL wouldn't have to put up all the money, just most of it. This deal may go through.

Pickering Packs it In

Well, if the foreign market hasn't been a bed of roses— eight sales in all since the 1960s—CANDUs have gone rather better back home; especially in Ontario which has nineteen of the twenty-one reactors operating in Canada. New Brunswick has one, at Point Lepreau, which has had a number of problems, and Quebec has one, Gentilly-2 (Gentilly-1 never came on stream).

The Ontario reactors have worked well until quite recently, when a series of spills and serious breakdowns at Pickering raised eyebrows, and tempers, across the province.

The first two Pickering units had to be taken out of service in 1983 after a problem with pressure tubes was signalled by the spill of 1,000 litres (220 gallons) of heavy water containing deadly tritium into Lake Ontario. This particular problem led to a three-year shutdown and a $1 billion repair bill. Soon after, 2,700 litres of heavy water leaked from the Douglas Point plant, since closed down. In October, 1983, there was a leak in one of the Bruce generators, causing a shutdown. Shortly thereafter, another Bruce unit shut down because of an electrical failure, and in February, 1984, a third Bruce unit went out of service because of the failure of a $7 switch. A few months later in May, Hydro had to shut down a fourth Pickering reactor, which had just been in service for two months, leaving only two of six units in operation, and a bill for $250,000 a day for coal-fired power to replace the friendly atoms.

When this rash of disasters broke, Hydro replied to its critics that the overall record of Canadian nuclear reactors is good—which it is—and that they may have their faults, but they are still better than other systems. Well, maybe. I know of no other systems that contain the potential to fry the neighbourhood for miles around, but then, I lack that simple faith which is required to think the nuclear way. What worries me most, though, is that with both Hydro

and AECL, the public is dealing not with government enterprises primed to look objectively at the nation's needs,
but with powerful corporations committed years ago to a
course of action which a large body of evidence is now
suggesting may lead to disaster. If we want muscular salesmanship, we don't need to fund it through a public corporation; we have beer companies to look after that need.

Government Policy was Simply Reversed

Again, my objection is that these companies are not playing
by the rules of either public or private enterprise. They
want the money, and the protections, of government, with
the freedom, and secrecy, of a private firm. AECL, when
it has one of its wonderful CANDU sales in the offing, insists
that it must be able to keep its negotiations secret—after
all, this is business, and we can't let the competition know.
But when the sale turns out to be a stinker, and the bills
come in, they are sent to the taxpayer. The nuclear industry—mines, manufacturers, and all—has spent, according
to AECL's figures, $30 billion in the past three decades,
and is currently generating $4 billion annually in economic
activity. Still, it has required the infusion of $3 billion in
subsidies. That's AECL's estimate; its critics put the amount
at as much as $5.4 billion.

A private firm that operated with AECL's go-for-broke
approach would soon be bankrupt, but the Crown faces no
such dilemma. The trade-off is supposed to be that a Crown
firm will represent public policy, but there is no sign here
that that is the case.

For example, AECL was supposed to order CANDUs and
let the private sector build them, but that policy didn't last
long. C.D. Howe, in 1956, said of AECL, "We simply act
as consultants for whoever wants to go into the business of
building atomic power-plants." In 1964, Charles M. Drury,
at that time Chairman of the Privy Council Committee on
Science, repeated the instruction: "Atomic Energy of Canada is not in—and indeed in my view should not get into—
the business of manufacturing and selling nuclear reactors." Indeed, that is the main business it is in, and always
has been in. J. Lorne Gray, one of AECL's early presidents,

made no secret of his scorn for Canadian industry—"The problems are beyond the normal industrial design office"—and, after a few tentative arrangements with Canadian General Electric, the Crown took on the job of building reactors itself. Government policy was simply reversed.

On the larger issue of pushing Canada so quickly down the nuclear road, AECL and Hydro did not reverse government policy, they formed it. Hydro provided the projections that seemed to justify massive expenditures on nuclear facilities which, once undertaken, had to be sustained. The lead time required to build a nuclear plant is about a decade, so decisions have to be made that will bear fruit long after the current government has gone to its reward. In the circumstances, what is required is some outside body of experts to provide impartial advice, but because of the Crown corporation approach, the expertise we get comes from those whose interests and careers are bound up in the creation of mega-projects. I don't mean to imply that Crown executives deliberately set out to hoodwink governments; they believe passionately in what they are doing. Rather, the difficulty is that they naturally see the good of the nation through the eyes of the corporation for which they work. What employee of any corporation is going to argue that what the world needs is less of the product he sells?

I don't object to Crowns wanting to do their job, and to increase its scope; it seems the most natural thing in the world. My objection is that there is no counterweight to them. Because Crowns are part of the government, they are invested with an objectivity they do not possess, and because they are allowed to keep much of their deliberations secret, we mistake their salesmanship for expertise.

This arrangement suits them very well. The Crowns seem to take the view that the public has no business meddling in their operations, except to provide funding. Lawrence Solomon, one of the energy industry's unkindest critics, says in *Energy Shock* that a former head of the Atomic Energy Control Board, asked at a royal commission hearing why his group hadn't informed the public about safety matters, replied, "Because I don't think . . . it is any of their business." I have never heard anything quite that aggressive from an AECB official, although one did tell me that he thought the public would rest easier if it didn't concern itself with safety. And he added, "So would I."

Both Ontario Hydro and AECL are muscular when it comes to defending their turf. They not only provide platoons of public relations officers and bundles of pamphlets to defend and explain what they do, they sometimes put direct pressure, in the best corporate manner, on those who speak unkindly of them. Solomon reports a case in which a New Brunswick teacher, whose grade four students asked a government PR man about radioactive waste, was threatened with the loss of his job and harassed by mail.

There is something amiss here. Crowns are not supposed to lean on the citizenry; they are supposed to be the servants of us all. Cling to that thought as we move into the next chapter, to examine the operations of the post office.

7
I Wrote A Letter To My Love, But The Damn Thing Never Arrived

"There is no plan."
Donald Lander, *president of Canada Post,*
to a House of Commons Committee, May 30, 1986

We live in a complex and difficult world, even those of us whom God has not chosen to be the president of Canada Post, but every now and then, an illuminating shaft of light will fall upon the surrounding landscape, and something will be made clear. For me, two shafts of light have appeared recently in connection with Canada Post.

The first came in late 1985, when Auditor-General Kenneth Dye handed in a report that showed how two Crown corporations were able to make money out of the mail service. Canadian Saltfish Corporation and the Freshwater Fish Marketing Corporation both act as market stabilizers, buying fish from private sources and selling it again. They operate on money borrowed from the Department of Fisheries and Oceans, which they return to Ottawa as the cash flows in. So what they did was to adopt the simple expedient of sending their cheques, sometimes worth more than $1 million, by mail (instead of by bank transfer or courier). They knew it would take anywhere from three to thirteen days for the cheques to make it from, respectively, Winnipeg—where Freshwater Fish hangs out—and Halifax—where the Saltfish Corporation is headquartered. This timely time-lag let them collect bank interest in the interim to the tune of $190,000. It seems a bit sneaky for one Crown deliberately to take advantage of the known klutziness of another Crown; but the Fish boys are proprietary corporations, which means they are supposed to pay their own way, and every dollar counts.

The second shaft of illumination arrived in late June, 1986, when Canada Post delivered its annual report to Parliament. That report made much of the fact that the post office only lost $184 million in the fiscal year ended March 31, a big improvement over the $395 million dropped down the chute the year before. But—and here is the part that caught my eye—the report also indicated that up to 30 per cent of the mail is now arriving late by the corporation's own standards, which are not exacting. To meet the corporation's standards, mail should be delivered within two days locally, and within three days if it travels to another major Canadian centre. The report showed that more than 80 per cent of the mail meets the local deadline or, to put it another way, you have a four-out-of-five chance of getting a letter across town in two days; however, your chances of getting a letter to a neighbouring city in three days range between 70 and 85 per cent. Incidentally, these numbers show up the post office in a better light than a survey conducted by the Institute of Corporate Directors in Canada, which sent a batch of test letters from Toronto to Oakville. They took an average of just under five days to arrive; two letters took nine days to stagger thirty-five kilometres. A reader cannot tell from the post office annual report if things are getting worse, because Canada Post is using "a new independent audited measurement system." But we can guess.

Mail Used to Move Between Cities in a Day. Remember?

When I lived in Ottawa, from 1963 to 1968, I used to mail manuscripts to my editor at the *Star Weekly* in Toronto almost every week. Normally, I would pop the envelope in the box in time to catch the 3:00 P.M. pickup. At about 11:00 A.M. the next day, I would telephone my editor and ask him what he thought of my work. Not much, he would say; so he would shove it back to me the next day, and I would curse and re-do it and shove it back to him. We operated for years on the assumption that mail moved from city to city in less than a day, and so it did. There was one constant from that day to this—everybody bitched about the post office then, and that hasn't changed—and two differences. Stamps were cheaper—four cents in 1963 for first-class mail, instead of thirty-six; and the post office was a government department, instead of a Crown corporation. As a government department, the post office cost $353,100,000 to run in 1967, brought in $305,400,000, and thus cost the taxpayer $47,700,000.

When I put all of this illumination together, I get something like this: over the years, the mail service has gotten much worse in Canada, although the cost of a stamp has multiplied ninefold. Now the business has been turned over to a Crown corporation, which is under instructions to cut the losses. It's proposing to do so by hiking the rates and chopping down the service.

In typical fashion, no one ever asked Canadians if we wanted it this way. Would we be prepared to pay forty cents, or even fifty cents, to mail a first-class letter if we could be guaranteed the service we had three decades ago? I would, but I don't know if Canadians generally would, because they have never been asked. They have been told that some of them would have to walk 180 metres (200 yards) for mail while others would continue to get it at their doorstep. They were told, in November, 1986, that 1,700 rural post offices would be closed and 3,500 others would be turned over to private contractors, with the staff either fired or kept on at reduced salaries. While governments spend hundreds of thousands per job to create employment elsewhere, they will save it by slashing positions already established. Canadians were told that if they live within four kilometres (2½ miles) of a main country road, they can no longer have the mail put in a box at the end of their laneways; they can drive to main route intersections instead. There, the mail will be stuffed into group boxes which, experiments have already shown, can in many cases be opened by anyone, with or without a key.

As part of Canada Post's new look for 1987, Canadians were informed that "special arrangements" will be made for senior citizens and handicapped persons who may not find these other arrangements to their liking. However, we were not told what the new arrangements would be. And we were not asked if, given the choice, we wouldn't rather pay something extra for a fairer more efficient system, in stamps or taxes or even, God forfend, by having our MPs give up some of their free-franking privileges (the post office moves 43 million pieces of government mail free each year).

When Canada Post unveiled its plan to reorganize its affairs late in 1986, it came up with a new, though so far unofficial, motto: "Like it or lump it." Doesn't seem adequate somehow.

It's bad enough for the post office to be hard-hearted, worse when it can't even advertise the efficiency such hard-hardedness is supposed to purchase. The process has gone so far that other Canadian corporations know they can make money by banking on the inefficiency of Canada Post. And that is, if I may say so, no way to run a railway—or a post office. In fact, we seem to have created the complete reversal of what a Crown corporation ought to be, in manufacturing something that is supposed to make money— even if it doesn't—rather than deliver a service. Whether this comes about as a result of high-level scheming, or whether Canada Post President Donald Lander had it right in the quote at the top of this chapter is beside the point. If we want a Crown corporation to make money, and we give it a monopoly; it will sure as hell make money, sooner or later. But if we want it to deliver a service, we ought to instruct it on its priorities, none of which will involve bleeding the taxpayer one way rather than another. It's that simple. We have to decide what we want the Crowns to do, and then make them do it. When we have a Crown boasting that it isn't losing as much as it used to, but the mail isn't getting through, something has gone agley, as old Robert Burns used to say.

Through Sleet and Snow and All That Jazz

We may be helped if we look back along the track of time, to see how we got where we are today.

Government couriers carried mail between Quebec City

and Montreal during the French regime, but that doesn't count as a postal service, because they carried private correspondence for free. We adopted a government service from the Americans. As early as 1639, the then province of Massachusetts established a post office, and the idea gradually spread to other colonies. There were no stamps, and the person who got the letter was supposed to pay the freight. If he couldn't, the postmaster, a local political appointee, would grumble, extend credit, and try to collect later. In 1692, the British government awarded a royal patent to a group of private entrepreneurs to run an inter-colonial postal service, but it did not do well. The complaints are now familiar: too expensive, and too slow. The British colonial administration took the service back in 1707, and ran it as a money-loser under various postmasters.

It was a chancy business. A notation in the Halifax *Gazette* of April 27, 1754, advised that, "If any Gentlemen, Merchants or others, wants to send any Letters to any foreign Port, they may depend on having their Letters carefully deliver'd to the Captain of the first Vessel bound for the Place to which their Letters are directed, by paying One Penny per letter . . . " to "Their Humble Servant, Benjamin Leigh." Been a long time since we've had Humble Servants behind the wicket.

In 1737, a trouble-making printer named Benjamin Franklin was appointed postmaster of Philadelphia, and he adopted a number of practices that were to become routine. That is, he moved the post office into his own printing-shop, hired a bunch of relatives on the government payroll, and used the system to send out copies of his *Philadelphia Gazette*, the circulation of which forthwith boomed. He also mailed out to his customers, at no charge to himself, copies of his *Poor Richard's Almanac*, thus giving force to one of Poor Richard's sayings, "God helps them that help themselves."

In 1753, Franklin wangled the job of Deputy Postmaster General of North America out of the British government, which meant that he ran the entire colonial system. The Postmaster General lived in England, and did nothing. Franklin paid bribes of £300 to obtain a post that only paid £150 a year, but he knew what he was doing. By 1774, when he was dismissed for his wickedness in fomenting the Amer-

ican Revolution, he was making £1,500 a year out of the
post, and turning over £3,000 a year to the British Treasury, which had never received a penny from his predecessors. I suppose it is too late to offer him Canada Post.

Franklin travelled all over the colonies, and even made
a trip up to Quebec, soon after that became a British possession in 1763, to look for ways to improve the service. He
and his partner, William Hunter, sank £900 of their own
money into establishing post offices and setting up routes.
Where it used to take three weeks for a man writing a letter
in Philadelphia to receive an answer from Boston, Franklin
cut the time to six days—a feat most Americans would be
glad to see equalled today. Besides systematizing the service,
the major change he made was to insist on the mail carriers
moving at night, as well as by day. Much later, New York
City would inscribe on the front of its main post office,
"Neither snow, nor rain, nor heat nor gloom of night stays
these couriers from the swift completion of their appointed
rounds," a line you can't repeat in public these days without
evoking a snigger. Actually, the New York people swiped
the line. Herodotus, writing in the fifth century B.C., described the messenger-carriers of Persia as travelling with
"a velocity which nothing human can equal," and went on
to say, "Neither snow, nor rain, nor heat, nor darkness are
permitted to obstruct their speed." Doesn't have the same
ring to it.

Franklin also established a monthly courier service that
connected Montreal and Quebec with New York, and a
trans-Atlantic packet service, but that was interrupted by
the Revolution. After the war, government postal services
were extended to the new settlements founded by the fleeing
United Empire Loyalists.

The Postage Stamp Enters the Fray

It wasn't until 1839 that Sir Rowland Hill hit on the bright
idea of having the letter-writer pay for delivery by selling
him a stamp; until that time, stamps were used as a tax-
raising scheme on all sorts of documents—which is why the
Americans didn't like them—but never on envelopes. The
penny post was born, and extended to the United States in

1850 and to Canada a year later. Here, it cost threepence, and the first Canadian stamp, designed by Sanford Fleming, was known as "the three-penny beaver."

Confederation saw the establishment of a Canadian federal mail service as a separate department. It quickly became—though no more so than other departments—a pool into which politicians could dip for patronage. When the Canadian Pacific Railway was completed in 1885, mail sacks began to move across the country each morning, on government contract. Daily mail delivery became a reality in 1886. The next year, Canada became a postal pioneer, with the establishment of what was called "imperial penny post," which, says historian George Brown, "allowed a letter to be sent anywhere in the Empire for two cents." Two Canadian cents. One British penny.

Peace, Progress and Patronage

For decades after that, the post office department ambled along, delivering the mail, building post offices, and handing out graft. Sir Hector Langevin, one of our early Ministers of Public Works, who had a hand in many of the post office contracts, formed a "Langevin Testimonial Fund" into which contractors often felt a compelling urge to pour money; but this was not peculiar to the postal business, it applied generally to public works.

Throughout most of this century, the civil service has been used as a place to park the friends of government, and postmasterships were among the easiest appointments to arrange. All that was required, whenever an election changed the political stripe of the government, was to bring a charge of political partisanship against the incumbent, which was never hard to prove, and throw the bum out. Between 1922 and 1938, when the mantel was thrown back and forth frequently between Liberals and Conservatives, 2,385 postmasters were dismissed, an average of 177 a year. Nearly all were dismissed on the grounds of partisanship. After 1938, when the Liberals had a stranglehold on power for twenty years, this practice stopped. You are invited to believe it was because the postmasters foreswore all political activity.

Despite its taints, the post office department ran smoothly enough, with six-day, twice-a-day delivery for most of the country. This meant a letter posted in downtown Toronto in the morning would be delivered in the afternoon. Of course, it was a simpler world all around; there was much less mail to move, and the system prospered in part on the backs of postal employees, who traded the security of a government job—permanent government employees could only be dismissed by an order-in-council—for low wages and long hours.

Enter the Unions

After World War II, most of the middle-management jobs in the post office went to war veterans, who apparently thought the place should be run on military lines. Their ascendancy corresponded with a post-war boom in the Canadian union movement, which finally extended, with much side-stepping and grumbling on the government's part, into the civil service. Unions were allowed, but there was no provision for collective bargaining, or legal strikes, until the postal unions came along.

Two unions became part of the system: one to represent the letter carriers who walk the beat; the other for the inside workers who sort and move the mail. Opinions vary, but it is my view that the unions were an inevitable, and necessary, response to the working conditions that prevailed in the postal department. The alternative view is that the unions caused the trouble. What cannot be denied, however, is that there was trouble in God's own plenty, and an air of paranoia, distrust, and distaste pervaded the operation. The department put cameras in the washrooms to catch employees dawdling, and installed peepholes through which to spy on workers in order to prevent theft and destruction of the mail. Later, when the unions did become established, the post office responded by stalling contract negotiations beyond all reason.

The unions reacted with bitterness and venom. In some post offices, a fringe with views zany enough to seem to justify some of the wild charges post office spokesmen were bandying about took charge of operations.

We were heading for a confrontation, and it came, in July, 1965, when both unions walked out. They had been asking for increases of $660 a year; at that time, postal clerks received a minimum of $2,190 to a maximum of $4,680. The government responded with an offer of $300 to $360, and wildcat strikes began in Montreal, Vancouver, and Toronto. Soon the whole system was closing down. Revenue Minister Edgar Benson reminded the unions that the strikes were illegal, but promised not to prosecute if the strikers would go back to work. They wouldn't, and soon there were 10,000 postal workers, out of a total of 22,000, off the job in illegal strikes that closed seventy post offices across the land. The government appointed a commission of inquiry, and asked the workers to go back on the job until it could report. The strikers complied everywhere but in Montreal. Montreal is a tough nut, in the postal unions. On August 4, the commission of inquiry, with a few frank things to say to both sides, recommended increases ranging from $510 to $550, and a referendum vote accepted this as a settlement everywhere but in Montreal. The Montreal postal workers refused to vote. They took the money, though, and went back to the job. The unions had won a clear-cut victory, and learned, regrettably, that belligerence pays.

The arrival of the unions led to a sharp increase in costs. One way out of this pickle, for the department, was to contract out an increasing amount of the work to independent entrepreneurs who were not subject to union jurisdictions, and who would perform work more cheaply than the government could. The *riposte propre* for the unions was to try to block any outside contracting, and, when that didn't work, to organize the outsiders. That is what led to the second postal mess, in 1969. The debacle involved *les gars de Lapalme*.

G. Lapalme, the company that gave *les gars* their name, was a fiction. A company called Rod Service Limited had been dealt the task of handling the postal trucking in Montreal—on a $3 million annual contract let without public tender. Its workers made an average $1.67 per hour, with seventy-five-hour weeks and no overtime. They organized with the help of the Confederation of National Trade Unions (CNTU), and after two strikes, won hefty raises, a forty-eight-hour week and overtime. Rod Service then went out of business, so the post office gave its contract to a new company, named for the two Lapalme brothers who were, in fact, merely business managers for the union. Then, on December 2, 1969, the government announced that the work would be dealt out to four new companies, none of whom was under any obligation to hire *les gars*. Their jobs had been dealt out from under them.

So they began a series of rotating strikes, protests, and harassments. Neither rain nor snow nor dark of night would keep them from screwing up the mail. One day, they loaded up their trucks, drove down to the main Montreal post office, surrounded it with their vehicles, locked them, and walked away. Some days they went to work, and some days they didn't. When they didn't, and the post office brought in private operators to do the work, their trucks were run off the road and smashed.

Another commission of inquiry was established, under mediator (now Senator) H. Carl Goldenberg. The commission's sensible solution was to drop the private contracts and integrate the truckers into the post office. The government accepted the report, but only offered jobs to 257 of the 427 truckers, at lower rates than they had enjoyed and with no union. The boys went berserk in a campaign that lasted six months and racked up a toll of 662 trucks attacked, 104 postal stations besieged, 75 people injured, 102 arrests, 7 dynamite bombings, and damage to 1,200 post boxes and 492 relay boxes. The total bill came to over $3 million, not counting the untold costs of constant mail disruptions.

The Lapalme boys marched on Parliament Hill, where Prime Minister Trudeau rolled down the window of his limousine long enough to invite them *mangez la merde*, which is not polite. They picketed the offices of the CNTU because they thought the parent union wasn't doing enough for them, and they kept Montreal's postal operations in a tizzy well into 1972. The CNTU eventually withdrew its support when it turned out that $20,000 it had raised for the strike had disappeared without adequate accounting, and *les gars* gradually drifted away. But they left behind a sour taste.

Automation Arrives, Trailing Trouble

Labour-management relations went from bad to worse; postal supervisors resented the younger, often better educated workers who, just to help things along, treated them with contempt. Sometimes it was deserved. A Calgary postal worker was given a written warning that "if your conduct does not improve, I will have to terminate your resignation." Another was told that he was incorrigible since repeated requests for improved performance had "proved no detergent." Should have washed his mouth out with soap.

This was the background against which management decided to get labour costs down by introducing automatic letter-sorting machines. The post office, with its genius for labour relations working on all cylinders, not only refused to consult the workers about the machines that would replace them; it refused even to concede that they had any right to be in on the discussion. In law, this was correct; as government workers, the post office minions were outside the scope of the Canada Labour Code, which provided for collective bargaining on automation issues.

Accordingly, there was the unilateral announcement that the machines would be installed, accompanied by the assertion that no jobs would be lost. In case anyone should ask why we needed the machines, the boss had an answer of sorts; everybody would be paid fifty cents an hour *less* to work on the machines than for manual sorting, even though the mechanical work is much more arduous. At a single stroke, the department turned all the inside employees—a group already predisposed to be hostile to automation—into an enemy of the process. The stage was set for a long, bitter, and brutal series of strikes.

Violent protests and wildcat shutdowns led to the establishment of an arbitration board in 1973. The board suggested the appointment of a labour-management committee to discuss automation, but the postal authorities stalled for two years before even calling the committee into session. All the while, automation proceeded.

In April, 1974, a group of Montreal postal workers staged a protest—the machines weren't due to be installed there for two more years, but they wanted to get their licks in early. Three hundred workers were suspended, and when a Montreal court issued an injunction prohibiting a recurrence, 2,000 fellow unionists walked out in protest. They went back to work on the strength of a promise that talks on automation would start, but when that didn't happen, they staged a slowdown in early 1975. Postmaster-General Bryce Mackasey decided to show the union who was boss by firing 27 workers, suspending 700 others, and importing 1,000 student strike-breakers to get the mail moving again. The usual results followed: union goon squads appeared, tires were slashed, homes vandalized, and scabs beaten. The students, remembering that they had homework, went home.

There followed more work stoppages, including a three-week total shutdown of the mail just in time for Christmas, 1975, and sporadic wildcat strikes, slowdowns, and plain bloody-mindedness that went on, and on, and on. Automation, which was supposed to sort everything out by providing more money so we could have happy workers and swift-moving mail, became a nightmare. After an expenditure of $1.5 billion, only 45 per cent of the mail was machine-sorted. The unions hadn't won, but they had made everyone lose along with them.

Canada Post is Delivered

Finally the government became convinced that it had to do something, anything, to break the charmed circle. Why not make the post office into a Crown corporation? Eric Kierans, when he was Postmaster-General, had suggested it back in 1968, and had actually got Cabinet approval for the change, although it came to nothing. That was just before the Americans changed their postal service from a department into a corporation and, after a shaky start, began to make money with it.

Thus we got Bill C-42, "An Act to establish the Canada Post Corporation," and on October 16, 1981, the post office shucked off the grubby cocoon of its past and emerged as a beautiful butterfly. The new corporation was enjoined to "operate a postal service on a self-sustaining basis while providing a standard of service that will meet the needs of Canada." Neither of which, incidentally, it has ever achieved.

The new corporation inherited assets worth $2.2 billion, 8,400 branches in 6,200 communities, 175 distribution centres, 29 mechanized plants, 6.2 billion pieces of mail to move every year, and the pot of poison that had been cooking for two decades. The place was 97 per cent unionized by now, and no employee in his right mind would, given recent history, stand without union protection. And if he would, there were all his brothers and sisters, breathing fire, to urge him to reconsider.

The law could make the post office into a company, and urge it to make money, but it couldn't wipe out the past or replace the people, on both sides, who were operating the place on October 17, 1981, just as they had been the day before.

Oh, there were changes, no doubt about that. The postal deficit, closing in on $1 billion annually, was trimmed back over five years to $184 million; productivity was increased, by a meagre 1 per cent among inside workers and 4 per cent among letter carriers, and there was a slight drop in absenteeism. But the financial improvement was achieved by cutting the workforce, which didn't help service, and jacking up the rates. A first-class stamp cost seventeen cents in 1981, and thirty-four cents four years later. Other rates went up much higher and faster, and soon businesses, including magazines and newspaper publishers, who depend heavily on the mails, to say nothing of mail-order catalogue companies, were screaming louder than ever. Mail revenue went up from $1.4 billion in 1981–82 to $2.1 billion in 1984–85, while overhead costs were actually cut by $95 million; the deficit shrank from $588 million to $243 million over those years.

But the service remained a mess. Contracting-out became a buzz-word, and the 5,000 rural sub-contractors who deliver the mail in the country were joined by others in small communities. Today, Canada Post actually only delivers the mail itself in thirty-six of the nation's largest communities. The post office was going to improve its service by getting rid of it. Costs were cut, in part, by Canada Post insisting on lower rates from Air Canada. It was going to get rid of its deficit by passing it on.

The President Quits

When the Conservatives came to power in 1984, they thought they knew what to do. Apparently they didn't: Michael Warren, the then president of Canada Post Corporation, handed back his job and a reported salary of $200,000 a year in mid-1985, because he said he could get no direction from the government. The latter appointed a committee which reported, duly, in November, 1985, and said that things were not going well. Absenteeism among postal employees was nearly three times the national average; mail volumes had risen a meagre 25 per cent over the past two decades; operating costs had jumped 75 per cent; and wages had more than tripled. While Canada and the United States had roughly equal postal productivity in 1972, by 1985, the Americans were nearly 50 per cent more productive than we were. And on and on, through two volumes of reporting to this dismally correct summary of labour-management relations: "Both parties appear oblivious . . . that the course they are on will in the end lead to the demise of Canada Post as we know it."

At last, we had an official assessment of what makes Canada Post tick—the death-wish.

The committee seemed to think we might get something out of copying the American system a little more closely. This opinion was based on a two-day visit to Washington and the fact that the American service now makes money. It makes money, in my experience, by doing what we now seem determined to do: hike the prices and cut the service. About the time the committee was asking us to emulate the Americans, I paid U.S. $23—more than four times the Canadian rate—to speed a parcel on its way by Priority Post from Sheridan, Wyoming, with delivery in Toronto guaranteed for the next day. My parcel crossed the border on its way to Canada nine days later. I couldn't get my money back, either; the guarantee doesn't apply to anything that leaves the United States. When I lived in Washington for two years, I got accustomed to receiving parcels meant for others, because U.S. postal machines have a tendency to smash any parcel that doesn't conform to their usual sizes. Automatic wrapping machines grab up the remains of said parcel and they are forwarded to the address on the nearest legible label. A friend of mine who runs a Washington bookstore quite often gets dirty laundry, homeward bound from university students, in place of the boxes of books he ordered.

The American system has also been marred by charges of corruption in high places. Thankfully, we have been spared similar experiences. In early 1986, Paul N. Carlin was dismissed as U.S. Postmaster General. Soon after, the corporation's vice-president, Carlin's likely successor, Paul E. Voss, pleaded guilty to receiving illegal payments in connection with the awarding of a $235 million equipment contract. He also pleaded guilty to embezzlement charges. Apparently he took the injunction to make money as something personal.

Canada's postal problems did not change when we dumped them into a Crown corporation and indeed, I cannot see that the move made the slightest difference, or ever will. The service is caught in an unholy bind; labour relations stink, and that makes the workforce determined not to have the post office succeed. With the service getting worse, people are trying to find other ways to get messages—especially parcels—through. Canada Post was designed to handle 50 per cent of the nation's parcel traffic; it handles less than 10 per cent, and loses money on that. The lower volumes create higher costs, so the service is cut again, in pursuit of that Holy Grail, a profit. Or even a slightly less Holy Grail, breaking even.

Now Ottawa is aquiver with a new idea; privatization. Or as the *Globe and Mail* asked on August 24, 1985, with splendid disregard for either common sense or grammar, "Should Post Office be taken private?", which sounds like something that would only be permissible between consenting adults. Well, I'm game. We've tried everything else. However, I have some questions. Should we have the massive, nation-stopping strike before or after the sale? Or will we find someone willing to guarantee all these jobs—62,000 currently—and thus avoid a strike? And if so, how is the poor, dim sucker who takes the thing on going to make money? I've got it. He can cut service.

We are back where this chapter began. The problems of Canada Post, perhaps our most crucial Crown corporation, will not respond to fooling with techniques. The Crowning of the post office hasn't done a thing, except to create an atmosphere in which the notion of making a profit has become substituted for the notion of providing a national service, even though both appear equally unattainable.

If I could solve this one, I'd lay down the implements of my craft and apply for the postal presidency. Donald Lander, the current incumbent, doesn't seem to know what to do with it, anyway. In setting up a Crown to move the mail, we seem to have made a wrong turn somewhere, although the reasons for disbanding the department seemed strong enough at the time. It appears that the form of a public service, whether it is to be a Crown or a department, is less important than the motivation behind it. If we are determined to make a mess of things, we will do so, whatever form we choose to use. That is certainly one of the lessons to be drawn from the sad saga of Via Rail, the subject of the next chapter.

8
You Can't Get There Via Rail

"Is no one in charge?"
Canadian Transport Commission
Report on Via Rail,
October, 1984

Canada is a nation in spite of itself, a place with too much geography and too few people, a country that can only be held together by the criss-crossing bands of transportation and communications. Right? Right. That being the case, you might wonder, why we would so arrange our affairs that our postal service—run by a Crown corporation—is a disgrace on its way to becoming a disaster, as witness the last chapter, and why our passenger rail service—run by another Crown—has already passed the disaster stage and is heading for oblivion. We have looked at some of the reasons why the Post Office evolved into an institution aimed at delivering less service for higher cost; it will be instructive to see the same process in operation in connection with Via Rail Canada Limited.

Via Rail was created by the federal cabinet in 1977, and has since absorbed more than $3 billion in public funds. The Canadian Transportation Commission study quoted at the top of this chapter, consisted of a series of searing indictments of the rail Crown. The report was prepared in response to complaints of 170 trains running late during the winter season; however, the CTC found that, "Via trains do not run late only in the winter time. They run late in the summer and in the spring and fall." A crock for all seasons.

Indeed, if you look at Via's financing closely, as the CTC did, it becomes evident that it would be cheaper, all things considered, if the people who run Via were to hand passengers who wanted to travel between Toronto and Montreal on the railroad $87 each as a bribe, to persuade them to go instead by bus, air, or private car. Really. Instead of those tinkly television ads in which the young couple—she winsome, dimpled, and clinging; he clean-cut, handsome and virile—flash across the nation in a trice, while music plays and rails hum, Via should show us what really happens on passenger trains. About thirty seconds of documentary, say, shot in the toilet—frozen and backed up—of a train stalled in the middle of the wilderness, with the steam pipes burst, the thermometer plummeting, and no word on when, if ever, the train will roll again. They might make another spot out of a scene involving my wife's aunt, an official in Transport 2000, the train-boosting consumer lobby. This one would show an aroused elderly matron confronting a bewildered conductor in a flash-frozen train staggering through northern Ontario. We could have a closeup of the matron offering to see the colour of the conductor's insides unless somebody, somehow, introduced some water into the passenger toilets. It was a scene full of poignant human drama, pathos, tension and, on the conductor's part, sheer terror. Where were the cameras?

Docudramas based on the reality of train travel, instead of terminally cute fiction, might persuade the last poor fools who insist on the virtues of passenger trains to think again. And with its ridership down to zero, Via could go decently out of business.

And yet, and this is surely the strangest thing about Via Rail, all over the world, people seem to be turning back to the passenger train. We are in the midst of what *The Economist* called, "The second railway age," ushered in by two events—the energy scare that began in 1973 and underlined the conservation potential of trains, and the development of new technology that will allow passenger trains to compete with airlines. "The world's railways are enjoying a comeback," as the *The Economist* rhapsodized. Passenger traffic is shooting up, from Cincinnati to Khartoum; the French, Germans, Italians, Algerians, Portuguese, Russians, Chinese, Japanese, Indians are all tumbling over each other to beef up their railways and invent newer, better trains. The British, in the hands of a Prime Minister who has staked out a position adamantly opposed to state-run enterprises, are nevertheless pouring more money into capital investment for British Rail than ever in history. Even the Americans, as we saw in Chapter 4, are refurbishing their decrepit system through government-owned Amtrak. This isn't a trend; it's an avalanche.

To go back to *The Economist* again, "Railways are not just survivors from the first industrial revolution . . . they have regained the confidence they need to survive in another century." You can't help wondering if the lads from *The Economist* will get out this way sometime. Via has a tagline to its commercials that goes, "Have you ridden the train, lately?" Those of us who answer in the affirmative could show the lads that in Canada, at least, we are willing to resist these faddish attempts to improve the train; we could show them a few trips that would turn rhapsody off at the spigot.

The fundamental reason other nations have gone back to the rails is that the train, in most circumstances, is cheaper, cleaner, and safer than the airplane, and infinitely superior in terms of saving energy and preserving the environment.

How Much is That in Seat-Miles?

For every gallon of fuel consumed, a jet aircraft provides seventy seat-miles. I like "seat-miles"; it has a nice ring to it. To arrive at seat-miles, you multiply the number of people moved a given distance by any transport mode, and divide this figure by the fuel consumed along the way. The private car is about twice as efficient as a jet aircraft, at 140 seat-miles per gallon. The bus will do seven times as well as the jet, while the train, at 1,000 seat-miles per gallon, is capable of more than fourteen times the jet's efficiency. Mind you, there is a trick to these figures, as to all figures. An empty train does not compare so favourably with a full airplane; the ratios only apply to "comparable load factors," that is, the number of passengers compared to the number of seats. By any measure, however, trains are much more efficient than any other form of transport.

They can also be just about as fast. The train is not the swiftest way to get from Montreal to Vancouver, and never will be; but if you're going from Ottawa to Montreal, or Toronto to Ottawa, or Windsor to London, it is the ideal solution. Or it would be, if we hadn't allowed our railway system to get into such appalling shape, with dirty, old, and unreliable equipment crawling along battered roadbeds. I have ridden on Paris-bound transcontinental trains that hit 200 MPH; I have flashed from Cardiff, Wales, to London, in seventy-five minutes; I have eaten a luxurious breakfast while skimming from Newcastle to Edinburgh at 125 MPH; and I have sat on a siding between Montreal and Ottawa for four hours, wondering why I hadn't hitchhiked instead.

In Europe, trains purr from city centre to city centre with almost-infallible timing, and some of them even make money. In Canada, trains are something you run through slums and into the red. I read a report on Amtrak the other day that noted, with horror, that when the government took over the system, "some cars were nearly thirty years old."

Welcome to the wonderful world of Via Rail, where the *average* age of rolling stock is greater than three decades. "The only railway in the western world," as Frank Roberts, former president of Via, once told me, "where the passenger cars are contemporaries of the DC-3. How many passengers do you think Air Canada would get if they were still flying DC-3s?"

While the Japanese can run trains at 300 MPH, and the French, Swiss, Dutch, Germans, and Italians are all accustomed to trains that average more than 100 MPH, Canadians still struggle with rickety coaches, wobbly tracks, intermittent timetables and dismal service. Even so, the obvious cost advantage of trains is so great that when Canadian National in a burst of whimsy, once actually began to promote its passenger service, ridership shot up. CN, naturally, stopped that foolishness at once, cut down the service, and jacked up the fares.

Canadians want to ride the train; God knows why, but we do. Cursing, we fight our way aboard; grumbling, we endure the appalling ride; mumbling, we are decanted into remote stations. Maybe there is a streak of masochism in the national bloodstream, which even Via's best attentions cannot eradicate. I once tried to make reservations well in advance for a trans-Canada trip by rail, only to be told I was too early. Call back, I was told, on May 1. When I called back, all the reservations I wanted were booked. I am not alone. On a single day in July, 1985, Via's Toronto reservations office received 9,148 calls—and missed another 2,928 that couldn't get through because the lines were jammed. As an irate customer wrote Via's customer complaints office, "They have tried over the years to discourage passenger travel, but the people just wouldn't go away." Seems a strange way to operate a business.

To understand how all this came to be, it is necessary to realize that Via Rail—everybody's fall-guy—was originally established to take some of the heat off another Crown corporation, Canadian National. When we left CN, back in 1923, it had just been formed (see Chapter 3) out of a passel of collapsing railways, handed a debtload of $2 billion, and instructions to get on with the job of moving passengers and freight. And, oh yes, it would be nice to make some money, too. From there it was all downhill.

CN was set up in competition with the Canadian Pacific Railway for both passenger and freight service, but the CPR was not burdened with all the political freight heaped on the Crown corporation. Railway politics have always been patronage politics, but it was easier to lay the weight on the CN than its private enterprise competitor. This applied to such direct and grubby political patronage as the appointment of station-masters and the assignment of freight contracts and to what might be called nobler political ends. For example, the railroad was forced to maintain service into communities where it was bound to lose money, as the normal extension of its national mandate.

It was also brought under the terms of the Crowsnest Pass Agreement of 1897. This was a deal under which the CPR received a subsidy of $3.4 million for building a line from Lethbridge, Alberta, to Nelson, British Columbia, through the Crowsnest Pass. In return for the subsidy, the CPR was to give preferential rates to grain and flour moving east, and the rates were to remain in effect "hereafter." The key rate under the agreement was a charge of twelve cents a bushel for carrying Prairie grain to west coast docks. At first, the CPR was able to make money on the Crow Rate, but by the 1920s, moving grain had become a losing proposition, and the CN—although it had no part of the original deal—was also bound by the Crow Rate. In the long run, it made no sense, not even for the farmers. The Crow Rate meant that the railways, required to carry huge grain shipments at a loss, had to charge higher rates elsewhere, and were loath to maintain and improve the service that was dragging the rest of the railway down. One account explains, with delicate tact, that the railways "refrained from upgrading and expanding their fleet of grain-hauling cars." Wheat delivery services, to put it more bluntly, were lousy. In this regard, CN and CPR were treated as if they were both Crowns, and the practical effect, as a royal commission reported in 1961, was to lumber the railways with an excess cost of about $6 million annually, and to ensure that the service provided was mediocre at best. The commission suggested there ought to be changes made.

In the blink of an eye, historically speaking, the royal commission's suggestion was translated into action; it was a mere twenty-five years later, in 1986, that the government announced that there would be a gradual abandonment of the Crow Rate.

However, in the CN's early days, the Crow was the least of the railway's worries. The CN and CPR competed vigorously with each other through the 1920s, when the West was booming. New farm settlements were springing up everywhere, and branch lines marched out to meet them. There were invasions and counter-invasions by each railway into the other's territory. As they spread into other lines, such as steamships and hotels, they competed there, too. Each railway built a large hotel in Halifax, although neither thought there was room for more than one. Even when the Depression struck in the 1930s, and the presidents of both railroads spoke out against "the tremendous waste caused by maintaining duplicate services in a country which can no longer afford to pay for duplication," competition was maintained. The CPR actually proposed an amalgamation, which CPR President Edward Beatty reckoned would save $60 million a year, but that would have meant, in all likelihood, a national monopoly for the CPR, because it was unthinkable to give it to CN. As a result, nothing whatever was done.

The railroads made money on passenger traffic, at first, because the rail provided an effective monopoly. Airplanes were scarce and costly, and the Trans-Canada Highway wasn't a reality until 1962. By that time, passengers were no longer a boon; in fact, the railways were discovering that the more passengers they carried, the less money they made. That, at least, is how the railroads figured it. When they started losing money on passengers, they divided the losses by the number of passengers and deduced that each passenger represented a book loss; ergo, more passengers, more losses. It could be argued—and frequently was—that if the services were better, more passengers would result and these losses would become profits, but the railways were not impressed. They preferred freight anyway; it was cheaper and less bothersome. Freight doesn't talk back when the toilets break down.

We're Closing the Line Between East Plonk and Old Fatso

CPR was in a better position than CN, because it was not a Crown; it backed out of the sparse short-haul runs to concentrate on medium-length, higher density routes, and the transcontinental. By the mid-1960s, however, even CPR was losing money on passengers, and trying to dump them, so in 1967, the government undertook to pay subsidies covering 80 per cent of the losses on passenger travel. By 1975, it was paying $160 million to CN under this provision, and both rail lines were itching to drop passengers altogether. To this end, they not only stopped replacing worn-out equipment—the last major purchases were made in 1957—they produced schedules that ranged from the bizarre to the intermittent, and generally did their best to make passengers wish they had stayed home. They won some victories. Passengers were removed from the famous, and money-gobbling, "Newfie Bullet," a railroad saluted in a Newfoundland folksong as the one where, when a man lay down on the tracks to commit suicide, he starved to death. Passenger service was also dropped in Prince Edward

Island, where the line had been so manipulated by politicians to ensure that it went through every hamlet that an 84-mile run wound 147 miles across the verdant landscape, dropping money every foot of the way.

As the decades rolled by, Canadian railroading took on a recurring rhythm in which the railways tried to shuck off their passengers, were beaten back by political interference—first through the intervention of MPs in Parliament, later through the more formalized interference of the Canadian Transportation Commission—and then given more subsidies in return for maintaining the service. It developed into a Canadian ritual, with movements as fixed and predictable as the mating-dance of the Blue-Footed Booby. One railroad or the other would announce that it was planning to close down the service between East Plonk and Old Fatso. It would produce figures, some of them marvellous concoctions, to show that passengers never did, never would, and never could, pay their way on this line. Local protestors would spring into action with their own figures to show— and it was often quite easy to show—that the railroad had cooked the books in its anxiety to get rid of passengers. The MPs from East Plonk and Old Fatso would get into the act, vowing by all that's sacred to lay down their lives for the threatened line. A Canadian Transportation Commission hearing would go into the matter, and recommend continuance of the service. The federal cabinet would accept the recommendation, and order the railroad to continue the service. The railroad would cry blue ruin. The government would dig into its jeans for more money, and the railroads, still complaining, would retire with their new subsidies.

I sat through a number of these events during the 1960s and 1970s, and I believe that with about ten minutes rehearsal to memorize placenames, I could give the evidence for both sides, write the Canadian Transport Commission judgment, and issue all the necessary press releases. In one of my favourite hearings, at Fredericton, New Brunswick, the Canadian Transport Commission simply shredded a study purporting to show that the Atlantic region should kill most of its rail service and go to airplanes and buses because, the study insisted, rail's share of passenger services was dropping across the four provinces. What the study never acknowledged was that a proximate reason for the drop was that passenger rail had been killed in two of the four provinces, P.E.I. and Newfoundland. In the other two, the only places where it had a chance to grow, it had grown.

However, the pattern that emerged over the years was clear. The railroads were caught in an intolerable bind. As other forms of transportation caught on, the number of passengers available to finance rail travel dropped. With them went the money to maintain and improve the service. As the service got worse, passengers were driven away, and the cycle repeated itself. There was an additional factor, as I have argued in an earlier book, *Paper Juggernaut*, and that is that the Department, later the Ministry, of Transport became the special preserve of a phalanx of bureaucrats who had little or no interest in rail, and who were mesmerized by air travel. These were the bureaucrats who produced the studies that showed what a wonderful success Mirabel would be as a second airport to serve Montreal. On the basis of their projections, the airport was built, and at a cost which has never been clearly determined—somewhere between $600 million and $1.4 billion. But the projected passengers stayed away in droves. On most days, you could fire a cannon through the place and never hit anything but a bemused MOT bureaucrat, fiddling with his pocket calculator and wondering what went wrong. The airport, which has officially adopted a white elephant as its logo (cute, eh?), continues to bleed money every year, is running at about 10 per cent of its capacity, and is burying most of its continuing losses in two Crown corporations and the Airports Revolving Fund. Mirabel is a monument to the dedication of a group of bureaucrats to air travel, and their scorn for the lowly train.

As Frank Roberts of Via Rail told me, "In the air branch of Transport Canada you have about 500 guys running around selling airplanes; for rail you have maybe 25 people who are not well-loved. That's the nub."

Via Rail Canada Inc.

Whoever was to blame, by the 1970s, passenger rail had become a cursing and a byword in the nostrils of transportation executives. CN and CPR were both coining money out of communications, hotels, real estate, and even a little something out of freight. Accordingly, the passenger services were allowed to run down. It became clear that the government could either let this process proceed to its natural conclusion (extinction) or step in. In 1977, it stepped in to create a new Crown, Via Rail Canada Inc. Its job was "to manage railway passenger services in Canada." CN was reconstructed, and recapitalized. The railway had started with a long-term debt of $2 billion which, by unceasing effort, it had managed to turn into $2.2 billion over the fifty-four years between 1923 and 1977. Interest payments on this debt came to $130 million a year. Then the accountants got to work, converted $808 million of this into equity, and gave the Crown a new lease on life. In return, CN agreed to pay the government a minimum of 20 per cent on net earnings annually, as dividends on this equity. In 1985, CN paid Ottawa $23.5 million.

Overnight, CN was kissed into a prince, and began to follow its written instructions from the Minster of Transport, which read this way: "It is the view of the government that CN should make every attempt to conduct its affairs with a commercial attitude and in a commercial manner." That being the case, there was no longer any reason whatever why CN should continue as a Crown; it ought to have been privatized at once, but nobody mentioned that when Via was in the throes of creation.

The new Crown took on the old one's passenger traffic, along with most of CPR's (although CPR retained some commuter traffic), and the trains to run it with. What Via inherited was a declining business, a lousy reputation, and several rail-yards full of decrepit stock, for which it paid $67 million. Since then, the corporation has received capital grants, in dribs and drabs, to buy new equipment, stations and repair-yards—but never enough to do the job properly. In all, it has received about $1 billion, less for the entire system than was sunk into Mirabel. And some of the money was not wisely spent. Between 1981 and 1985, Via paid out $225 million for a fleet of "light, rapid, comfortable" (or LRC) trains that turned out to be even more prone to break down and conk out than the 1957 clunkers it inherited. Via officials kept explaining that the U.S.-made LRCs were just going through the kind of breaking-in problems to be expected with any new technology. That may have been true, but it was cold comfort for abandoned passengers. In 1984, the Canadian Transport Commission noted, "Via possesses two fleets; the largest being old, conventional equipment which is expensive to maintain and is unreliable, and a much smaller new fleet (LRCs) which is also unreliable and expensive to maintain."

The passenger cars, the report went on to say, biting its lip, "are functionally obsolete both before and after they receive maintenance." Via doesn't have enough equipment, which means that when something breaks down, it takes time to replace it, so schedules become mere guesswork. Even when it has the trains, Via cannot be sure it can run them. It is at the mercy of track maintenance programmes, carried out by CN and CPR in the summer—high season— and if a passenger train and a freight train are on the same track, it's the passenger train that must pull off and wait for the freight to pass. CN and CPR have their own priorities, and quite properly put them first. While the passengers wait, there is a good chance they will be par-broiled because, just as Via's old steam-heat tends to fracture in the winter, its air conditioning tends to pack it in during the summer. To buy a new set of trains for the Toronto-Montreal corridor, where 52 per cent of Via's passengers are carried, and where alone it has a chance to make a real profit, would cost $2 billion.

Via is not going to get $2 billion—in part because it is a Crown, without friends in the pits where bureaucratic infighting takes place and the money is doled out.

Via is the opposite of say, AECL or Ontario Hydro; it is a Crown stuck with the disadvantages of distance from government, and yet compelled to follow political directions. In 1981, the federal government simply lopped off 20 per cent of Via's passenger traffic by a Cabinet order which was not announced until Parliament had started its summer break, and MPs were unable to raise objections. Via heaved a sigh of relief; the lines lopped were all money-losers. Then, when the predictable screams of outrage built to the frenzy, Via was told to restore most of the dropped lines again, but not told how to make them pay.

Then They Cut the Subsidy

From the first, Via has been trapped, with not enough money either to buy new equipment or keep the old stuff rolling, and it didn't, and doesn't, even own its own tracks. Instead, it pays the other railroads "trackage fees" for the right to run its trains on their rails. There is probably someone in the world who understands exactly how these fees are arrived at; cynics believe they are drawn out of a hat, and no low numbers are put into the hat. CN, a Crown, consistently refused to disclose to Via, another Crown, what cost data is used as a basis for its charges. Trust us, they said, and with that, Via had to be content.

All we know for sure is that Via pays CN for using its trackage and maintenance much more than Via is able to collect from its customers for train tickets. In 1985, Via paid its sister Crown $350 million, and that year collected its all-time high for total passenger revenue, $201 million. Hard to make money that way. CN, a consistent money-loser before Via came along, now makes a profit, thanks to its Canadian Rail subsidiary ($105,532,000 in 1985), but Via doesn't, can't, won't. The loss has gone out from under the CN shell and now nestles under the Via shell. The railway lives on subsidies, which hit a high of $632 million in 1985.

So the government is going to cut the subsidy. That'll fix 'em. In mid-1985, Finance Minister Michael Wilson announced that the government would cut its support of Via to $400 million by 1990. That was when it was announced that the money-losing services which Via had managed to shed, to the dismay of its customers, were to be restored. Oh, yes, and Mr. Wilson said the system would now be run on a "use it or lose it basis." What this means, translated, is that Via is to hoist its fares and cut its service to try to balance the books and if the customers don't like it, and stay away in even greater numbers, the railroad will go to the great siding in the sky.

That is why the Canadian Transport Commission wanted to know back in 1984 if there was anybody in charge (the commission paid for its lip; although it did yeoman service trying to make sense out of Canada's nonsensical transport policy, in 1986, it was given notice it would be closed down). The answer is no. There never has been anybody in charge. Via was formed in haste, without thought, to solve an immediate problem; it was never fully discussed in Parliament before it came into being; its administrative structure was never made clear, nor its relationship to government. It existed for nine years without even the passage of a law to sort out its place in the scheme of things. As I write this, the law is tabled, although not yet passed.

Via was handed the passenger rail portfolio of both CPR and the CN, but it lacked either the moxie or the clout of CN, its sister Crown. Maybe that is worth looking at for a moment. CN has always been up to its hips in politics. When the Liberals were looking for a place to nestle Jack Horner, the Alberta MP who crossed the floor to join them, and then was defeated at the polls, they made him chairman of CN. When he resigned to become Grain Transportation Administrator, they appointed another Liberal, Betty Hewes of Edmonton, in his place. And when the Tories came to power in 1984, they fired her. All perfectly straightforward; the kind of thing purists deplore and Ottawa insiders understand by instinct. CN is a political creature; whether shops are closed in Moncton and opened in Winnipeg, whether rural lines are chopped in Alberta or added in Quebec, whether freight rates are held, lowered, or increased, these are all political decisions. CN knows its way around Ottawa, and has a solid base of law and bureaucratic expertise to work from. Via has neither; from the start it has been suspended between heaven and earth, like Mahomet's coffin.

All that is to change. The National Rail Passenger Transportation Act, expected to pass in 1987, will at last make an honest woman of Via. The new act spells out the corporation's role; assigns its duties, to provide "a safe, modern, efficient, and reliable network of rail passenger service"; and hands it an eviction notice.

Every route is to be assigned a proportion of its costs which must be recovered in passenger fares, and any route that doesn't meet its quota wil be readjusted—either the service cut down or fares pumped up—to make it conform. Within two years of the day the legislation comes into effect, the entire Via system must be able to operate within the smaller deficit—$400 million—that will then be available. If not, once more fares are to be raised or services dropped.

The New Equipment will go Where it's Least Needed

Remember Procrustes? He was the gent who went into the hotel game by stretching or amputating the limbs of travellers to make them conform to the dimensions of his roadside bed. One of our early motel operators. He did not get a lot of return business. Like Procrustes' hapless travellers, Via has been measured for the bed. There are some compensations. There will be another infusion of funds for equipment—$87 million for 30 locomotives, and $500 million for 130 doubledecker coaches. However, the new stuff will not go into the main commuter corridor between Quebec City and Windsor, where 50 per cent of the passengers are to be found. These folk will have to make do with the old stuff. The new goes to the transcontinental service because, as a senior transport official told Greg Weston of the *Ottawa Citizen*, "Imagine the howls from Westerners if we said to hell with them and instead put another bundle into Via just for Quebec and Ontario."

It's reassuring, somehow, to know that politics still calls the shots.

There will also be $235 million more for maintenance facilities, and Via will take over passenger stations from the other railways, instead of leasing them. Finally, the fees paid to CN and CP for running the Via trains will be renegotiated, downwards. The pea will be moved at least partway back under the CN shell.

However, even with these improvements, Via won't make it; it hasn't a hope in hell. If Via had been dealt enough money to provide swift and effective service in the late 1970s, and if it had been given a clear mandate, vigorous leadership, and access to the inner workings of government so that it could at least argue its case, there is a good chance that Canada would be in the process of joining the rest of the advanced world in a passenger railroad revival. But with its current reputation, out-moded equipment, and disastrous background, Via cannot possibly do what the government wants done in two years. In twenty, perhaps; in two, no. Most of the new equipment won't even have arrived when the deadline expires; we still have a long way to go with the clunkers now in service.

So the cards will have to be re-dealt. The government may decide simply to let passenger rail die. That is what it has already done in P.E.I. and Newfoundland. Not likely, though. Canadians love the train, an affection which editorialists ascribe to our silly sentimentality and railway buffs put down to the fact that the train is still the most effective mode of mass transport we have. Public opinion surveys show that up to 80 per cent of Canadians want high-quality passenger trains, and two-thirds are against any cuts.

When the time comes, the real alternatives for the government will be to forget the stipulations attached to the new legislation, extend the deadline (the most likely development, by far) or stick to its word, and start hacking at the lines while raising the rates. This latter option will cut passengers further and faster and leave the decision-makers to make up their minds as to whether to collapse Via and try another route, or to hope that, by that time, it will be possible to kill rail passenger service. (It won't be.) Privatizing the corporation won't work, and I've never heard it seriously suggested; you couldn't give it away. Maybe they will turn the whole thing back to CN; that would be fun.

Via represents a Crown whose corporate status has done it little good; it has not been protected from the vagaries of politics, or able to use its independence—what independence?—to carve out a special niche for itself. What is to become of it, God only knows.

Whatever anyone says of Petro-Canada, the subject of the next chapter, no one can accuse it of Via's brand of futility.

9
Carrying The Can For Petro-Can

"Every time we do something, we get dumped on."
Wilbert Hopper, *Chairman of Petro-Canada*
quoted in Saturday Night, June, 1986

The lobby of the main Petro-Canada building in downtown Calgary is awesome. Hell, the whole thing is awesome; two huge, red buildings, sheathed in imported granite plunked down in the middle of a city whose denizens seethe with rage every time their eyes are affronted by what they inevitably call, "Red Square." Inside, the awe is enlarged when you walk across a space that looks as if it would do nicely for the Calgary Stampeders to practice place-kicks in, and fetch up against the corporate plaque. Not, mind, one of those little brass squares that tells you that here in 1903 a humble service-station attendant squirted his first oilcan. Nuts to that. We are talking Plaque with a capital "P." In a space that soars for half-a-dozen storeys above your head, there is suspended an entire airplane, of the kind early petroleum explorers used to fly into the bush in search of oil. No one from Petro-Can flew into the bush in that airplane; it is a symbol of the history of the bush exploration Petro-Can didn't do, an attempt to link the new kid on the block to the other guys.

As you stand there in the silence—for much of the building is innocent of tenants—the thought may flit across your mind that Petro-Canada may be rich, but it is not necessarily smart. Is it judicious for our oil company to show off this way? I remember in one visit to Red Square coming away with a memory from my third year in high school. There was a kid in my class who was stinking rich, with his own car, an allowance that would choke a horse, and no common sense. Every time we went anywhere, Charlie would try to pick up the tab. "This is on me, guys," he would say, "I can bear the freight." And he would laugh. We let him hang around because he did, after all, have a car, and we let him buy the sundaes and milkshakes at Boone's soda-fountain— we were proud, but we weren't crazy—but we never liked him. Fat-mouthed show-off, was the general view. Old Charlie thought he could buy his way into anything, but he had no class. And he was always whining. "Nobody likes me," he would say, which was perfectly true, and "Everybody's always picking on me." True again.

It grieves me to feel the same way about Canada's Crown oil company—fat, loud-mouthed, spoiled brat—because in principal, I have always believed we ought to have our own oil company. In practice, I saw having our own oil company as this nation's inevitable reply to the Seven Sisters who rule the oil world, and I still see it this way. Perhaps it will make me feel more kindly towards Petro-Can if we review the reasons the Canadian government brought it into being. They were perfectly good ones, and what has gone wrong since—wrong in my view, anyway—will, I hope, tell us something about the use and abuse of Crown corporations in the Canadian context.

"Petro-Canada," and I am quoting now from Marsha Gordon's *Government in Business*, "was established in response to concerns raised about the world oil crisis of 1973–74." Fair enough, but it doesn't catch the flavour of the thing: it's like saying that Adam bit the apple because he thought it might please Eve; there were other temptations, and other considerations. An American study, performed by the staff of the U.S. General Accounting Office, comes a little closer when it says, "Canada's reliance on foreign-owned oil companies both for information on its resources and most of its oil and gas production greatly disturbed the Government and the Canadian public."

We had been lied to, and that concerned Canadians, and

we had been shown that we had very little control over our own energy resources, and that scared the hell out of us. Petro-Can was the result.

To understand what happened it is necessary to realize that cost has never had anything to do with the price of oil. Almost from the first, price has been manipulated by oil companies and governments, with the oil companies, until recently, having the upper hand. During the 1950s and 1960s, international oil firms produced Arabian light crude— the bell-wether grade—for ten cents a barrel, and sold it for an artificial price of $1.75 to $1.98. They were able to do this because the world oil market was dominated by seven major oil companies—the Seven Sisters—who moved 98 per cent of the oil onto the international stage. They had access to large volumes of crude, mostly in the Middle East, which they were able to sell to their own refineries at fictitiously high prices, and then retail in closely controlled markets. They took off most of the profits abroad, where they paid little or no tax, but they made a good living here, too, because they had a stranglehold on the market.

The National Oil Policy, Which Wasn't National

For many years, it made sense to these companies to supply Canada's eastern markets with the oil they produced in the Middle East for ten cents a barrrel, rather than the product of Oklahoma or Alberta, which cost almost ten times as much to produce. It also made more sense to supply Western Canada with Alberta oil. The Alberta oil cost more to produce, but less to move. Canada was split in two by what was, ironically, called "the National Oil Policy." In fact, it was an international policy. The consumer benefitted because oil prices were kept lower than they might have been had we followed the U.S. lead, which was to restrict imports from any source that might threaten the oil firms' stable market.

Because of the wide variations in cost for oil sold for, essentially, the same price, oil for decades has had two prices, the real cost of producing a barrel of the stuff, and the "posted price," an artificially high figure at which this oil would be sold on the open market, if such a market had existed. (It does now, "the spot market".) Tax revenues and royalties in the Middle East were paid on the basis of the "posted price" and it was this amount the oil companies charged their subsidiaries, and that is how they ensured that they would make profits beyond the reach of the tax-man. In short, oil has always sold for a fictitious, oligopolistic price, sometimes called a "monopoly rent" price.

The first revolution in the oil world occurred when the Middle Eastern states began to cut themselves in on the action by nationalizing their own resources during the 1950s. One after another, they set up government-owned corporations to take charge of the energy industry. They were beginning to get fed up with such incidents as the British-owned Iraq Petroleum Company plugging up wells capable of producing 50,000 barrels a day so the Iraqis would have no hint of how much oil they actually owned. By and large, the Arabs wanted to sell as much oil as possible at the best possible price, whereas what the oil companies wanted was to control the price and production to suit their own needs.

In 1959, apparently because the Russians were threatening to break the company cartel by selling oil at below the posted price, Exxon, the world's largest oil company, abruptly dropped its posted price. A contemporary account explains that "the price began to gravitate towards cost," which is one way of putting it. Exxon did not bother to consult with the Arab countries, who owned the oil; it simply informed them after the fact. That meant an abrupt drop in revenues for every Arab oil-producing nation, and they were not pleased. When Exxon did the same thing again in 1960, they were furious. Government revenues all over the Middle East plummetted, and the major oil nations called a conference in Baghdad in September, 1960, to decide what to do about it. That conference issued a demand to the oil companies to maintain prices—that was the short-term solution—and, more significantly, resolved to form a co-ordinating organization to deal with the oil giants.

The Organization of Petroleum Exporting Countries—OPEC—was born. OPEC was not, at least at first, merely a way to screw up prices; it was a defensive mechanism brought into being by the helplessness of the Arabs to deal with a long-established cartel. Now the Arabs had control of their own oil, and an organization to bargain for it on the world stage. What they lacked, and to a large extent still lack, is the expertise to explore, exploit, ship, and market the stuff into the western world. That remained the task of the Arab-American Oil Company, Aramco, a firm composed of Exxon, Standard Oil of California, Texaco, and Mobil. Aramco was formed back in 1936 to handle Middle Eastern oil, a task it continues to perform.

OPEC Turns off the Tap

OPEC is a cartel whose purpose is to control oil supplies and regulate prices. It is not a very successful cartel because cartel members do not always stick to the agreements they make, and because higher oil prices brought competition from non-OPEC members. Aramco is a consortium that does the marketing for the Middle East product. As we moved into the 1970s, both had a stake in the smooth operation of international petroleum markets, and in increasing the price of oil. Canada had nothing to do with any of this. With 95 per cent of our oil industry in foreign hands, mostly subsidiaries of the Seven Sisters, we were simply the exploited hinterland: Arabs without even an OPEC to fend for us.

Then the boom came down on us. Crude oil is brought onto the world market only as it is required, since it costs so much to move and store. What is more, the process of refining and distribution is enormously complex, and requires constant estimates of requirements in various geographic areas for different kinds of petroleum. The same refinery that produces gasoline also produces heating oil, diesel and jet fuel. It it no easy matter to measure how much of each will be required in each area of the market in a changing economy. The positioning of refineries, the building of pipelines, the supply of oil tankers, the production level of each refinery and its division of production among the dozens of products to be marketed all determine how much oil is available at a given time in a given sector of the market. And so, although oil is the second-most common fluid on the planet—second only to water—the potential always existed for a minor disruption in the market to become a major disruption in supply.

That is exactly what happened in 1973. With an economic boom running, world demand had soared, so much so that the total world production was being moved onto the market. Aramco normally maintained a reserve of 10 per cent of requirements, but even that was called into use. The United States lifted its long-lived import quota system, and that added a new dimension of demand.

At the same time, the Middle East was drifting into another war, and the Arabs were castigating the West, especially the United States, for backing Israel. Middle Eastern leaders threatened no fewer than fifteen times to use oil as a weapon to bring the Americans in line, but the administration of President Richard Nixon paid no attention. It was otherwise occupied, with Watergate.

On October 3, 1973, Egypt launched an attack on Israeli forces along the Suez Canal. On October 17, the Arab oil ministers met and agreed to cut oil exports by 5 per cent, and to recommend an embargo against "unfriendly nations." On October 19, King Faisal of Saudi Arabia learned that the United States had decided to provide $2.5 billion in arms to Israel, and ordered an immediate cut of 25 per cent in oil production, along with an embargo on the United States and other western nations friendly to Israel. Other Arab states followed Saudi Arabia's lead.

The job of administering the embargo was given to Aramco; which meant a company dominated by American firms was instructed to enforce a cutoff against the United States. Aramco did its job so successfully that Aramco President Frank Jungers was able to report in a cable, which unfortunately became public, that the Saudis had indicated "great satisfaction with Aramco" for the way it carried out its role.

The amount of oil blocked from the market was not large—no more than 2.5 million barrels a day worldwide—but the effect, in a tight market, was major. Refiners who had no assured supply, because they were not connected to the Seven Sisters, were forced to bid at OPEC auctions, and prices soared. Oil which had moved at U.S. $2.41 a barrel during 1972 sold for U.S. $17.34 on December 14, 1973, in Iran; in Nigeria, nine days later, it hit U.S. $22.60.

Despite the repeated rumblings from the Middle East, the North American oil companies had not built up any supply of crude, nor had they established refineries to process North American oil to replace the endangered supply. The energy of governments and companies seemed to have been devoted to talking about oil rather than moving it. Mobil ran commercials on television to show that the world was running out of crude. Continental ran newspaper ads which estimated the "overall reduction of crude products in the United States at some 2,700,000 barrels a day, or 15 per cent of total requirements." Actually, the U.S. shortfall was less than half that. Gulf Oil weighed in with a claim that America's inventory of petroleum was running out. The U.S. Federal Energy Administration decided to take action by dispatching 200 public relations officers "to inform the public about the oil crisis."

"A True Act of Deception"

That crisis, which lasted from October 19, 1973, until the embargo was lifted on March 18, 1974, existed mainly in the mind. Oil imports in the United States were actually higher during December, 1973, than they had been a year earlier (although they later dropped). On March 1, 1974, there was more gasoline on hand than there had been a year earlier, and supplies of home heating oil and kerosene were actually 21 per cent higher than the previous year's figures. But the gasoline was not refined, or not at the pumps where it was needed, and the public perception turned a minor and temporary shortage into a world-shaking event. All over North America, there were lineups at the pumps, shutdowns in the factories, and heat cutoffs in schools, shopping centres, and offices. The oil was there, but it wasn't where it was needed; in fact, the refineries were not even operating full-out. During the winter of 1973–74, American refineries ran at just over four-fifths their capacity, withholding, in effect, almost 20 per cent of the available supply. Christoper Rand, a former oil company employee, argued in *Making Democracy Safe for Oil* that "if the nation's refineries had been running just at the level which they could have attained without eating into stocks, there would have been no cause for cutbacks, gasless weekends, damped thermostats, talk of rationing, or zany price hikes. In other words, the American oil industry had combined with the Arab oil embargo in a true act of deception at the expense of the American consumer."

And the Canadian consumer, let's not forget him. We didn't reach the heights of panic available to Americans, but then we seldom do. We had no cases like the California incident in which a man, who thought he had not been served in turn in a gas-station lineup, went home, got a gun, returned and killed the attendant. But we did have earnest speeches from our leaders on energy conservation. As a result, the Christmas lights on Parliament Hill were shut down to preserve energy, thermostats went down, sweaters went on, and we accepted a series of price-hikes at the pumps that otherwise would have brought us out in droves, bellowing with rage.

When I was researching the crisis in 1984, for purposes of a magazine article, I talked to Dr. Michael Canes, vice-president of the American Petroleum Institute in Washington, who told me, "This was a fear-driven shortage." Edwin Rothschild, director of the Washington-based consumer group, Energy Action, agreed, but he thought "it was the oil companies and the government spokesmen who provided the fear. The shortage was not real, but panic turned their extravagant talk into self-fulfilling prophecy." And *The Energy Report* of the Harvard Business School— hardly an anti-industry source—commented, "It became clear that the real crisis was one of price, not supply."

What that meant, in Canada, was that we were being hammered by a created crisis over which we had absolutely no control. When the dust settled and the oil began to flow again, a barrel of Saudi Arabian light had multiplied four-fold in price. And consumers had been conditioned to expect more price hikes. After all, we were running out of the stuff, weren't we?

The first beneficiaries of the crisis were the OPEC nations, but the oil companies also managed to pick up some loose change. On January 1, 1974, OPEC's share of each barrel of oil was raised from $1.77 to $7.00. The oil companies' role was to pass on the increase and take a little for themselves on the way past. Every billion helps. Profits for the major firms increased by between 30 per cent and 100 per cent in 1973, then soared another 60 to 130 per cent in the first quarter of 1974. The jump in prices was also multiplying the value of oil in the ground; the value in American dollars of U.S. fossil fuel production went from $18.8 billion in 1970 to $45 billion in 1976, and $160 billion in 1981, although the amount produced actually went down. The oil companies kept saying how mad they were at the Arabs, but it was hard to understand why.

It was a Time of Brave Talk and High Prices

We were into the era of energy conferences, conservation drives, and insulation sales. Meeting halls across North America rang with brave talk of "energy alternatives" and the magic elixir, "energy independence."

In Canada, the National Oil Policy ensured that the eastern half of the country was dependent on imported crude (which came through a pipeline that originated in Portland, Maine), and was subject to the embargo. But we suffered, even more than the Americans, from a plethora of disinformation. As a senior official in the U.S. Energy Department put it to me, "There is a lot of lying going on."

"Lying" is such a harsh word; let's call it shading the figures. In the late 1960s and early 1970s, when Canada's foreign-owned oil companies were pushing for exports, we were told that we ought to get rid of the stuff while we could. In 1971, Energy Minister J.J. Greene, speaking from figures supplied by the oil industry (there were no other figures), estimated that Canada had "923 years of supply for oil and 392 years for gas." The numbers sounded so exact, they impressed the hell out of us. Also in 1971, Trade Minister Jean-Luc Pepin made a speech in which he said that, "in maybe 25 to 50 years, we'll be heating ourselves from the rays of the sun and then we'll kick ourselves in the pants for not capitalizing on what we had when oil and gas were current commodities." The Imperial Oil Annual Review for 1972 trumpeted, "Our present energy reserves, using present technology, are sufficient for our requirements for several hundred years." In 1973, Energy Minister Donald Macdonald said, "there is probably more than enough energy resources to meet domestic requirements at least until the year 2050." Like Pepin, he thought we ought to sell the stuff soon, and so did Premier Peter Lougheed of Alberta. In fact, he was pretty damn sore over the fact that oil wasn't being shipped out faster: "Alberta cannot agree to having to keep its oil in storage for tomorrow in order to serve a slow-growing Canadian eastern market, or to have its oil available for some kind of emergency," said Premier Lougheed. To even the dimmest intellect it was clear that all the wise men, both those inside the industry and those responsible for regulating energy supplies, were satisfied that we were up to our ying-yangs in oil and gas. On that understanding, we signed long-term agreements to ship natural gas to the United States, and we started shipping petroleum south, as fast as we could. Between 1965 and 1973 oil exports to the United States increased fourfold.

Then we had the oil crisis and, by jiminy, there wasn't so much of the stuff sloshing around after all. In fact, we were running out, and if we didn't act soon, we would freeze in the dark. In 1974, the National Energy Board, the same board that had approved the increased exports to the United States, announced that "Canadian oil supplies would be inadequate to serve traditional Canadian markets . . . by 1982." There was talk of rationing, and predictions of oil at $65 a barrel. The oil company commercials, referred to above, drove home the point; instead of being a drug on the market, oil was a non-renewable and vanishing resource.

The same experts who had been telling us to get rid of oil before it became worthless were now telling us to hold onto it for dear life—and explaining to us that, in the circumstances, it was only understandable that we should pay more for the precious fluid. So we did. By the time OPEC, the oil companies, and our own governments were finished with us, we were paying *twelve times* as much as we had before the exercise began, and thanking our lucky stars that the price wasn't even steeper. Of course, all this was before we discovered a new oil glut which, by 1983, was running at 13 million barrels a day.

It was against this background that the decision to establish a national oil company was taken. The process began in fact, even before the energy crisis broke in 1973, and was propelled—life is strange, isn't it?—by a policy proposal from the New Democratic Party. This proposal, which went back to the party's founding in 1962, stated that Canada should have a national oil company—everybody else did, didn't they? And the NDP had kept on passing resolutions to this end. Nobody cared; Canada was firmly in the grip of the Liberal party, Pierre Elliott Trudeau, prop., and the Liberal party thought a national oil company was a dumb idea. Still, just to reassure itself that it was on the right track, the Liberal government, in 1971, ordered a study of the oil industry to see what all the fuss was about.

The firm hired to do the study was the Arthur D. Little Company of Cambridge, Mass., and the Arthur D. Little Company turned the bulk of the work over to one of its up-and-coming executives, a bumptious, bouncy, energetic Canadian geologist named Wilbert H. ("Call me Bill") Hopper. Bill didn't think much of state oil companies since they were too likely to have to follow political decisions, and he cited the case of Italy's state firm, ENI, which had been forced to locate refineries in depressed southern Italy to serve regional development goals. His study didn't say "Nuts to that," because it was a high-toned study, but it lined up the case pro and con a Crown oil firm in such a way that it seemed—as the Liberal party had thought all along—to be a pretty dumb idea. So a state energy company was put on the back burner for the time being. After all, we had lots of oil, didn't we? The NDP was told to go soak its head.

If this were an old movie melodrama, this would be the part where the piano used to hit the low notes, and the sub-title read, "Came the dawn. . . ." There is nothing like an election for opening a government to new ideas, and the election of 1972 was a lolapalooza in this line. The Liberal majority of 1968 was gone, and the Trudeau administration was clinging to power with 109 seats to the Conservatives' 107. It was dependent for its political life on the NDP, so the same Cabinet that had earlier given the notion of an oil Crown the old heave-ho was suddenly saying, "Just a darn minute, here; maybe what this country needs is a state-owned oil company, and we're surprised somebody didn't think of it earlier." So they commissioned another study.

We get another new Energy Policy

In June, 1973, the Trudeau government ordered a major review of Canadian energy policies, and Bill Hopper's 1971 paper was given a good workout. *An Energy Policy for Canada—Phase 1*, which is what the new study was called, listed ten arguments in favour of a state firm, and eight against; however, altogether it was a fairly convincing argument against the concept.

Advocates of the idea said, "Darn it all, anyway," and the NDP kept pushing, but without success until—a drum-roll please—the energy crisis broke in October, 1973. Now it was clear to everyone that Canada had allowed itself to become utterly dependent on foreign oil companies, whose first responsibility was to their own stockholders, not Canadian needs. It was also clear that Canada could not trust the foreign firms who operated our oil industry to give us full and frank information about what was going on. Whatever drawbacks might be associated with a Crown corporation, it could be no worse than standing around biting our nails while foreign governments and foreign firms played football with the Canadian consumer.

Although many in their party favoured the Crown approach, the Liberals might have held out had they possessed a parliamentary majority. But they did not have a majority, and the NDP threatened to bring the government crashing down unless it would agree to the creation of a national oil company. Remember the old poem about the girl who, "Vowing she would ne'er consent, consented"? On December 6, 1973, Prime Minister Pierre Trudeau rose in the House of Commons to announce "a new national oil policy. The objective of that policy, to be reached before the end of this decade," went on the Prime Minister, "is Canadian self-sufficiency in oil and oil products."

The Company Would not Displace Private Firms. Uh, huh.

Significantly, one of the means to that objective would be "a publicly owned Canadian petroleum company principally to expedite exploration and development." This company—the one we ought to have had, rather than the one we have—was not "intended in any way to displace the private sector." We were about to see another example of a Crown launched for one purpose becoming something quite different.

Bill C-8, "An Act to Establish A National Petroleum Company," was introduced in May, 1974, just before the Liberals were defeated on their budget. The company-in-waiting became part of the 1974 election campaign. The Liberals were for it, the NDP claimed to have fathered it, and the Tories were against it. The Tories were thrashed, and the Petro-Canada bill played a part in that defeat. Canadians felt instinctively that they had been trifled with during the oil crisis, and that ownership of a national oil company might keep them from being trifled with again. The notion that the national oil company might itself do the trifling occurred only to cynics.

The election returned a majority Liberal government, which had little trouble passing the enabling legislation. Royal assent was given on July 10, 1975. Petro-Canada (the full title, a name that works bilingually) commenced operations in January, 1976. It had a five-year budget of $1.5 billion, $1,004 billion in the kitty, the result of the government's purchase of $580 million in common shares and $423.8 million in preferred shares, and the government's shares in companies it had been purchasing in the oil industry—45 per cent of Panarctic Oils, 15 per cent of Syncrude Canada, the Alberta tar sands project, and the government share of the co-operative Arctic venture, Polar Gas. The legislation creating Petro-Can, as it quickly became called, set out five objectives for the company:

1. To engage in exploration for and development of hydrocarbons and other types of fuel or energy;
2. To engage in research and development projects relating to fuel and energy resources;
3. To import, produce, transport, distribute, refine, and market hydrocarbons of all descriptions;
4. To produce, distribute, transport, and market other fuels and energy; and
5. To engage or invest in ventures or enterprises related to the exploration, production, importation, distribution, refining, and marketing of fuel, energy and related sources.

These were pretty broad tasks. In fact, the legislation was

framed widely enough to let Petro-Can do pretty much what it felt like, although few people dreamed that what it would do would be to turn itself into another giant oil corporation, just like all the others, and settle down industriously to sticking it to the consumer. But that is what happened.

Petro-Can came out of the chute running, with Maurice Strong, a former corporate executive and Liberal, as chairman, and bouncing Bill Hopper, the non-state enterprise man, as president. In 1976, Petro-Can bought the Alberta and British Columbia assets of Atlantic Richfield for $342 million, which gave it oil and gas production in the West. In 1978, it bought Pacific Petroleums Limited, controlled by Phillips Petroleum of the United States, for $1.5 billion, which considerably increased its western oil and gas holdings. That was the largest merger to date in Canadian history; Petro-Can became, at a stroke, the largest Canadian-owned oil company and the seventh-largest petroleum firm in the country.

That same year, Strong departed for a job with the United Nations, and Mr. Hopper became acting chairman and then chairman and chief executive officer. The man who didn't think much of Crown oil companies was in charge of one; but the joke was on us, because, as it turned out, he ran the Crown much like a private company. This fact did not appear evident for some time. Indeed, everything was going as planned; Petro-Can was getting into exploration, up north and offshore, buying out foreign firms, and beginning to make its presence felt in the oilpatch. Pacific Petroleums, as it turned out, owned refining capacity and 426 gas stations scattered between western Ontario and Victoria, B.C. Nothing much, less than 4 per cent of the Canadian retail market. Still, there it was, why not give it a try? So Petro-Can put up its own signs on the gas stations and was suddenly in the downstream end of the oil business. (Everything up to the refinery is "upstream," selling the stuff is "downstream.") There was nothing in the legislation to prevent this, and the general public perception, that Petro-Can was there to give us a "window on the industry" and to push frontier energy development—to boldly go where no oil company had gone before—didn't come into play. Other oil companies were getting a bit restive—Had they heard wrong, or had Prime Minister Trudeau said flatly that Petro-Can was not to be a commercial competitor?—but who cared about them?

The Tory (Joe Clark Type) Interlude

Well, the Tories did, bless them. The Progressive Conservatives knew when free enterprise was being traduced, and when they stumbled into power in May, 1979, they quickly set up a Task Force on Petro-Can, with instructions to tell it how to "privatize"—it was a new word, then—the company. The Task Force said the government should create a new government agency, not a Crown, to take over the "public sector activities and assets of Petro-Canada." Frontier exploration, tar sands, negotiating state-to-state sales, all that sort of thing, should be turned over to this agency. The company's conventional oil activities would be transferred to a new, private Petro-Can and the shares in this company distributed to every Canadian, as a gift of the Crown.

However, there was a problem. The Task Force report, dated October 15, 1979, arrived on Prime Minister Joe Clark's desk exactly 22 days before the Ayatollah Khomeini took power in Iran. Soon, we were into another oil crisis, more shortages, more lineups, and predictions of worse to come. Bill Hopper, never a soft-spoken man, put in his two cents' worth with a comment that, "Not only are there prospects of a chronic shortage of crude oil in world trade, there is the absolute certainty that all governments will use all their available means—everythng from gold to guns—to obtain their needs."

Privatized, but only sort of

Well, shucks, if we were going to have a war over oil, it would be stupid to sell Petro-Can, wouldn't it? In December, 1979, the Clark government, modified the Task Force report. Petro-Can would be privatized, but only sort-of. The government would retain 30 per cent, give away 50 per cent to the citizens, and sell 20 per cent. Before this could be done, however, the Conservatives were defeated, the Liberals returned, and we had the National Energy Programme (NEP), which would save us all.

The NEP was announced in October, 1980, with the stated aims of protecting the Canadian consumer from the full force of international price hikes and securing Canada's energy independence by bringing the oil industry under national control. In 1979, 82 per cent of all Canadian oil moved through foreign firms; we would reduce that to 50 per cent and make this nation independent of OPEC, or anybody else, by developing our own resources. We had to do something; according to the background documents released with the NEP, by 1990, we would be paying $9.3 billion to finance our oil trade deficit.

But there was, thank God, a solution, a strength that flowed out of the very shortages that were so threatening. Oil prices would keep on rising; the world price—we had this based on our very best statistics, and now, by golly, we even had our own oil company to keep track—would go from $22.69 a barrel in 1979 to $58.50 in 1983, and up from there. With all this money to play with, all the government had to do was to deal itself into the game, scoop some of the new riches away from the oil companies, use some of the excess to keep Canadian oil prices down, spend some more to buy deeper into the industry, provide tax breaks to inspire exploration, and pocket the rest. Nothing to it.

After much debate with the oil-producing provinces, a deal was arranged to structure this dream. In September, 1981, a federal-provincial conference struck a four-year energy agreement under which Canadian prices would escalate in six-month stages to $57.75 a barrel in 1986, which would still be only 75 per cent of the world price, predicted to be $77 a barrel by that time. In fact, the price would go right on leaping upwards as far as the eye could see, at an annual rate of 13 per cent. On this platform of growing riches, we would construct the New Jerusalem of oil.

The new wealth would be divided up among the federal government (25.5 per cent), the oil industry (44.3 per cent), and the provincial governments (30.2 per cent). Everyone would be happy—with the possible exception of the consumer.

About the time this deal was hammered out, a worldwide recession struck, and the demand for oil sagged. Concurrently, the higher prices and tax breaks for oil exploration brought new oil welling out of the land—and the sea—and the 1986 price hit, instead of $77, $14. Dear, oh dear. Once more, Canada had convulsed itself into a new energy policy based on assumptions that turned out not to be worth a bucket of warm spit.

Never mind, on the basis of the NEP, Petro-Can was on the move again. In 1981, it purchased the Belgian-based oil giant Petrofina Canada. The price paid was either $1.4 billion, the figure used at the time; $1.61 billion, the figure calculated by Dominion Securities Pitfield in a 1984 study (this is the figure Petro-Can showed in its 1981 annual report, made up of $825.5 million paid out to the end of that year, and an "estimated" $787.4 million to be spent later); "around $1.7 billion," the figure used by industry analyst Peter Foster, or some other goodly number. As noted earlier, the details of this deal were effectively concealed from the Auditor-General of Canada, who is not, incidentally, Petro-Can's auditor. Petrofina was a major marketer, especially in Quebec; indeed, Foster argues that the real reason for the takeover was that "most of Petrofina's gas stations were in Quebec."

The Petrofina purchase was paid for straight from the federal treasury, via the Canadian Ownership Account, a tax the government had thoughtfully tacked onto oil and gas in 1981, so it didn't cost Petro-Can a dime. All the company had to do was to issue convertible notes to Ottawa which could later be turned into shares. In the Atlantic Richfield deal, Ottawa had donated a meagre $100 million, with the oil company borrowing the rest, and Petro-Can had to borrow the entire $1.5 billion for Pacific Petroleum.

Petro-Can was rapidly turning from an oil exploration company into a major retailer, but nobody seemed to notice. In 1983, Petro-Can bought BP Refining for $416 million, which made it a major retailer in central Ontario. The press release describing this sale at the time said, "Petro-Canada indicated that this acquisition would complete its refining and marketing business."

Gulping Gulf

Just kidding, folks. Just a little joke between tycoons. In October, 1985, Petro-Can acquired the western down-stream assets of Gulf Canada Limited, including 1,800 service stations. This was part of a complex, on-again, off-again deal involving the Reichmann brothers of Toronto, who had purchased these assets as part of another deal, but who didn't want the service stations, only the oil and gas reserves owned by Gulf. Bill Hopper had a tough time making the federal cabinet, now back in the hands of Conservatives as a result of the 1984 federal election, swallow the Gulf deal, but a rationale was finally worked out—the arrangement would "round out" the company and make it easier to sell to private industry when the time came. This purchase cost $887 million, although Peter Foster insists that, with everything into account, the final bill will come to "more than $1 billion."

Today, Petro-Can, with assets of more than $9 billion, only produces 6 per cent of Canadian oil, although it is our third most important producer of natural gas. But it has 3,890 service stations, more than any other company in the land. It has spent $5 billion in public funds. Its exploration programmes have not been a success (it wrote off $865 million in drilling costs in 1985), and have more than wiped out all the paper profits it has made since its inception. The Crown we set up to find oil isn't having much luck in that line, but it is going like gang-busters in the oil-selling business, where there was never a shortage of participants.

Let's See if We've Got This Right

Before he assumed the lofty office of Finance Minister, Michael Wilson accused Petro-Can of mis-stating its profits, and Auditor-General Kenneth Dye pointed the finger at the company for hiding information from Canadians. Curbing competition and thus raising prices is the charge levelled at Petro-Can by the Investigations Branch of the Department of Consumer and Corporate Affairs, while Dominion Securities Pitfield accuses our national oil Crown of spending more than it needed to. Dominion Securities' analysis of the company states the Petro-Can's assets were acquired at values much higher than those reflected on previous owners' balance sheets. Hey, nobody's perfect.

We created a Crown to keep us informed on the oil business, boost exploration, encourage research, and to stay away from the jobs that were already being looked after by the other oil giants. What we got, ten years and $5 billion later, is a secretive giant that looks much like any other oil company and is now oriented to new magic phrase, "the bottom line."

Now it would like to be privatized. Bill Hopper told *Saturday Night* in June, 1986, "I'm very much onside with the notion that now is the time, since this instrument has done its job, to sell it off."

Maybe we should; it is hard to imagine a single advantage we have gained for our $5 billion, except a modicum of exploration—most of it paid for, not through Petro-Can, but by exploration grants. We are better informed than we used to be about the oil industry, but that has nothing to do with Petro-Can either. It is the result of regulations passed during the first energy crisis, which require extensive reporting from all oil firms operating in this country. We didn't need a Crown to get a grip on oil, just a little common sense.

Petro-Can has certainly improved Canadian control in the oil industry, but seems to have lost sight of why we needed that control. We needed it to protect ourselves from the pricing practices of Big Oil; what we got was our own oil company showing Big Oil how it's done.

We can get some insight into how far Petro-Can has strayed from what was intended by delving into a series of internal memos, which we were certainly never intended to see.

These memos outline the process by which our Crown corporation bought into a French company, hired an affiliate of that firm to undertake research in Canada, the results of which are now being shared with France, and then collapsed most of its own research group.

In the late fall of 1984, these memos show, Petro-Can purchased 27 per cent of a French firm called Internationale de Services Industriels et Scientifiques, S.A.—ISIS for short. It paid 81 million French francs (about $17 million) for this minority interest. ISIS owns 82 per cent of another French company, Institut Français du Pétrole (IFP). This is a major research and development company, with a 1984 research budget of close to $160 million. In January, 1985, Petro-Can committed itself to hiring IFP to undertake research into a floating production system for use in developing offshore resources. This is work that would seem to form part of the natural functions of Petro-Can's own research group; offshore production is one of the areas in which they had become expert. The project is described this way:

> Floating production systems may be used to develop the oil deposits discovered on the Grand Banks of Newfoundland. Such systems may incorporate flexible conduits to move the oil from wells or other seabed-based facilities up to some sort of floating production platform.
>
> It is proposed that an IFP project team examine the engineering and environmental design criteria for a Grand Banks Floating Production System and proceed to advance technology in the required areas. The work will be directed to produce novel concepts and approaches which offer operational and economic advantages over conventional technology.

The arrangement with IFP provides for an annual review of "current development objectives," and each side is required, "subject to the rights of third parties, [to] make available to the other selected relevant studies, reports and other information relating to Projects and potential Projects." Furthermore, IFP is required to spend at least 27 million francs—$5.7 million—on research projects that both parties agree to, with a minimum expenditure of 7 million francs annually—about $1.5 million.

Petro-Can will be getting some research for its investment, but it will also be required to share information it has, including that on offshore oil development. In addition, it is required to sponsor and pay for research projects performed by IFP, such as the floating production system study.

By March 7, 1985, Petro-Can had approved more work by IFP than its research budget would allow—the documents don't show the numbers—so a new schedule was drawn up, allotting $375,000 to the floating production system project. These were great jobs if you could get them. The draft budget shows the French employees being paid at rates ranging from $103 an hour for the project manager to $52 an hour for a secretary.

While this was being patted into place, Petro-Can's own group of researchers in this area were "realigned," in the quaint phraseology of the internal documents. Many were laid off, others were reassigned. In some cases, highly trained scientists were turned into salesmen, and sent out to peddle natural gas. About sixteen or eighteen jobs were directly involved.

Why would we dump our own researchers and hire foreigners? The rationale appears in a February 12, 1986, memo: "The Executive Council believes that we must manage Petro-Canada's existing businesses for maximum performance in the short-term. This program of 'getting back to basics' involves knowing the existing asset base and maximizing the cash generation from those assets."

This directive goes directly counter to the company's description of itself in the document, *Canada's National Energy Corporation*, produced by Petro-Canada Public Affairs, which asserts, "It [Petro-Can] must, therefore, balance the business principle of maximizing profit with other considerations to reach goals in the national interest. That requirement from time to time leads Petro-Canada into activities in which Canadian jobs and business opportunities, regional development, or long-term energy security may be more important factors than only maximizing the short-term return on dollars invested."

Forget that jazz; it all belongs to the old Crown. In the new Petro-Can, it makes perfect sense to dismantle your own research group and sub-contract the job to others.

There is not a word in either the 1984 or 1985 annual reports of Petro-Can to indicate either this research arrangement or the purchase of shares in ISIS, although the acquisitions of BP and Gulf are trumpeted. In the 1985 report, a section on "Building an International Position" mentions activities in China, Colombia, Indonesia, Spain, and Papua New Guinea, but France is not mentioned, despite the size of the investment there.

If you want to know if a public company can spend $17 million without it coming to anyone's attention, the answer is, Oh, my, Yes, provided the company we're speaking about is a Crown. And if you want to know how much original research, and how many Canadian jobs in a high-tech field could be secured by the expenditure of $17 million in capital, plus annual injections of money for individual research projects, the answer is, Quite a few.

Incidentally, the floating production study was supposed to begin on August 1, 1985, but didn't get under way until September 30, two months late. Two Petro-Can employees were assigned to monitor it—with $20,000 allotted to cover two trips to Paris for each of them. It's a dirty job, but somebody has to do it. A memo dated October 15, 1985, makes it clear that things were not going as planned. IFP wasn't doing the work—it had in turn sub-contracted it to two other companies in which ISIS owns an interest—and was instead "acting as the study co-ordinator and perhaps providing some limited technical direction." But that wasn't the nub of the complaint; it was that "IFP et al were encouraged to stress conceptual work over merely assembling standard production system components," but that wasn't happening. There was "an IFP tendency . . . to conduct a standard engineering exercise."

All that money spent, and the job still wasn't being done the way it should be.

What appears to have happened with Canada's Crown oil company is what, by this time, we ought to expect; an instrument formed for national policy purposes, and given independence to operate in the commercial world, has become just another corporation. Why should we pay $5 billion for that? Let's sell it.

The thing that will stick in my craw, though, is the notion that the Canadian taxpayer—to say nothing of the Canadian consumer—should have sunk all that money into a company so that someone else can walk off with it. Petro-Can will not be sold for what we paid for it, unless every analyst outside Red Square has it wrong. It will be sold at a loss, and then turned into a profit-maker for private shareholders. In the year ending December 31, 1985, it lost a whopping $769,335,000—but with its $9 billion in assets, it has a net worth (all the assets less liabilities) of $3.6 billion.

This is one of the nation's largest companies and in private hands, which is where it will no doubt wind up, it will make potfuls of money for somebody. But what has any of this to do with the reasons for which we established it in the first place?

It will be a relief, in the next two chapters, to look at some Crowns that, however disastrously they perform economically, at least do serve public purposes.

10
CBC, Why Not Take All of Me?

"Sail on, O CBC, sail on!"

Max Ferguson, *1967*

It was the Auditor-General, Kenneth Dye, who ratted to Parliament: The CBC had just lost or misplaced $57 million, or maybe it was more, or less. It was pretty embarrassing. The Crown corporation had stalled turning in its annual report for two months past the 1986 deadline, but even with the delay, Mr. Dye said, "I was unable to complete my audit."

The CBC had installed a new accounting system—the latest thing in computerization, of course—and in the process had managed so to screw things up that the dear old corp., in Mr. Dye's words, was "unable to maintain adequate accounting records and control." Thus, there was a large amount of money unaccounted for. Oh, it was around somewhere, maybe stuck in the back of a drawer, maybe drifting around in the innards of the computer. Nobody was saying the money had been *stolen*, mind, it just couldn't be *located*, an entirely different matter.

Well, we couldn't have this, Canada's most visible, prestigious Crown—and, at a billion dollars in annual expenditures, one of her most expensive—behaving in a slapdash, amateurish way. So CBC President Pierre Juneau was shoved out in front of the curtain to make a speech.

Juneau asked for another $40 million, and make it snappy.

Otherwise, he said, he would be forced to take action, and cut valuable services. The CBC-FM radio stereo network could be deep-sixed, for example, unless Parliament coughed up quickly.

Hand over everything in the till, or I'll shoot myself in the foot.

You have to admire the birds who run the CBC; their accounting may be shaky, but by God, they've got brass. Fussbudgets may wonder about what they did with the money we gave them last week, but that isn't the issue; the issue is that they want more next week, or we will come to regret it. And—this is what makes the cheese more binding—they are right.

Not right that it is okay to drool away millions of dollars without proper accounting—no one can defend that, and in due course, heads will roll—but right that the service is indispensable to this nation, and must be maintained, nay, extended and improved, although whether that requires more money remains to be seen.

The CBC is Canada writ small, with all the bumps, warts, character, and potential for disaster, and for greatness, the nation itself contains. It is a monolith, a gross, swollen, ugly, misshapen, wrong-headed brute of a thing. But it is *our* wrong-headed brute of a thing. The bloody old CBC, bless it. If we didn't have it, we would have to invent it. It's the nation's whipping-boy and the nation's lifeline. It affronts us, and it defines us. It drives us to the telephone, bellowing with rage, and it pulls us to the edge of our chairs, crooning with joy. It is an aspect of this country that sets us off clearly, irredeemably—and thankfully—from the United States, probably the only thing, aside from Wayne Gretzky, that thinking Americans wish they had invented.

Now if it could only get its act together, and do in television what it has done in radio, we would learn to love the monster, God rot it.

The CBC was born in desperation, has survived by leaping over the potholes of catastrophe, and lives under constant threats—threats imposed by its enemies, occasionally; public indifference, more often; and its own stupidities, most often. In one sense, it is the perfect Crown corporation because it serves a function that cannot, and will not, be provided by private enterprise. In another sense, it is our worst Crown corporation because its demands are incessant, its blunders palpable, and its arrogance immeasurable. Like other Crowns, it wants power, but not responsibility. It demands independence, except that it wants unlimited access to the public teat; it insists on its integrity, except that it cannot apparently look after its money; and it wants everyone to understand that it is above politics, except that it is up to its hips in politics every time a news broadcast hits the air. It is most of the good things, and all of the bad things, that can befall a nation that uses government corporations. It differs from other Crowns only in this—that every Canadian has an opinion about the CBC, and knows quite a lot about it, and how it operates, for good and ill. And that is, perhaps, the best thing about it of all.

The CBC was born, as we have already seen in Chapter 3, out of the sure knowledge that unless Canada took charge of her own airwaves, they would be usurped by the United States. The Americans had three networks linked coast to coast; we had a handful of private stations, broadcasting locally. In the United States, licences to broadcast were cheap and easy to obtain; in Canada, the government allocated frequencies stingily. When they could get them. When commercial broadcasting began in the early 1920s, only six clear radio channels were allotted to Canadians, and then the Americans appropriated every clear channel on the ether, including the six already being used by Canada. We were simply blotted out. Our government went down to Washington to demand that the Americans vacate a dozen spots for our use, and the Americans replied with a rude noise. Finally, they allotted us six channels—taking seventy-seven for themselves. When we wouldn't accept this lopsided arrangement, negotiations broke off, without any deal being struck. It was then open season for American transmitters to beam across the border, drowning out the local signals. This was not a game in which we could play tit-for-tat, since the total Canadian broadcasting power at the end of 1920s amounted to less than fifty kilowatts. U.S. stations broadcast 680 kilowatts.

Canadian radio stations huddled together at one end of the dial. In Toronto, in 1925, there were seven radio stations (three owned by newspapers, the others by Bell Telephone, Eaton's, Marconi, and Westinghouse), but they shared two broadcast frequencies, which meant they had to take turns on the air.

Finally, and most crucially, up until 1925, no commercials were allowed in Canada, except for brief credits to the sponsor, while Americans were already hearing the glories of soap suds, toothpaste, and floor wax. Strong networks were built on the sale of commercials, and dominated the airwaves on both sides of the border. In 1925, a "Radio Popularity Ballot" conducted by the Toronto *Telegram*, listed seventeen U.S. stations ahead of any Canadian one. About the same time, *Maclean's* magazine reported that "nine-tenths of the radio fans in this Dominion hear three or four times as many United States stations as Canadian." The nation's broad distances and thin markets defeated us, and many people believed that it made more sense to develop the Canadian regional markets as offshoots of American broadcasting. In Montreal, CFCF became an NBC affiliate, while CKAC, owned by *La Presse*, joined CBS. In Toronto, CKWG, backed by the *Telegram*, became part of NBC in order, as the newspaper put it, "to put programmes on the air which it would bankrupt any Canadian station to provide." The affiliates—does this sound depressingly familiar?—filled between 40 and 60 per cent of their airtime with American shows. "Canada," wrote broadcast historian Austin Weir, "was fast becoming a mere satellite of American broadcasting."

God Created the CBC. Who Else?

According to Sandy Stewart's history of Canadian radio, *From Coast to Coast*, the CBC was then created—this will come as no surprise to the corporation brass—by God. Not directly, of course. The churches began to catch on to radio as an effective instrument for spreading the Good Word, and religious groups took over stations in Montreal, Toronto, Saskatoon, Edmonton, and Vancouver. One of the Toronto stations called CFCX was run by Jehovah's Witnesses. Now it was considered okay for Toronto Baptists from the Jarvis St. Church to operate CJBC—after all, the Catholics had a station out of St. Michael's Cathedral—but not okay for Jehovah's Witnesses to do the same. Things became more complicated when one of the Witness stations was rented out to the Ku Klux Klan in Saskatchewan. Howls of outrage poured into the offices of Pierre Joseph Cardin, who, as Minister of Marine, was in charge of the air (ships, radio, airwaves, get it?). Cardin began to switch the frequencies of various stations, bumping four Jehovah's Witness stations off the air. One of the switched frequencies went to Gooderham and Worts, a distillery, and all hell broke loose. In the House of Commons, J. S. Woodsworth, MP for Winnipeg North (and a Methodist minister), demanded to know who had appointed Mr. Cardin as national censor, and when the minister would start censoring the Orange Lodge and the Catholic church. The freedom-of-religion argument led to a noisy debate about the role of government in controlling the airwaves. The debate became so acrimonious and complicated that Mr. Cardin decided to take the forthright, manly way out. He dumped the whole mess into the lap of a royal commission.

The Aird Commission was named for its chairman, Sir John Aird, president of the Canadian Bank of Commerce, an implacable—everybody thought—foe of the notion of public broadcasting. However, the evidence introduced before the commission made it clear that if there was to be any broadcasting in Canada by Canadians—religious or secular—government would have to take a hand, to cope with the entrenched American influence. When Aird visited New York and heard NBC executives speak of Canada as part of their territory, he was affronted; and when he visited London and heard BBC executives explain how their system worked, he was convinced. It would cost a lot of money to build a transmission system and provide programming that could compete with the Americans, and since private Canadians showed no disposition to come up with the money—the CPR and the Canadian Manufacturers' Association both developed plans for national networks, but the funds were to come from the public purse, only the profits would be private—a government network was the only solution. This was especially true since broadcasting would have to be provided in two languages, and made available to remote areas where commercial radio could never begin to break even. (Brief pause to point out that nothing has changed.)

In September, 1929, the Aird Commission reported, in nine succinct pages, in favour of "some form of public ownership, operation and control, behind which is the national power and prestige of the whole public of the Dominion of Canada." The report recommended seven high-powered radio stations across the country, linked through a national system to be called the Canadian Radio Broadcasting Company. It would be financed by a $3 annual licence fee on subscribers, and a $1 million annual subsidy. In those days, a million dollars was a respectable pot of money.

Most people were in favour of the report, and the Liberal government prepared enabling legislation. But before the legislation could get into the House of Commons, the Great Depression hit. Mackenzie King called an election, in 1930, and was defeated. Not to worry, all the best Tories were for public broadcasting. Former Prime Ministers Arthur Meighen and Robert Borden both backed a public network, as did the new Prime Minister, R. B. Bennett, who said, as he introduced the Canadian Broadcasting Act of 1932, "No other scheme than that of public ownership can ensure to the people of this country, without regard to class or place, equal enjoyment of the benefits and pleasures of radio broadcasting."

The CRBC is Born. And Dies.

Only one vote was cast against the bill, which established a three-man Canadian Radio Broadcasting Commission (CRBC), to run the radio stations and regulate broadcasting. It was a mess. The first chairman, Hector Charlesworth (the editor of *Saturday Night* magazine, and something of a bigot), insisted on censoring all Jehovah's Witness scripts, which revived the religious controversy and embarrassed the Canadian Radio League, then, as now, the major lobby for public broadcasting.

There was also considerable resentment over the annual licence fee—two dollars, rather than the three recommended by Aird. Canadians objected to paying to listen to the radio when Americans didn't have to, so they just refused, and collecting the fees became a nightmare. (The notion was later junked, and the CBC received parliamentary appropriations to cover its deficits.)

But the CRBC might have survived if it hadn't made itself a patsy for the Conservative government during the 1935 election campaign. This campaign was enlivened by a series of radio dramas devised by the Tory ad agency—although no one was told that—featuring a Mr. Sage, a folksy porch-sitter who spent his time bad-mouthing the Liberals. The plays were broadcast nationally, and the Tories loved them. The Grits did not. The Liberals laid formal complaints before Chairman Charlesworth, who insisted that, in the last four plays of the series, a sponsor be named. He was. The public was told that the plays were being broadcast courtesy of one R. L. Wright. What they were not told was that he was an employee of the Tory ad agency.

This sort of stuff is okay if you win the election, but the Conservatives did not. When Mackenzie King came back to power in 1936, he hastily disbanded the CRBC and, following the advice of the Canadian Radio League, established a Crown corporation, the Canadian Broadcasting Corporation, which emerged on the world on November 2, 1936. The rest, as they say, is history.

Which is to say that, for the next fifty years, the CBC grew, politicians kept trying to interfere with it, and investigating and broadcasting commissions kept trying to work out its rights, duties, and relationships with private broadcasting.

For twenty-two years, the CBC was both the Crown responsible for public broadcasting and the regulator responsible for all broadcasting—including the granting of licences and receiving of complaints. This meant that, for example, when Conservative leader John Diefenbaker thought he was being ill-used by the public networks during the 1957 and 1958 federal elections, he was invited to address himself to, yup, the CBC, which told him to go soak his head. This is known as preserving the integrity of the Crown corporation.

When he came to power in 1958, Mr. Diefenbaker wasted little time in implementing a report of the Fowler Commission to separate the broadcast functions of the CBC from the regulatory ones. He created the Board of Broadcast Governors (BBG), with two goals in mind. One was to

press for more Canadian content in broadcasting, a recommendation of the Liberal-appointed Fowler Commission; the other was to bring the CBC into line by giving its
referee's whistle to the BBG. Neither attempt was partic-
ularly successful.

Mr. Diefenbaker stuffed the BBG with political appoint-
ees, but they didn't have much luck bringing the CBC to
heel. They were too busy defending themselves against
claims—many of them valid—of favouritism in the granting
of broadcast licences, and howls of outrage from private
broadcasters, Tories to a man, who didn't want to meet the
BBG's guideline for Canadian content—55 per cent. Since
we were now in the world of television—the first broadcast
was in French, on September 6, 1952, followed by English
two days later—the content rules were taking money out
of the pockets of the private broadcasters who had backed
the Conservatives in the first place.

Broadcasting has Been Studied More Than Teen-Age Sex

Not only that, the CBC argued that the BBG had no right
to tell it what to do and, in a tug-of-war over whether it or
CTV would broadcast the Grey Cup football game in 1962,
stopped just short of open defiance of the regulator. (In
the end, the broadcast was shared with CTV as it still is.)

So we had some more investigations—I can't prove it,
but my guess is that Canadian broadcasting has been in-
vestigated more often than teen-age sex—and (what else?)
another series of recommendations in 1965. That led to
the establishment of the Canadian Radio-Television Commission (CRTC), set up in 1968 to (guess what?) regulate
Canadian broadcasting and beef up Canadian content. It
was headed by an aggressive gent named Pierre Juneau
(the Juno awards are named for him), who went on to
become a prime ministerial aide, a cabinet minister (briefly),
a Liberal candidate (disastrously), and then president of the
CBC. Was this a political appointment? Is ice cold?

Politics has always bedevilled broadcasting in Canada,
and always will. Prime Minister Pierre Trudeau, on a number of occasions, tried to bully the CBC into submission—

or, if not submission, at least silence—and Prime Minister Brian Mulroney has tried to turn the network into his personal cheering section. But neither succeeded, and while there was a lot of anguish over the Juneau appointment within the corporation, no one has ever been able to point to any overt influence anywhere on the narrow political front, that is, on party politics. On the broader policy front, the CBC is fast losing the battle, especially in the crucial field of television.

The CBC's board of directors has always been heavily political, with patronage appointments to party hacks far out-running merit appointments. This ought not to matter much, since the CBC, like most Crowns, is essentially run by its management. When the corporation comes under fire, however, it becomes crucial, and disastrous. When the Conservatives began to hack away at CBC revenues, in 1985 and 1986, causing the demolition of much fine regional programming, and delaying the replacement of the corporation's mouldering capital plant, the directors stood around with their thumbs in their cheeks and their minds on nothing much at all. Mavor Moore, a gifted writer and director, and long-time CBC observer, was stung to write, "Appointment by patronage leads boards of trustees to abdicate down or up—to hand their power over to those who know the territory, the operating staff, or to give it back to the government of the day. The present CBC board of directors cannot, apparently, make up its mind which way to abdicate." So the service is dismantled while its guardians collect their per diems and follow the party line. Perhaps they think the CRTC will step in.

The CRTC Sings: I'm a Yankee-Doodle Dandy

Broadcast regulation is, as it has always been, quixotic, uneven, and highly political. The CRTC, given the task of enforcing broadcast rules (especially content rules), seems to have its mind on other things. No broadcaster, to my knowledge, has ever lost his licence for refusing to live up to the commitments he made when the licence was issued. The CRTC simply issues papal dispensations after the fact. When a broadcast licence comes up for renewal, no outsider is allowed to bid for it—or to argue that he could do a better job. The licence holder reapplies, apologizes for what he did during his last term—or boasts about it—and walks away with his renewal.

While the CRTC has never been political in the partisan sense, its crucial decisions, especially in television, have vital political implications in the broad sense. The CRTC decided, not only to license the importation of whole American networks on cable, but then to license more private Canadian stations in major urban markets. In neither case was any compensation exacted to support Canadian broadcasting; in both cases, the effect was, in the phrase of CBC executive Mark Starowicz, "Americanization by privatization." Every time a new broadcaster appeared, the American content on Canadian airwaves went up. For example, the creation of the private Global television network was apparently motivated by the CRTC's desire to see how many American game shows could be crammed on the air before something gave. Global recently promised to provide more funding for Canadian drama, which will be nice if it happens. It also produces an excellent early-evening news broadcast. For the rest, it is a wasteland.)

Finally, in 1982 came the licensing of pay television, and the CRTC handed out licences to two national and three regional pay-TV networks, all of them private. They collapsed into one national service which has said several times that it has no intention of meeting the commitments made in regard to Canadian content when the licences were issued. Instead, it is filling out the service with three services dominated by American material—the Nashville Network, the Cable News Network, out of Atlanta, and the Sports Network, which does at least cover Canadian sports in between large slabs of the American ones. The CRTC beams. The regulator has taken the most political decision it can take, to abandon Canadian airwaves to the United States, and send us all back to 1932. Here we go again.

Canadians watch an average of twenty-three hours of television per week, and a Canadian child, by the time he or she reaches the age of twelve, will have watched 12,000 hours of TV, 10,000 hours of it American network programming. That 10,000 hours, Starowicz points out, represents more time than the child will have spent in class.

Twenty-eight per cent of English language television available in this country is Canadian, and, in prime time, 23 per cent of all programmes available are Canadian. There are more hours of American newscasting available to Canadians than Canadian, and for every hour of Canadian drama on TV and cable, there are twenty-four hours of American.

No other nation on earth has allowed itself to be so culturally swamped. We are a Third World country in broadcasting, but that is not the fault of the CBC. In the circumstances, there is a certain bitter irony in the argument that the CBC ought to import more American programmes because they are cheaper than producing our own, and thus help cut costs. Or there is the alternative—make the CBC hustle for more commercial dollars.

When he was chairman of the CRTC (which is now called the Canadian Radio-Television and Telecommunications Commission), Pierre Juneau ordered the then CBC president, Laurent Picard, to cut the number of commercials on the network in half, because, he said, commercials have "a definite influence" on CBC programming choices. When Juneau became CBC president, he decided that what the network really needs is commercials. He explained to Matthew Fraser of the *Globe and Mail* that "someone who is running a corporation always knows more than someone who is on the outside," a thought that apparently hadn't occurred to him when he was instructing Mr. Picard. Actually, I think he may have had it right in the first place, when his concern was not trying to find the dollars to keep the huge, rickety machine going, but looking at its role in Canadian broadcasting.

The mission of the CBC—if you will accept so lofty a word as "mission"—has not changed. It is one of the few Crowns we have where the intention of its founders has never wavered nor been suborned. What it was, it remains, both a symbol and a bulwark of Canadian culture and Canadian identity. It is, God knows, flawed, but it has not become, at least not yet, just another company out scratching for a buck, the way Petro-Can has; its public purpose remains valid.

That will not be the case if the CBC decides, as Petro-Can, the CN, and the Post Office have all decided, that what it really has to do is to pay its way by imitating its private enterprise competition. There is a role for the CBC as keeper of the national flame; there is no role for it as importer of "Dallas" and "All My Children." Private broadcasters are perfectly capable of buying all the imported junk. Indeed, they argue, correctly, that having the CBC in the bidding simply makes these programmes more expensive.

Aha, the CBC replies, but if we didn't carry all this stuff, and all the commercials that go with it, it would cost even more to run the CBC. Perfectly true, too. The question then becomes, are Canadians willing to pay for a public broadcasting network that is not merely an imitation of the Americans? Maybe not, but I think they are, and I think the pattern to follow is the pattern of CBC radio.

CBC Radio is Wonderful. Then There is TV.

In 1975, commercials were removed from CBC radio. At the time, this was considered a radical step because it would lead, and did lead, to higher costs. It is true that radio advertising revenue was not exactly swollen; the gross annual take at the time was $3,376,000, and the net—with agency fees and other expenses paid—was $3,007,000. Not really much. Just the same, foregoing this revenue gave the network a different sound, and reinforced its programmes which are—in my view, and the view of the people who give away prizes for such things—measurably superior to anything on private radio, or anything offered on the American private networks.

CBC radio is wonderful. The people who run it are somewhat strange, but the product is distinctive, in every sense of that word. Network programmes like "Morningside," "As It Happens," "Sunday Morning," "Quirks and Quarks," "Ideas"—the list is nearly endless—are unlike anything consistently produced elsewhere. For any Canadian working abroad, the shock of recognition when you run across one of these programmes while twiddling the short-wave dial is instantaneous and gratifying.

On the other hand, the daily fare on CBC television is virtually indistinguishable from that offered on the private networks or the imported networks, with rare exception.

American radio has not been able to shove the CBC off the air for the simple reason that the Canadian product is better. Not merely different, but better. Crudely put, CBC radio knows what it is doing and CBC television does not, and the difference has nothing to do with policy, or politics, or anything else but dollars.

Time to look at the dollars, briefly. News stories like to refer to the CBC as a "billion-dollar operation," and that is not so far wide of the mark. If you add up the parliamentary appropriations for the corporation and the money it makes and spends on its own, the total comes to just over a billion dollars annually.

In 1983/84, for example, the CBC earned $179.1 million from TV advertising, another $13.3 million from other sources—syndication, cassettes, that sort of thing. It spent $1,005,700,000. Parliament—you and I—made up the difference, $813.3 million. This was paid out in two chunks, $742.1 million for operating costs and $71.2 million for capital allocation.

I have used 1983/84 because it is the latest year, what with all the tomfoolery at the CBC, for which I can lay my hands on internal figures. In recent years, the rules have changed; instead of, in effect, giving the CBC a blank cheque by simply picking up (while grumbling), the bill for its losses, government now tells the corporation what it is prepared to appropriate for capital and operating costs. The figures have been cut sharply over the past two years. In 1984/85, the corporation got $871 million. In 1985/86, it was allocated $896 million, then abruptly ordered to slash $75 million, which took it back below, in real dollars, where it had been in 1983. In 1985/86, it got $846 million (not all of which, I emphasize, has been properly accounted for), and for 1986/87, it is to get $870 million. With inflation, it is getting less and less in real-dollar terms each year, and in 1987, has less buying power than it had in 1978.

If the CBC is full of fat, as we keep reading, you may wonder why the cuts cannot be simply absorbed. The reason may become clearer if we look at 1983/84 spending.

The corporation disposed of just over $1 billion, but that did not all go to produce "The Journal." Transmission and distribution cost just over $127 million, to start with. Then there was the operation of 6 domestic networks—English

TV, AM Radio and Stereo, and French TV, AM Radio and Stereo. These cost about $400 million. Then there were 30 regional TV stations, 18 English and 12 French, along with 46 regional radio stations, 31 English and 15 French—another $232 million. Then came such specialized programme services as Northern TV, the House of Commons service, Radio Canada International and closed captioning for the deaf—$28 million. "Other" costs, including engineering, commissions, and corporate management services ate up $179 million. That's a total of $966 million; payments to freelancers, talent fees, and royalty payments not shown in the regional or network costs pushed the figure to just over $1 billion.

A Study Said the CBC is Efficient. Honest.

Is there waste in there? Almost certainly; there always is, but the difficulty is that there are no ways to cut costs substantially without cutting into services. It is a rule of management that the people who make the decisions about where the cuts will fall are usually the ones who do the wasting, so when they reach for their sharp pencils, it's someone else who gets the point. In the CBC, when the government demanded a cut of $75 million in 1985, it was regional programming—which has no powerful defenders at CBC headquarters—where the pain was felt most.

It isn't as if there is money lying around the corridors. The only thorough outside study of CBC management, undertaken eight years ago, was done by a management consultant firm, McKinsey and Company. Called "The Efficiency of the CBC Compared to Other Broadcasters," the study concluded that the corporation "is an efficient and productive organization compared to other broadcasters" and, surprisingly, that the CBC carried out its mandate "with fewer resources than could the aggregate private sector." Where the CBC is inefficient and costly, it is mostly because, as in the North, it is required to carry out tasks the private sector would not take on. And because of its national reach, it actually gains some efficiency over what might be expected from private firms. Finally, compared to other public broadcasters, in England, Sweden, Japan, France, or Australia, "the CBC produces about twice as many hours of television programming per employee."

No one who works at the CBC, as I do from time to time, will accept the argument that it is cost-effective, but apparently it is no worse than the others, and better than some. And in recent years, the corporation has had to pull in its belt, which either improved efficiency or slashed the service, depending on where you sit.

With money in such short supply, for the CBC to muddle up its own accounting procedures as it did last year is unforgivable, but that has almost nothing to do with whether it is "worth it" to keep the corporation going. The argument against preserving the CBC, or selling off its major bits to private industry, is not so much an argument against the Crown as an argument for giving up and handing the place over to the Americans, lock, stock, and barrel.

The CBC costs us about $400 a head per annum—I am dividing a billion dollars by 25 million Canadians. This is about a quarter of what we spend on smoking, and if we cannot afford it—a frequent argument—then we cannot afford the messy business of being a nation.

But if we are going to spend this money, we ought to get the genuine article and not an imitation of the private networks or American TV. This brings me back to my argument about following the radio route on TV. In 1983/84, TV commercials earned the CBC $100 million—but $41.5 million went out again in commissions and selling expenses. To put it another way, TV commercials return less than 20 per cent of the $500 million it costs to run the television networks, regional and national, in English and French; the other 80 per cent is a subsidy to the advertiser. This is not to say that ads are cheaper on the CBC—they aren't, but because the CBC is required to perform such non-commercial services as broadcasting into the North, and serving communities where ads can never pay off, its costs of programming are higher, while its rates are the same as those of the private networks.

Private television can make millions out of the same ads. This is not as tricky as it seems; the private stations just fill up with imports and re-runs. It costs the CBC $500,000 to produce an episode of "Seeing Things," and CTV $40,000 to rent an episode of "Remington Steele." Reruns of "Leave It To Beaver" retail for $100 a pop.

The solution is not for the CBC to cram up with ads and imports, but to leave that to the private stations and concentrate on the things that make it unique rather than those that make it an expensive imitation of the other guys. Dropping commercials out of TV would cost us perhaps $2.50 per person per annum, and my guess is that most of us would be happy to pay the price. We might even be willing to pay more for better programming, if it comes to that.

What we will not do—and this is the thing that neither the CBC nor its regulators seem to be able to get through their fat heads—is to go on paying more for the same old stuff we can get without cost on CTV and Global.

I have a plan—every red-blooded Canadian has a plan—for the television service of the CBC. Mine is a simplified version of the proposals made by the Caplan-Sauvegeau Task Force on Broadcasting Policy, which reported in late 1986. The Caplan-Sauvegeau Report was almost universally praised and will probably be almost completely ignored by the policy makers, so I don't intend to outline it here. Anyway, my plan is simpler.

It begins with an acknowledgment that the broadcasting audience is being fragmented—which means that programmes and whole networks have to be designed for selected audiences. The mass audience of yesteryear is gone, and a good thing, too. Audience fragmentation means we can afford to aim high, with at least part of our television broadcasting. The other base for my plan is the acknowledgment that, since Canadians pay for the service, they are entitled to what they want (within reason), even if what they want is mostly junk.

So we split CBC-TV into two networks. The first, the primary network, goes back to what it was supposed to be in the first place, a totally in-house produced source of programming, with no commercials, no foreign programming, and no sports.

Then we establish a second network, operated by a much smaller group of professionals. It would produce sports, but aside from that, would buy all its programming from the Canadian private sector, and from foreign producers—

in the United States and the United Kingdom, primarily. It would carry as many commercials as it could get away with. It would contract with the first network to pick up "The National" and "The Journal," and perhaps some of the best of the public affairs series, to run after they were broadcast on the first network. It would earn all the money it could, and turn a large share of the takings over to the first network to support, on television, the quality of programming we now get on CBC radio.

I don't know whether, between them, the two networks would wind up in the black. Probably not, but for much less money than we're spending now, we could have one network devoted to excellence and one to bucks, and the second could lessen some of the financial pain of the first.

With the CBC, as with the other Crowns, we don't have to make money, but they must at least serve a public purpose. Certainly that is the case with the Crowns in Atlantic Canada, whom we will meet in the next chapter.

11
The Tender Trap

"Though judged on ordinary business criteria IEL has proven a fiasco, it has been beneficial to Nova Scotia."

Roy E. George,
The Life and Times of Industrial Estates Limited, 1974

Standing on the shores of the Strait of Canso, with the stacks of a Crown-owned heavy water plant in the background, it is possible to ruminate on the folly of such operations. For years, this plant produced heavy water, which could neither be sold nor used, and stacked it in containers. Just up the way, at Glace Bay, stood another heavy water plant, also Crown-owned, also doing the same thing. One hundred million dollars a year sunk into stacking water. It seems crazy, and the decision to close the plants, finally taken by the federal Conservatives in May, 1985, seemed sensible. But don't say so aloud. I did, to a mild-looking gent who, like me, was waiting for the lift-bridge at the Cape Breton end of the Causeway to come down so we could cross to the Nova Scotia mainland. He took my head off. He had worked in the plant, for thirteen dollars an hour, and now he had no job. Now he was heading for Halifax, where he hadn't a hope in hell of getting work at his age—mid-fifties—so he would probably spend the rest of his life on unemployment or welfare. He said he was used to hearing people knock the operations of Crown corporations in this end of the country, but the smart-asses who did so ought to remember, he said, that without the Crowns, there were really only two things for a body to do. And what were they?, I asked.

"Move," he said, "or die."

I said ah, um. He had a point. It is easy to deplore, denounce, and decry the Crowns, but for a large sector of the nation, they represent the last best hope. They may lose money, indulge in weird management and lousy public relations, hide important information from the taxpayers, and lend their good offices, and budgets, to scalawags from time to time, but at least they are doing something. And therein lies the tender trap of government enterprise, especially, but not exclusively, in Atlantic Canada. There appear to be two major kinds of government investment here; the desperate gamble to take over and attempt to revive failing concerns and the equally desperate gamble to attempt to establish new concerns in the teeth of the odds. Anything that has half a chance—the grocery business, for example—will already be owned, up and operating at a handsome profit by one of the area's ruling clans; it is the dregs that draw the Crowns. Once in, the intervening government is trapped. Now it is directly responsible for the jobs represented by its gamble. Having mounted the tiger, it faces the difficult problem of how to get down intact.

This situation leads to what I think we can fairly call "The Atlantic Speech." This is the speech given by federal political leaders as soon as they look out of the airplane window and notice the rain, the fog, and the gang of local voters on the tarmac looking hopeful but truculent. The speech starts with a hymn to free enterprise, in which the virtues of go-getting entrepreneurship are painted in glowing colours. This goes down well. The speaker than works himself up into a sweat over the need to cut down on red tape, bureaucratic bungling, and government regulation of all kinds. This draws polite applause. Next, the sturdy independence and self-sufficiency of Atlantic Canadians are brought to our notice, and we learn that these people take second place to no one when it comes to all this good stuff. The applause strengthens. Finally, the speaker announces a new lump of cash for Devco or Sysco or whatever may be the nearest large industry on the public teat, and swears on the grave of his fathers that jobs there will be preserved.

The applause becomes thunderous. The scene will be re-enacted at every Rotarian luncheon, provincial dinner, or bunfight the federal politician attends until he retreats to Ottawa, with his wallet—pardon, your wallet—in tatters and the satisfying feeling of a job well done.

The first federal politician who stands up in Atlantic Canada and tells the locals that what most of them ought to do is to move somewhere else will be praised for his blunt outspoken ways, and then ridden out of town on a rail.

You will get something of the Atlantic flavour when you realize that there is actually a Cape Breton song, moony and sweet, called "Let's Save Our Industry," which praises the joys of heaving coal and pouring slag. Picture, if you can, a crowd of the chaps from Canada Post in Ottawa standing around under the window of the Postmaster-General on a starlight night, carolling the pleasures of life in the stamp works.

Sysco is Sacred

Sysco, properly the Sydney Steel Corporation, has been belching smoke and losing money in downtown Sydney, Cape Breton, for decades. Founded in 1901, it did well under private and foreign ownership for many years, but began to lag behind as other more modern plants took over the industry after World War II. When its parent company, Dominion Steel and Coal (a subsidiary of the British conglomerate, Hawker Siddeley, de Havilland's sometime parent), proposed abandoning it in 1967, the province of Nova Scotia stepped in and took over, to preserve 4,000 jobs. In form, it is a provincial Crown, although most of the money is laid out by Ottawa. Since 1967 it has run up a debt estimated at $300 million, and absorbed $239 million in federal grants. It also dropped another $63 million from the provincial coffers—not counting interest and depreciation charges, which don't appear on public accounts—between 1980 and 1985. In the meantime, the jobs went down to about 1,200. The company hit a bit of a crisis in 1984, when it became clear that it would take more millions to update it so it wouldn't lose even more money in the future. Besides, as the insiders knew, but the public didn't, Sysco was systematically polluting its own neighbourhood, and heaven knew what clearing that up would cost. (About $70 million, is the latest guess.) At this point, the Halifax *Chronicle-Herald* telephoned a Toronto steel analyst, Jay Gordon, to ask him what he thought should be done with the company. From the safety of the other end of a 1,500-mile-long telephone line, Mr. Gordon spoke in trenchant terms: "Close down the whole mill," he said, "Sydney Steel is a disaster no matter what happens." As for the workers, "those guys should be put on permanent vacation and sent their cheques in Florida."

Lawsy me, what a fuss. Not only was Mr. Gordon attacked hip and thigh—"stupid, irresponsible, harmful" were among the printable comments—the newspaper was lambasted for bringing the subject up in the first place. Some things are not discussed in polite society. It was not so much that Mr. Gordon had things wrong (there were a couple of small errors in his analysis) as that closing the mill was not an option to be considered. John Callaghan, speaking for the United Steelworkers, said that to suggest the possibility was "a stupid thing to say because the city would collapse." Well, if you think about it coldly, the expenditure of somewhere around $600 million to hang onto 1,200 jobs doesn't seem really smart.

So what happened? Well, in 1986, the federal Conservatives, those hard-headed businessmen, in a joint operation with the provincial Conservatives, free-enterprisers to the core, plunked down another $150 million to buy an electric arc furnace for Sysco. Premier John Buchanan actually wanted an oxygen furnace, but that would have cost much more, and Mr. Buchanan is nothing if not reasonable; so, to save money, he gave way grudgingly. He was attacked by the provincial Liberals, who thought he should have held out for the oxygen furnace because it would bring more jobs. Canadian National was lined up to buy steel rails from Sysco—it would have preferred to buy them elsewhere, but we weren't having any of *that*—and Nova Scotia looks forward to many more happy years of losing money with one of its favourite Crowns. Unless—rumours began to fly again at the end of 1986—the whole thing is scrapped, and despair rekindled.

Devco: a Crown With a Regional Mission

Sysco was not designed to lose money; that's just a happy coincidence. Sysco's sister Crown, the Cape Breton Development Corporation (Devco) actually made money one year, although it has since reformed. Devco is unique; it is the only federal Crown created to serve the economic well-being of a geographic area, rather than a particular industry. Whatever else is said of Devco, the fact remains that it does serve Cape Breton; there may even be some virtue to the local argument that if Devco is abandoned, we might just as well tow Cape Breton out into the Atlantic and let her sink.

Devco was born at the same time as Sysco, in 1967, and for the same reasons. A group of coal mines in the Sydney area that belonged to the Dominion Coal Company (like Sysco, an offshoot of the Dominion Steel and Coal Company) were in trouble. All the coal mines were in trouble; this was not unique, but 80 per cent of Cape Breton's coal came out of the Dosco mines around Sydney. They had been studied to a fare-the-well, by three royal commissions, subsidized to the teeth, and were still losing money. Only five mines were working, the labour force was down to about 6,500, and the coal seams, stretching three to four miles out beneath the sea, were becoming more and more expensive to mine. Coal from the United States, cheaper to dig and to transport, was taking over the Ontario and Quebec markets—which were shrinking, anyway, with the increased use of oil and diesel. Federal subsidies of about $8 a ton, or $3,000 annually for each mine-worker, were not enough; the company teetered on the verge of bankruptcy.

Dosco announced that it was going to close the mines unless the federal government came up with more financial support, and when Ottawa said it would, Dosco said it was pulling out anyway. Panic struck. The steel industry was already in trouble, and there wasn't anything else. So the government set up a special study by a Montreal consultant, Dr. J.R. Donald, and asked him what to do. He flirted with the notion of allowing the mines to close, thereby having done with the problem, but rejected it. Instead, he proposed that the industry be nationalized, as the Sydney Coal Corporation, and slowly extinguished. Ottawa would, ho, ho, not be stuck with the business forever; the mines would be run down to about 3,000 employees over six years, then to nothing in the following decade. While this was happening, a second Crown, the Cape Breton Development Corporation, would be created as a partner to the Sydney Coal Corporation, to promote industrial development and provide employment for those eased out of coal.

The government accepted Mr. Donald's basic idea, but couldn't resist fooling about with it, and when An Act to establish the Cape Breton Development Corporation became law in 1967, both sides of the job were shoved into a single company; there was no Sydney Coal Corporation, only Devco, a company divided, as it has been ever since, between two divisions and two tasks. The Act provided that the plans for closing the mines would be timed to coincide with the "broadening of the base of the economy of Cape Breton Island." For every new job created outside coal, you could scratch one inside. The United Mine Workers, who had been opposed to nationalization, changed their minds when they saw that clause. They didn't believe there was going to be any broadening of the base of the economy; their jobs were secure forever.

There was one of Those Wonderful, Catch-all Clauses

Ottawa provided $45 million, $20 million to develop new industry and $25 million to update the mines, and undertook to make good on Devco's losses. Nova Scotia put in $10 million for economic development. In return, neither government ever exercised, or chose to exercise, much control. Even after the original $30 million set aside for industrial development had disappeared, with little to show for it, all that happened was that Ottawa took to providing new lumps of money, about $6 million annually, which the corporation spent as it saw fit. The Act had one of those wonderful catch-all clauses allowing it to "do all such other things as the Corporation deems incidental or conducive to the attainment of its objects," under which it could have blown the whole wad setting up a redlight district, and maybe made money. Not that it ever contemplated anything so wicked. What it did instead was to pour a whole lot of money into Sysco, for starters. It bought the steel company's decrepit coke ovens, renovated them and ran them for five years, while selling the coke to the steel plant at below-market prices. (Coke ovens are used to turn ordinary coal, which cannot be used in steel-making, into coke, which can.) This cost about $35 million, and then Sysco, the ungrateful whelp, turned around and charged Devco $10 million because the coke ovens broke down for a time, delaying steel production.

Devco also set out to provoke, inspire, and finance anybody who had a good idea for an industry on the island, and, what with one thing and another, found itself in oyster farming, fishing, sheep breeding, beef production, maple syrup, boat building, wool milling, food processing, metal casting, lumber milling, and the manufacture of sashes and doors. Oh, yes, and one of its ventures built modular homes. It leapt into the tourist industry and financed a steam railway, a golf course, beaches, marinas, and restaurants. Some of these were good and suitable projects—Devco worked hard at separating the loony from the merely unusual— but what they all had in common was that, without outside help they would never have been mounted because they were unlikely to stand on their own. Even when they flopped—and oh, my, many of them flopped—they represented a brave attempt to break the circle of dependence. Yet the complaint can always be made that they simply drew the circle tighter, by making dependence more inevitable than ever. If you were aiming to open a restaurant in Cape Breton, would you want to face competition from a neighbour on the government rolls? Nope; you would ask for a handout yourself.

In the coal business, Devco did bring many improvements. Its mines established an enviable safety record and a productivity record that doubled between 1968 and 1978, and by 1985, hit 5.3 tons per miner, up there with the best mines. The cost—$100 million. There were no profits to pay back this investment, in part because much of the output was contracted to a provincial Crown, the Nova Scotia Power Corporation, at firesale prices. Coal sold to Scotia Power rose 11 per cent in price between 1979 and 1984, while other prices were jumping 41 per cent. A federal

Crown was subsidizing a provincial Crown, shuffling the
losing pea from shell to shell.

Along the way, the notion of closing down the coal business disappeared into one of the deeper shafts. The energy
crisis of the 1970s, which temporarily made coal a valued
commodity, provided a stay of execution, and even when
coal prices slid back down, the jobs provided continued to
justify keeping the mines going. In 1984, a year after the
company was to have folded its tents and silently stolen
away, the big news was about replacing lost mining. There
was a tragic fire in Glace Bay colliery No. 26, which cost
one man his life, and Devco $50 million, as well as putting
1,326 miners out of work. Back went the government to
its bottomless purse, and soon there were commitments to
ladle out another $324 million to start two more mines, and
provide 900 of the missing jobs. The company payroll will
soon be back up to 5,000, and the $324 million promised
so far is just a down-payment. One of the new mines, Lin-
gan-Phelan, will cost about $221 million to develop; the
other, Donkin-Morien, which has been under way in fits
and starts since 1978, is somewhat chunkier and more am-
bitious. The estimate there is closer to $800 million.

Devco has always been plagued by management problems, many of them stemming from its split roles, with half
of its heart in coal mining and the other half in everything
from shearing sheep to boiling maple syrup. In 1983, a
scathing internal memo prepared by the Treasury Board
popped into the newspapers and told a tale of sloppiness
and neglect. The company consistently failed to provide
accurate projections about costs, production and losses, the
report said. The coal division was spending millions more
every year than it was reaping in sales, while the industrial
development division was seen as a bottomless pit, pouring
out public funds for little return.

The report led to a shakeup. Devco president Steve
Rankin resigned, to run as a Liberal in the federal election
of 1984 (he lost). His replacement, Joe Shannon, dismissed
four vice-presidents, closed down three industrial subsidiaries and announced a new five-year plan to restructure
the entire operation. Then, in May, 1985, Mr. Shannon
announced that he had done his job. The company had
actually declared its first profit, $9.8 million, for the fiscal

year 1984–85. Mr. Shannon returned to private industry. His replacement, Derek Rance, was soon to announce that the profit was one of those blips that appear on radar screens. In 1985–86, Devco would be back to losing money.

For the future, we have the solemn promise of the federal Department of Regional Industrial Expansion, which oversees Devco, that there will be more money forthcoming. By golly, said the Conservative government in Ottawa, with a little more shrewd spending and a new sense of direction, we can turn this thing around. At this point, old Devco watchers headed for the exits. We have seen this part before.

And yet, what would you have them do? It would take teams of economists, with a couple of necromancers thrown in, to determine whether the money consigned to the flames in Sysco and Devco is money well spent. How much larger would the unemployment and welfare rolls have been without this pair? Roy George, a long-time student of the company, pays Devco one of those left-handed economist compliments when he writes, "Though it has not led Cape Breton to an 'era of progress' . . . its achievements in coal seem quite good compared with what the public expects from a public organization." While George notes the customary Crown scorn for control to go with the money provided—"Though there was the semblance of fairly tight control on the activities of Devco, in practice it has been allowed to do very much as it has thought best"—he concludes, "But assuming that an activity has to be undertaken by public authorities because it is unattractive to private enterprise . . . the Devco experience suggests that the Crown corporation framework can work fairly well."

"Fairly well" is not a rave review, but it must be said of both Devco and Sysco that, compared to some of the other lulus launched by Nova Scotia, they are models of sobriety and restraint.

Industrial Estates Limited

It is one of the interesting phenomena of this nation that a government that is recognizably right-wing in its politics can lay down larrups of socialism that would bring shrieks of outrage from the business community if left-wingers tried it. Thus, when Robert L. Stanfield, Nova Scotia's Premier and Canada's version of American Gothic, stepped up in 1957 and announced the establishment of Industrial Estates Limited (IEL), Canada's first-ever development corporation, everybody—well, everybody who counted—admitted that it was a swell idea. Nothing socialist or left-wing about it. What it would be was a corporation "to promote, diversify, and develop industry in Nova Scotia." Solid, reputable businessmen were put in charge, and they ensured that the public money invested—$159 million drifted out of the public coffers and into seventy-seven different industrial ventures during IEL's first dozen years—would go only on solid, worthwhile projects that were bound to pay off. Like Clairtone.

The Clairtone Saga. Not for the Faint of Heart

Clairtone Sound Limited was going to make high-quality stereo sets in Nova Scotia, and initially would produce 1,000 jobs, and twice that many with inevitable expansion. But the company, despite the infusion of $7 million from IEL, was perpetually short of funds. This led to another of those hard-headed business decisions; backed by IEL, Clairtone would go into the car business, buying Canadian Motor Industries Limited, to assemble Japanese cars in Canada. If you ask why a radio company thought it could get out of trouble by going into the automobile business, about which it knew very little, you reveal yourself as lacking that simple faith which the poet Tennyson asserted is more than Norman blood. IEL was not so scornful; the province put up another $1 million for Clairtone to study the car business. While this project was still being developed, and with the stereo plant not yet in operation, Clairtone jumped into colour television sets. By 1967, Clairtone hadn't done much except lose $6.7 million, and its bankers were getting twitchy. Frank Sobey, IEL's president at the time—and the scion of one of the province's great financial families—reportedly suggested pulling the plug at this point. But it was too late; the tender trap was already sprung. As Garth Hopkins wrote in his book-length profile of Clairtone, "The people of Pictou County believed in Clairtone. . . . To refuse further government investment . . . would be politically damaging." So IEL took over the company, ran it for six more years, and *then* let it go bankrupt. The total provincial tab came to $20 million.

Then there was Deuterium Canada Limited, the heavy water plant at Glace Bay, whose mournful operations were visited in Chapter 6. IEL lured the company to Cape Breton, poured out $100 million in subsidies and then, when the venture threatened to fail, bought it up and converted it into a Crown corporation.

Well, the damn thing wouldn't work. A process designed originally to use fresh water was adapted to the salt water locally available, and that did dreadful things to the plant's innards. IEL was in something of a swivet until, in 1971, it hit on the happy idea of unloading the whole mess onto Atomic Energy of Canada Ltd. Isn't that what federal Crowns are for? So another pea shifted shells, although AECL did not buy the heavy water plant outright. After all, it already had such a plant at Point Tupper. Instead, AECL leased Nova Scotia's plant from it, and invested another $200 million to rehabilitate it. It was not until 1978 that the federal Crown bought the provincial one outright, for $65 million. At that point, the plant had lost $140 million for the province, so at least some of that was repaid by federal taxpayers.

That was about the time when nuclear sales plummeted, and heavy water became a drug on the market. Now AECL owned two plants in Nova Scotia turning out a product it couldn't sell. So AECL went into the heavy-water stacking business until 1985, when the whole operation was closed down. But, say, if heavy water ever comes back in style, we'll see who's been wasting public money. One scheme I've thought of would be to drain all the light water out of the Atlantic and replace it with heavy water; ships would float better. I'm thinking of setting up a Crown corporation to study the notion.

You will have noted that by the time all this foolishness was done, the provincial Crown had managed to stick a federal Crown with the cost of its folly. Perhaps IEL isn't quite so hopeless after all, although the outfit seemed to have a penchant for dumping public money like a sailor on leave. Certainly it had some stunning failures; but there were also notable successes. Volvo Canada Limited and

Michelin Tires were both installed in Nova Scotia with the aid of IEL, supplemented by regional development grants from Ottawa, and both have expanded and provided continuous jobs ever since. And at least IEL has nothing on its books with quite the flavour of the Bricklin experience in neighbouring New Brunswick.

The Bricklin Saga

Provincial Holdings Limited, the New Brunswick Crown, was designed to follow the IEL pattern; it would solve provincial unemployment by luring in outside companies, most of them American. Aren't Americans rich? With the enthusiastic endorsement of Premier Richard Hatfield, another strong Conservative, and thus free of the taint of socialism, the province went into the auto-manufacturing business. And kissed $23 million goodbye, with the aid of a hustling, handsome, larger-than-life Arizonian named Malcolm Bricklin.

The government decision to back Bricklin was based on a report that took only three weeks to produce, was prepared entirely with figures provided by Malcolm Bricklin, and promised a return on investment of 18 per cent—perhaps as much as 29 per cent—annually, over twenty years. This estimate grew from the leadpipe certainty that the company could produce 10,000 copies of a dashing new luxury car in its first year of operation, and 32,000 four years later. At $5,000 each—a lot of money in 1970—the cars were expensive, but they had doors that opened upwards, like a gull's wings. There were a couple of tiny missing parts to the report, such as the part that explained how to bond fibreglass to acrylic, which was required to make the body of the car, but which nobody knew how to do, as well as a breakdown of the car's technical specifications, which did not exist. Nor was there anything much on Bricklin himself, who was really more of a salesman than anything else. But, hell, if you spend all your time worrying about petty bureaucratic details, you never get anything done. New Brunswick took the spacious view, and began ladling out money.

The province started out modestly enough, with $500,000

for a 51 per cent interest in the company—which was really shrewd, because New Brunswick would have control—and loan guarantees of $3 million. To get things off on the right foot, Bricklin hired his father, Albert, for $60,000 a year; his mother, Gertrude, for $30,000, his sister, Barbara Jonas, for $37,000; her husband, (as legal advisor, fees unrecorded), and Malcolm's uncle, Ben Bricklin, for a meagre $18,000. Malcolm himself drew $120,000. And they say Crown corporations don't create jobs.

There were problems—heavy staff turnover, soaring costs, lagging production—the usual things. In 1972, with the car scheduled for production in a year, I wrote a story about the Bricklin enterprise which was not kind. Not long after, I was on a campaign airplane carrying Robert Stanfield (by that time, federal leader of the Conservatives) to Fredericton. Premier Hatfield, who had come out to greet Stanfield spotted me deplaning and told me he wanted to talk to me. We had dinner together and he told me, more in sorrow than in anger, that I represented the kind of Central Canadian thinking that wanted to keep the Maritimes a poverty-stricken ghetto. I lacked vision, he said; I had no faith, and I was determined to sneer into the ground anyone who wanted to get up off his behind and take a chance for New Brunswick. It was good strong stuff, and meant to sting. You don't backtalk premiers, especially when you figure they will pick up the dinner-tab (he did), and when Mr. Hatfield got to the point of asking, What would I have the Maritimes do? I was so remorseful I could barely finish my steak. I mumbled something to the effect that if the province was going to sink all this money into a venture, it ought to have more direct control of the production process. The Premier told me I was talking nonsense. You couldn't interfere with the company, he maintained; you'd kill it.

Later, he put this argument more formally to H. A. Fredericks, who wrote a book called *Bricklin*. "Political interference with management and disclosure of information that other companies can keep confidential can make it impossible for government-supported companies to compete and survive," is the way he put it to Fredericks, and he said much the same to me (I didn't make notes; I was busy

eating). A couple of days later, I came up with the answer—
always the way, isn't it?—that lack of political interference
and non-disclosure of information can achieve the same
end.

Which it did, of course. By the time the government
called in an auditing firm in 1975 to sort out the damage,
the auditors said the job couldn't be done. Bills could not
be traced, and records had not been kept. About all that
could be determined is that the wholesale cost of the car
would be about $9,000, instead of the $2,200 stipulated in
the original agreement, and only about 6,300 would be
built, not enough ever to make a profit. In the meantime,
Malcolm Bricklin had moved on to finer things; he was
working on a bigger and better car which would retail for
$25,000, and the province was picking up the tab for this
without the formality of having agreed to do so. New Brunswick was also paying most of the costs of General Vehicle,
Bricklin's parent company, which it did not own, as well as
executive travel budgets of $27,000 a month.

So the government pulled the plug, wrote off its losses
at $23 million, closed up the plant, and all the Bricklin
relatives went back to Arizona.

These Things are Like the Gambler's Itch

There will be more of these, you know. They are the one
thing we will never run out of. Prince Edward Island tried
to give the tourist industry, its major employer, a helping
hand by encouraging the development of a luxury hotel in
downtown Charlottetown with the aid of provincial subsidies in 1982. There was a nasty battle between the local
developer and the hotel chain that agreed to manage the
property, more money was spent than anyone ever intended, and before you could say "bailout," the developer
and the chain were suing each other, while the hotel began
to sink into the sand. By this time, the hotel had absorbed
$30 million—including $17 million worth of loan guarantees from Ottawa. In the end, the province did the only
thing it could do: in 1985, it bought the hotel from the
receivers for $5.1 million down and another $5 million to

come. The alternative would have been to write off both the jobs and the investments to date. Happily, it was able to resell it to CP Hotels.

With hindsight, it's easy to say that PEI ought not to have gone into the hotel game unless it knew what it was doing, and yet, all it ever wanted was to create jobs for its people. These things are like the gambler's itch to governments. I know I've blown the rent money, but with one more roll of the dice I can at least make back my stake. So the money goes down and dammit, it's snake-eyes again. But the government that refuses to gamble, that sits on its hands and hopes for the best, delivers its people to the hands of fate. The poorer the region, the higher the stakes. In Atlantic Canada, spending by governments accounts for 80 per cent of the region's combined gross provincial product. Much of this is funnelled through provincial Crowns because, as Bill Belliveau of Infomarketing Limited told a regional economic conference in Halifax not long ago, "a solution that relies on the private sector would fail, because we hardly have a private sector."

Newfoundland: Not Stupid, Just Desperate

That is the consideration that caused Newfoundland to stumble into such fiascos as Come by Chance; not stupidity, but over-eagerness. In Newfoundland, the problem has not been so much the creation of losing Crowns as the sellout of provincial resources to private companies, like John C. Doyle's Canadian Javelin, which, whenever they made money, departed with it. Churchill Falls, the giant Labrador Hydro project, was handed to private entrepreneurs by the Liberal government under Premier Joseph Smallwood under such conditions that, as one economic study showed, "the more successful Churchill Falls became, the more Newfoundland would lose." When the Liberals were replaced by the Conservatives, the new administration threatened to nationalize the project, and eventually worked out a deal to purchase it from its private owners. Today, Churchill Falls is jointly owned by two provincial Crowns, Hydro-Quebec and Newfoundland and Labrador Hydro. And it makes money.

Another Crown—or near-Crown—that makes money in

Newfoundland is Fishery Products International, known locally as FPI. It is a curious bird. In the early 1980s, when the fish business was going belly-up all over the Atlantic region because there were too many small companies and not enough markets, the federal government set up a royal commission to investigate the industry, and it actually came up with a workable plan. Shove some of the companies together, said the royal commission, give them some funding, and try again. So that was done. What emerged, in 1984, were two giant fish companies. One, National Sea Products, known to its friends as Natsea, is based in Halifax, and owned privately. The other, FPI, based in St. John's, is partly owned by the federal government, partly by Newfoundland, and partly by the Bank of Nova Scotia.

Because of the re-financing, and because the new firms emerged just when health-conscious North Americans were beginning to renounce beef for fish, both companies are now making money. FPI made $25.6 million in the first half of 1986, whereas each of the six companies that were cobbled together to form it had been sinking fast. Natsea made $16.4 million during the same period, where it had lost $3.7 million in the first six months of 1984, before the reorganization. Both companies benefitted from government largesse; FPI got $255 million from Ottawa and the province; Natsea's reorganization cost $155 million. The only difference is that, in the case of Natsea, the Halifax elite put up some of the money, whereas for FPI, it all came from governments and the bank. Both are robustly successful firms today, and among the largest employers east of Montreal. Could a private company have succeeded in Newfoundland? Ask a local, and he'll point out that there are no private firms in St. John's wealthy enough to have taken on the job. FPI is to be resold to the private sector, now that it is healthy again. That's fine, but it was the Crown interlude that made this possible.

That is why, in Newfoundland, you don't hear much talk about getting the government out of business; what the locals want is more government in business, and that is likely to mean, in the long run, more Crowns. Sigh. However, if we are going to be lumbered with Crowns, we are going to have to have them run on somewhat different lines than, say, Clairtone or Bricklin. If a government decides that a venture is worthy of public funding on political and social grounds—to provide jobs—that is quite a different matter than either merely pouring out grants to private industry or throwing it into a Crown, with few questions asked, and hoping for the best. In Chapter 13, we will look at what some of the rules ought to be; for now, it is time to turn our attention to the other solution to troublesome Crowns—privatization.

12
Privatize Me In Violet Time

"Even though you are a Crown corporation in a mixed economy, you have to operate under the rules of the private sector. Otherwise the private sector can't survive. So the question arises, why not be part of the private sector?"

Claude Taylor, *president, Air Canada*
August 18, 1984

The Senior Official of Her Majesty's Treasury straightened his tie, flicked an imaginary speck of dust from his cuff, glanced nervously around the room, peered out the window where crowds of tourists bearing umbrellas embossed with snappy slogans thronged Parliament Street, shuddered, glanced furtively at me beneath lowering eyebrows, and asked me to repeat the question.

"Certainly," I said brightly, "How do you spell 'privatization'?"

The S.O. of H.M.T. wore the trapped look of a senior British bureaucrat who has acceded to the request of a colonial for an interview in good faith, and now finds himself closeted with a nut-case. "Harrrumm," he said. He had undertaken to fill me in on the details of Britain's privatization programme, which has been buzzing along—if you believe the official documents he could see bulging from my briefcase—for more than seven years. If I didn't even know how to spell the thing, we were in for some tedious spadework. Sighing, he began, "P as in Peter . . . "

"No, no," I cut him off, "all I mean is, do you spell it with an 's' or a 'z'?" I handed him two official releases from his own department. "You see, you spell it both ways." I smiled at him, winningly, I thought.

He looked pained. I got the impression of a man trying to resolve to himself what the punishment would be for donking a visiting journalist over the head with a flower pot and burying the remains in St. James' Park; rejecting that and wondering whether it would be rude to ask a visiting journalist what the hell difference it made; rejecting that, and resolving to be polite at all costs.

"*Zed*," he said. "I think." He paused. "No, *Es*," he said, fumbling through his papers and coming up with one that said "Privatisation in the United Kingdom—Background Briefing". He nodded vigorously, "Definitely *Es*."

I thanked him. He rolled his eyes. It was going to be a long day. But I had a sound reason for asking; in the three years I have been working on this book I formed the notion that the preferred solution to the problem of Crown corporations, namely, to sell them off to the private sector, is being conducted by people who don't really know what is involved. Not even, to put it at its flattest, how to spell the process. Privatization doesn't appear in the dictionary, yet; mine goes from "privative, *adj.* causing privation" to "privet, *n.* any oleaceous shrub of the genus *ligustrum*," without bothering its pretty head about privatization. Just to set the record straight, the British appear to favour "s," while Canadians lean to "z." The spelling wasn't the only thing the S.O. of H.M.T. didn't know.

He didn't know what proportion of the shares of British Petroleum, the most spectacular of Britain's privatizations so far still belongs to the government (31.7 per cent). Or whether any other group owns anything like that much of BP (no). Or whether, when the British calculate the gains from privatization at over £8 billion, anyone bothered to subtract the earnings these companies would have made for the government had they not been sold (no). Or whether more new "nationalised companies" had been formed since the selloff programme began; in short, are they creating them as fast as they sell them? (The British call their government enterprises "nationalised" companies, even though many of them weren't nationalized at all, but created from scratch; "Crowns" is better.) The S.O. of H.M.T. promised to look into all these things and send me the details, but I had a feeling he wouldn't, and he didn't. In common with most of the enthusiasts for privatization, he was more concerned with how well the programme is going than with fiddling details. But it is the fiddling details that ought to tell us whether privatization is really the way to go.

Counting the Take on British Petroleum

Take British Petroleum. Britain's largest company was a mixed corporation when Mrs. Margaret Thatcher and the Conservatives took over in 1979. At that time, the government held 51 per cent of the stock—down from 68.3 per cent in 1977. Labourites had already been selling out what they always refer to as the "family silver" or "the national birthright." In 1979, when "the boss," which is how senior British bureaucrats refer to Mrs. Thatcher, determined to sell off the nationalized industries, BP was put on the market. In the course of three sales through 1983, the government cleared £827 million, while reducing its share to 31.7 per cent. In the three years 1983, 1984, and 1985, BP made over £10 billion in profit. The public's share of that was, at least on paper, about £3.17 billion; viz., 31.7 per cent. With a holding of 51 per cent, the take would have been £5.1 billion, or £1.93 billion more—the smaller shareholding meant that the taxpayer foreswore more than twice as much as the sale of the shares brought in. These figures are dodgy, because we don't know what the exact numbers would have been in different circumstances, but it is at least arguable that far from making money, the sale of BP shares has cost money. However, the government is still the largest shareholder, so if the industry falls on its nose, it will wind up a lesser loser than it might have been, for whatever comfort that may bring.

Then there is Enterprise Oil, which holds the North Sea properties of British Gas Corp., and which was put on sale in 1984. The government had it chalked up for a £270 million sale in 1984, but a depressed market resulted in the sale of only two-thirds of the shares, at the minimum tender price of 185 pence, a total of £82 million, in what Stanley Orme, energy spokesman for the opposition Labour Party, correctly called "a disastrous flop." The entire issue was guaranteed by a group of British stock firms who, in effect, bought the shares from the government and tried to sell them on the market. They had to absorb any they couldn't sell, and wound up with about £195 million worth of shares they didn't want—and a bad temper. There was another complication; three-quarters of the applications for shares came from a single corporation, Rio Tinto-Zinc. The realization that one company would acquire, at firesale prices, control over an asset with excellent long-term growth prospects in the crucial energy sector, put the government in a tizzy. So the cabinet stepped in to cut Rio Tinto-Zinc's share down to a maximum of 10 per cent of the company. That, not surprisingly, infuriated London's financial leaders, who accused the government of changing the rules at the end of the game to thwart a perfectly legitimate market coup.

The More-or-Less-Virgins

In the Enterprise sale, as in most others, the government retained one "golden share," worth one pound, which carries special rights and responsibilities. In the case of Enterprise, these rights include a veto on any attempt to sell the company's fleet of ships, or "any disposal of the entire undertaking." In the case of British Aerospace, sold in 1981, the golden share carries the right to prevent foreign ownership of more than 15 per cent of shares carrying voting rights. With Jaguar, sold in 1984, one share carries the right to prevent any one person or group, regardless of nationality, controlling more than 15 per cent of equity. In other cases, the single share carries the right to appoint directors in proportion to the stocks held by the government, but not to vote the stocks. These golden shares, which make perfect sense, nevertheless underline the ambiguous nature of some of these "privatizations"; while letting go, the government continues to hold on. It has created a new form of corporation, the more-or-less-virgin.

What happens is that the strong ideological push to get rid of the firms, coupled to a sinking feeling about what will happen when the process is done, tends to create a lot of shilly-shallying.

For example, after the sale of Jaguar, which brought nothing but good news—sales soaring, jobs climbing, exports leaping, and a profit after years of losses—the government resolved to rid itself of money-gobbling British Leyland, the giant car and truck maker. Britain got stuck with BL in the usual way, to preserve jobs when the private company threatened to go under in 1975. Over the next decade, the government sank more than £10 billion into the firm, which continued to hold onto jobs while losing money. Then, BL was put on the block, and immediately drew interest from both the Ford Motor Co. and General Motors. GM wanted to buy 49 per cent of the Land Rover division, while Ford had its eye on the Austin Rover division. However, the prospect of selling a British household name to foreign interests inspired outrage not merely in the breasts of Labour MPs, but in those of Mrs. Thatcher's backbenchers, and both deals were scratched. If they ever go ahead, they will be attended by all sorts of qualifications about jobs, purchasing practices, and trade with the European Economic Community; that will be a golden share with a deep and lasting shine to it.

Buy a Bank and get a Billion-Pound Bonus

One of the monumental foulups on the road to privatization in Britain occurred when the government decided to give away—not sell—the Trustee Savings Banks, in 1985. Her Majesty's Treasury, twirling its lorgnette, handed down a ruling on the banks; although they were part of the national savings banks system, which the government owned, they didn't, according to the Treasury, belong to anyone. This meant that whoever bought the Trustee Savings Banks' shares would own, not only about £800 million in retained earnings, but the proceeds of the sale itself. The shares were reckoned to be worth about £1 billion; if you could come up with that, you would get it back, plus the money you put up for the shares. The government wouldn't get a plugged nickel out of the process; just the satisfying feeling of a job well done.

This brilliant stroke was stymied when a couple of the banks' depositors went to court with a claim that if the banks didn't belong to the government, they must belong to their own depositors, who should share in the proceeds of any sale. In August, 1986, that case was finally adjudicated by the House of Lords, which ruled that the Treasury had been talking through its hat. The banks belonged to the government, and nobody else but. In the meantime, the lads in charge of privatization in the Treasury had been lining up a sale on the basis of the earlier ruling, and it is not too much to say that the money men in the City (London's financial district) were licking their chops and reaching for their wallets, while singing the praises of Mrs. Thatcher and her wonderful brand of economics. When the House of Lords gave out the bad news, you could hear jaws dropping from Chancery Row to Marble Arch, and the sale was hurriedly called off. It will be rearranged, but for how much, and to whose benefit, is still uncertain as I write this.

I don't mean to give the impression that the British privatization programme has been a washout; there have been some notable successes, but even in these cases, there has been a price to pay. One of the great triumphs has been British Telecom, the communications company which went on the market in 1984, and was snapped up—at £2.5 billion—by eager buyers. No, I misstate myself; 50.2 per cent of the company went on the market; the government still owns 49.8 per cent. The reason British Telecom shares were so eagerly awaited was that the company has always been a gold mine. In 1983, it made a profit of £1,031 million, almost double its take two years earlier.

Once it was a private company, more or less, British Telecom stopped the old practice of subsidizing domestic calls by higher long-distance charges, and hoisted telephone rentals by 8.5 per cent for homes and 9 per cent for business, about twice the rate of general increases in the cost of living. Profits soared by another 49 per cent; the chairman, Sir George Jefferson, got a pay raise of £27,000, and the consumer, paying for all this, was left to ruminate on the joys of owning-not-owning a telephone company.

Some You Win

The British Telecom sale underlined what everyone already knew, that it is easy to persuade investors to pay for corporations that are energetic, well-run, profitable, and which happen to be government owned, like British Gas sold in early 1987; somewhat less easy to persuade them to part with cash for those concerns, like the National Coal Board, that are a constant drain on the public purse—to say nothing of being a pain in the public ass.

In many cases, the privatization process has revitalized companies by moving them out from under the heavy hand of government. Cable and Wireless, a major international communications company, quadrupled its profits between 1981, when it was sold, and 1985. Another privatized firm, National Freight Consortium, a trucking company, went from profits of £4.3 million to £28.8 million in the same period. The company is now 83 per cent owned by employees, their families, and pensioners. Employees who invested in shares of their own company at £1 saw them jump to £16.6. That makes for willing workers.

In other cases, privatization has demolished consumers by moving them out from under the protective hand of government. One garbage-collecting firm sold into private hands laid out a schedule that called on the trucks to pick up trash at an average speed of 8.7 miles an hour. This is the heave-and-run school of garbage-gathering. A private cleaning and repair firm took over a school-cleaning contract and put a new seal over a school's floors without removing a mess of cigarette butts and a puddle of child's vomit. A private street-cleaning contractor took over from public enterprise, and handed out plastic garbage bags to residents, with instructions to clean the junk up themselves. A road maintenance contractor was discovered to be using child labour.

Even ideological purity—and the Thatcher government has lots of ideology—strains at some of the prospects that lie ahead. Britain is resolved to sell off the ten water authorities in England and Wales, which would give the Treasury a quick fix of about £5 billion (the Thames Water Authority alone will fetch £2 billion). It is inconceivable that the government would allow such sales without retaining control over so vital a product. The hope is that the authorities, with the spur of profit, will operate more efficiently and invest in more modern water and sewage facilities (some are Victorian), so that better services will be forthcoming for equal or even less cost. That may be so, but it is going to be a neat trick to balance the public interest against private profit without the kind of government intervention the exercise is supposedly designed to end.

Rolls-Royce with a "For Sale" Sign around its Neck

When I asked the S.O. of H.M.T. if there would be any exceptions to the privatization programme, he had a crisp answer ready: "No." The Post Office, BritRail, British Airways, British Gas, Rolls-Royce, the National Bus Company, all, all are on the auction block. The difficulty remains that while many Britons—not the unions, but others—would sing hosannas on the day the National Coal Board is slipped across to some unsuspecting sucker, they are not so pleased to see something as cherished as Rolls-Royce with a "For Sale" sign around its neck.

As a privately owned company, Rolls-Royce declared bankruptcy in 1972, so the good old Treasury stepped in and took over. The car division was spun off to private hands as Rolls-Royce Motors, while the government kept the engine division, and poured millions of pounds into developing the RB-211 jet airplane engine, now one of the finest in the world. At the same time, staff and overhead were cut. Jobs fell from 57,000 to 38,500, unit costs were cut by 30 per cent, and sales improved up to 300 per cent. In 1984, the firm made an operating profit of £162 million and was ready to be returned to private hands. It is now an attractive candidate, but anyone who trots around to buy it is going to be made to feel like the young swain who calls on his date only to be met at the door by a tough-looking father with a keen interest in his intentions towards the darling daughter. Of course, if he wants to take out the ugly sister, British Shipbuilders, well, bless you, my son, and here's money for cab fare. That's the unshakable dilemma of privatization; it is sometimes the wrong ones that are easy to sell, and it is sometimes the wrong kind of suitor who turns up, panting, at the door.

British Airways, however, is swooning to be sold, and there will be a fight for it. The company made an operating profit of £303 million in 1984–85, and £205 million in 1985–86, in the teeth of ferocious world competition. What carried it through, besides tight management, was preferential treatment by the British government in handing out and maintaining air routes. Without its effective monopoly on some routes, the airline would soon drop into the class of losers, and the pushing and shoving that has already taken place over the sale is centred on the conditions a privatized line will face, more than the price. No government will kiss these profits goodbye in a hurry, or consign them to anyone who looks like a suspicious character.

Tom Kierans, president of the Toronto stock firm, McLeod Young Weir, is probably the world authority on privatization in Britain; he steered the sale of British Telecom onto the market. He is also a true-blue Tory, and former key advisor to Ontario governments. In a study done for the Institute for Research on Public Policy, he pointed out that the natural sources of funds for companies that go on the auction block are firms that are already too large, and are more concerned with "paper entrepreneurship"—takeovers for the sake of spinning dollars, not creating wealth or work—than they are with promoting efficiency. Relating the British experience to Canada, Mr. Kierans wonders what good would be served by having huge conglomerates take over the Crowns and write the expense of the takeovers off on their income tax. "The spectre of conglomerates . . . financing growth as it were out of the Consolidated Revenue Fund raises troubling issues," Kierans wrote. Actually, the whole Canadian experience in privatization so far raises troubling issues.

The Bricing of British Columbia

One of the first examples of privatization we had was orchestrated by the Social Credit government of British Columbia, in what was either a warm-hearted gesture or a desperate campaign ploy in 1977. The Socreds decided to dump four major resource corporations, which had been turned into Crowns by the New Democratic Party in its brief turn at the B.C. wheel, into British Columbia Resources Investment Corporation—BCRIC (pronounced "brick"). The government received a promissory note from BCRIC for $151,500,000; then the company gave the province 15 million shares in itself, and the promissory note was torn up, while the shares were distributed, free, to 2.4 million British Columbians. This burst of generosity gave birth to a new word—"bricing"—meaning to give away shares in a publicly-owned corporation, thereby (this part is not in the official definition) winning an election. At the same time, residents were allowed to purchase up to 5,000 shares of the company each, in what a study by the Ontario Economic Council called "the largest single equity distribution to date in Canadian history." The shares had a nominal value of $6, so the effect was that everybody got $12 in free shares, and that helped sell the other shares. British Columbians cheerfully poured out $450 million for shares, which are now worth $1.30 each on the market. The government did not mean to strip the suckers of hundreds of millions of dollars, but that is how it has worked out.

Free at last to pursue its destiny among the giants of free enterprise, BCRIC promptly fell on its nose. It was a bad time for resource companies. Losses worked their way up to a spectacular $470.8 million in 1985. Most of that was a one-time write-off of assets. Still, it meant that BCRIC had managed to lose more in one year than its entire remaining equity base ($310.1 million). A lot of BCRIC shares have joined Confederate money and Snake Island Oil bonds in attic trunks.

Then we had the brave attempt to privatize Petro-Can in 1979, during the Progressive Conservatives' brief hiccup of power, discussed in Chapter 9. By the time that was done, Petro-Can was bigger, but no less governmental, although it remains an attractive candidate for the private sector, if we can ever agree on to whom, when, and for how much?

The Liberals, when they resumed power in 1980, foreswore the privatization plans of the Conservatives, and for the next four years went on merrily creating Crowns. Then came the election of September 4, 1984, in which the Tories under Brian Mulroney swept to power with the strongest parliamentary majority in Canadian history, and a firm commitment to clobber the Crowns. Now we would see action.

In *A New Direction for Canada: An Agenda for Economic Renewal*, a study paper released by the new government in November, 1984, the party's thinkers made it clear that privatization was a priority. It had become the international buzz-word, not only in Britain, where the trend started, but in France, West Germany, Italy, Argentina, Brazil, Mexico, even, ye gods, in the Soviet Union and China. Despite the snares and pitfalls, the process has so many instant advantages—quick cash, for starters, the reversal of a trend to government control which has clearly gone too far, for another—that it seemed almost inevitable that Canada would follow the international example. The Tories, ruefully remembering the Petro-Can fiasco, had set up an eight-man task force under Senator William Kelly, which prepared a hit list of Crowns to be de-throned, and detailed plans on how to do it. The task force report was kept secret, naturally—we couldn't have the peasants discussing what was to happen with their property—and that led to some confusion. What was for sale? For how much? Under what conditions? Nobody knew, although the newspapers were full of potential candidates. A new cabinet committee was established to deal with the subject, and we eventually got a minister of privatization (currently Barbara Macdougall); but of coherent philosophy, there was none. While Transport Minister (now Deputy Prime Minister) Don Mazankowski was exploring options for the sale of Air Canada, to come on the market in 1985, Prime Minister Brian Mulroney was having second thoughts. In an aside to reporters on quite another subject, he announced that "Air Canada is not for sale." If not, why not? Nobody knows. In 1987, the planted stories in the newspapers suggested the sale was back on; but, at a guess, any sale that takes place will be surrounded by enough conditions to still the passion in all but the most ardent suitors.

Whim Takes Over

With a clear and coherent plan, privatization is tough; the British had found that out. When the plan is abandoned, and whim takes over, it can be deadly. Sinclair Stevens, the Minister of Regional Industrial Expansion, was determined to sell off the major holdings of the CDIC—Canadair, de Havilland, Eldorado Nuclear, and Teleglobe Canada—and in October, 1984, announced that the divestiture would be

well under way "within six to twelve months," that is, by
mid-1985. There were some policy problems—would Teleglobe retain its monopoly over international telephone
communications?—but these would be worked out as the
money rolled in. De Havilland was finally pushed out into
the hands of Boeing in late 1985, in a deal that leaves the
government still potentially responsible for up to $400 mil-
lion in debt. Canadair went to Bombardier in a better-
managed transaction, as we saw in Chapter 2. Mr. Stevens'
deadline came and went, with the privatization candidates
still hanging around the edge of the dance floor, looking
winsome.

However, the Canada Development Corporation was
forging ahead on its own to get privatized. In May, 1985,
the CDC sold shares in one of its subsidiaries, Canterra
Energy, for $14 a share; a year later they were trading for
$6.88, and there were a lot of unhappy bunnies with Can-
terra stock in their portfolios. In September, 1985, the CDC
put out 23 million of its own shares—most of the government's remaining portfolio—under an installment-buying
plan that would make it easy for small investors to partic-
ipate. You would pay half the current stock-market price
down, and get a receipt. Then you would pay the other
half, turn in your receipt (unless you had sold it to someone
else to make a quick profit), and pick up your share. Just
before the deal was announced, the price of common shares
in CDC was driven up to a fifty-two-week high of $11.50.
That set the price of the public issue; two payments of $5.75
each, one to be paid at once, the other on September 16,
1986. Right. Then—isn't it a caution the way these patterns
repeat?—the shares began to tumble, until they hit $6.25
in late August, 1986. Now, those who had paid $5.75 were
going to have to pay another $5.75 for a share worth a little
bit more than they had already forked out for half of it.
Buyers on the Toronto Stock Exchange were pronouncing
their opinion by offering to buy the $5.75 receipts for sixty
cents. Or investors could kiss the whole thing goodbye. At
this writing, it looks as if most opted to pay the second
installment, leaving the government richer by $120 million.
It is still, by far, the largest shareholder in the CDC, and
has, all unintentionally, emptied the pockets of the trusting
in the name of a privatization which still hasn't taken place.

Meanwhile, back at the cabinet, things were at last stirring. Loto Canada, the Canadian Sports Pool Corporation, and Canagrex, a Crown established in 1983 to export agricultural products, were simply abolished in mid-1985, in all but name. Good work, too. They were all seen, quite correctly, as mere patronage pools for the Liberals. The Tories would make do with their own patronage pools. About the same time, the Canada Museums Construction Corporation, which was having horrible problems with cost overruns, was absorbed into the Department of Public Works. There was no sound reason why it should have been created in the first place. These were all new Crowns, whose passing left scarcely a ripple.

Then, still in mid-1985, the government actually passed The Crown Corporations Dissolution Authorization Act, which eliminated four Crowns. They were:

1. CN (West Indies) Steamships, which had been inoperative for decades;
2. Società a Responsibilità Limitata San Sebastiano, which had been created for the sole purpose of dodging taxes in the Vatican; it owned the Canadian ambassador's house in the Papal See, which was transferred to the government;
3. St. Anthony Fisheries, a company that only lasted one year, and whose purpose was to buy fish; it was replaced by the much larger Saltwater Fish Corporation; and
4. Uranium Canada, which you may recall as a company that held uranium stockpiles for Eldorado Nuclear. It had long since passed its holdings to Eldorado.

The net effect of all this was that the Consolidated Revenue Fund picked up $9 (yes, nine dollars). George Baker, the Liberal MP from Gander-Twillingate, told the House of Commons, "The principle of this bill is a big zero."

Despite all that huffing and puffing, and the obliteration of seven Crowns, we hadn't actually privatized anything. Finally, we had lift-off. After a nasty fight among the Treasury Board secretariat, which was supposed to be running things, the Department of Regional Industrial Expansion, and the Department of Supply and Services, the government made its first sale. For $27 million, Northern Transportation Company Limited, which runs barges on the Mackenzie River, was sold in August, 1985. Whew. It was a money-maker—$3,355,000 on operations in 1983. But never mind the money, at last we committed privatization in public.

Then Canadian Arsenals, the government munitions-maker, was sold, in December, 1985. The buyer was a Montreal company, SNC Group, and the selling price was $92.2 million. Was this a fair price? Who knows? The deal, which went through five separate rounds, was so surrounded by secrecy that about all the public ever found out was that Canadian Arsenals had made either $8.5 million (it said) or $6 million (the Auditor-General said) in 1983–84. The Auditor-General also said that "when public assets and shares . . . are to be disposed of, MPs are entitled to precise qualitative and quantitative information." Such a fussbudget.

The de Havilland sale for $155 million, announced with Canadian Arsenals (and detailed in Chapter 2), wound things up for 1985, except that, of course, while all this was going on, another $887 million was being sunk into Petro-Can (see Chapter 9). Nothing more happened until August, 1986, when as we have already seen, Canadair was dealt off to Bombardier for $120 million.

Ready for a Box Score? The Envelope, Please

Within the first two years of its mandate, the Conservative government had succeeded in privatizing four (count 'em) Crowns, and taken in $514.2 million (I am allowing the full $155 million the government negotiated for de Havilland, although it may wind up paying out, not taking in; I have assumed a gain of $120 million from CDC shares, the National Transportation Company's $29 million, $92.2 million for Canadian Arsenals, and $120 million for Canadair). Then there was the creation of at least one new Crown, to study international relations (remember?), so we are down to three Crowns, net, privatized, and seven pulverized. In the meantime, of course, we had stuck another $887 million in Petro-Can, to buy part of Gulf, and Petro-Can appears to have created at least four new subsidiaries (newly listed by Statscan). So that is, let's see, ten down, five up. In two years, five Crowns have been removed, while our investment in Crown corporations has gone up by another $372.8 million. It's going to be a long haul. Although we can expect some major sales through 1987, we don't know, yet, what the final tally will be before the Conservatives go to the polls again. They would certainly like to bring in some quick money, and the way to do that is to sell something like Teleglobe Canada, but whether that is in Canada's best interest is doubtful. (Between 1982 and 1985, Teleglobe earned $232.6 million in profit and paid $205.8 million in income tax.) At the current rate of progress, we may get down to perhaps 300 federal Crowns by about the time the sun becomes a nova, and we cease to worry about trifles.

The Provinces Had Their Moments, too

The privatization process actually began, you recall, in the provinces, with British Columbia's disastrous Bricing operation. Pretty soon most of the provinces were trying for a piece of the action, although, as with Ottawa, results have not been impressive. We have had many brave words from throne speeches and budget speeches over the past five years, but the process is a little like the song in *Pirates of Penzance*, where the policemen keep bellowing about going out to beat up the pirates, and the chorus keeps reminding them, "Yes, but you don't go."

Ontario bought into Suncor in 1981, taking up 25 per cent of the company for $650 million, which, with the cost of borrowing, represents about $1 billion now. It seemed like a good idea at the time; Suncor is into exploiting the oil sands of Alberta. Trouble is, it now costs more to produce oil from the sands than the market will pay. The opposition Liberals voiced much scorn over the Suncor purchase, and proposed privatizing the thing. Once they took the Ontario helm, they called in Dominion Securities Pitfield to have a look, and in mid-1986, Dominion Securities Pitfield advised the province to stuff the shares under the mattress and hope for the best. On the market, they would fetch somewhere between $87 million and $169 million. "It is our recommendation that Ontario not dispose of the shares at this time but maintain the matter under continuing review," the report concluded. If Suncor is to be privatized, it will be sometime in the future.

Gritting its teeth, Ontario went ahead and privatized its

Urban Transportation Development Corporation (UTDC).
More or less. UTDC was designed to develop rapid transit
systems and streetcars. Over a period of fourteen years,
$163 million in public funds was put into UTDC, of which
$67 million represented shareholder equity—that is, it was
money that hadn't vanished, money that was still there.
While UTDC lost money on operations, a total of $17.8
million, it made a profit of $12.3 million in 1984. This was
not a dog. However, the public mood being what it is, the
Liberals—state enterprisers—resolved to sell what the Tories—free enterprisers—had wrought. They put UTDC up
for bids, because, as Premier David Peterson said, "We have
talked to a number of people in the business who feel that
UTDC could grow and expand if it had a private component."

Nothing wrong with this, or with putting out for tender
a company developed with public funds—except to those
of a strong ideological turn of mind. In economic terms,
the distinction between investing in a corporation, then
delivering it to the private sector in hopes of getting more
jobs back from it, and simply handing grants to private
investors, is not crucial. Anyway, for good or ill, Ontario
decided to sell and approached twenty-one potential buyers. Only two showed any signs of interest. By the time the
sale was completed, Lavalin of Montreal had agreed to pay
$30 million down, and $51 million in all. However, Ontario
agreed to give Lavalin a $20 million debenture to be held
for twenty years, with the interest to be paid in the form
of 25 per cent of net profits on new earnings of the corporation over the period. So, Ontario gets $10 million?
Well, no. Lavalin will receive $10 million as a management
fee for taking over existing UTDC contracts, which takes
care of that. Then the province puts up all direct labour
and materials costs for some manufacturing projects, plus
a fixed amount of $2.75 million monthly per month for
eighteen months—a total of $49.6 million—to cover over-
head. The province is also responsible for nearly $500 mil-
lion in performance bonds for existing projects. It will also
supply performance bonds for any new GO train or Via
Rail contracts concluded by the restructured firm.

Ontario still owns 15 per cent of UTDC. What it ended
up doing was parting with control of a corporation into
which it had put $167 million for nothing down and $20

million to be paid out of profits, while retaining all the important risks, and throwing somewhere over $50 million into the hopper besides. It has privatized the profits and publicized the losses. Clearly, this was the best deal that John Kruger, Ontario's privatization consultant, could work out, but you have to wonder why anyone would bother.

In June, 1986, the Ontario Liberals also garrotted IDEA Corp., a venture capital Crown created by their Conservative predecessors. IDEA was launched in 1981, given $91 million to invest over five years, and told to go out and help emerging technologies to become business ventures. After five years, IDEA was supposed to be making enough money that it wouldn't need any more government support. At least, that was the idea. Well, you know how these things are. There was a battle among cabinet ministers over who would get to give out the goodies—sorry, administer the programmes—and in the end, two ministries came to administer one Crown. Then there was a battle over the corporation's lush offices, and another battle over investments in old, mature firms instead of new, venturesome ones, and a shuffling of presidents, and a claim, unfounded, that the husband of a Liberal cabinet minister had profited from an IDEA deal and, what with one thing and another, it just seemed like a good notion to turn out the lights at IDEA. When that was done, $41.5 million had been invested in fifty-eight ventures. These projects were turned over to another Crown, Ontario Development Corp., which might have taken on the job in the first place, and saved time. The headlines trumpeted another privatization, but nothing of the sort took place.

And so it goes. Saskatchewan announces proudly that it has privatized Saskatchewan Oil and Gas Corporation, in January, 1986, for $110 million. Actually, the government retains 60 per cent of the company, and nobody else is allowed to own more than 4 per cent. Of the $110 million received from the share issue, $75 million went into government coffers, and $28.7 million into Saskoil's treasury (the rest financed the sale). So Saskoil went out looking for other companies to buy. Or, as Jim Lyons of the *Financial Post* put it, "With bulging pockets . . . it is hunting for bargains to enhance its long-term prospects as oil industry economics squeeze companies less robust." Oil industry experts write like that. To put it more plainly, the Saskatchewan government having cashed in part of one of its companies will use the money to buy some more. This is privatization Prairie style.

Quebec Denationalizes Booze: Sort of

Privatization Quebec style has also been vigorous, but confusing. The Parti Québecois, in a desperate bid to bolster its fading popularity before the 1985 election, undertook to sell the province's 360 liquor stores to the private sector— not the warehousing, or distribution, just the retail outlets owned by the Société des Alcools de Québec (SAQ). The proposal was immediately attacked by the unions, who suggested that private owners would immediately fire long-time union employees, and hire relatives, and by the Liberals, who said it would never bring in enough money to be worthwhile. But the government persisted, and put 129 Montreal-area stores on the market in mid-1985. By the end of July, it had sold 58 outlets, many of them to co-operatives of former employees. No bids whatever were received on 63 other stores. When the Liberals swept to power in December, 1985, the whole project was put on hold pending the results of a study by Pierre Fortier, who had been put in charge of a newly created privatization portfolio. It is a poor and backward government that lacks such a portfolio these days. This study suggested a more comprehensive privatization, to include the entire SAQ, arguing, correctly, that the PQ plan had not involved privatization at all; it was merely "a franchisation plan." They were McDonaldifying booze. So that is now under study. In the meantime, many of the groups who were hung out to dry by the new policy have launched lawsuits to make the government live up to its contracts or buy them off.

However, the Quebec Liberals are plunging ahead with privatization, in one form or another. An advisory committee report tabled in July, 1986, and titled, rather grandly, *From the Quiet Revolution to the Year 2000*, suggested the sale of ten "strategic" corporations, ranging from such money-losers as Rexfor, a forestry giant and Quebecair to in-and-out runners like Soquip (oil and gas), Soquem (mining), and Sidbec (steel).

Actually, Quebecair and Soquem were already on the market. Soquem, which owns gold mines in northern Quebec, and makes money, will be turned into a mixed corporation, at least to start with. A new company, called Cambior, will be created and shares representing 60 per cent of that will be sold to the public, while Soquem holds onto the rest. It is going to take a while.

In fact, the only Quebec firm actually privatized during the first year of the Liberal government was a sugar-beet plant in St. Hilaire, Raffinerie de Sucre de Québec, which sold for about $10 million in cash and a $40 million debenture to a private rival, Lantic Sugar. As Pierre Fortier noted when announcing the sale, it was not so much a privatization as "a liquidation," which cost 100 jobs and left sugar-beet farmers in the area without a local market.

There was another sale, in August 1986, of Quebecair to Nordair Metro, for $10 million. One of the conditions of the deal, according to the original announcement, was that jobs would be maintained, but within two weeks of the sale, 307 layoffs were announced, although 123 of those dismissed were to be offered other jobs.

The Caisse: Vive la Différence?

In the meantime, no one has suggested privatizing the Caisse de Dépôt et Placement du Québec, the looming giant that keeps gobbling up parts of private concerns to add to its swelling portfolio. The Caisse was founded in 1965, to manage the contributions of eleven pension and insurance plans, including the Quebec Pension Plan. Instead of sitting on its money, or lending it all out to governments (although it did some of that), or just buying bonds and clipping the coupons, the way most pension funds are content to do, the Caisse opted to buy equity stocks in Canadian companies in pursuit of its mandate to "generate a profit through sound investment and to support Quebec's economic development." The corporation's 1985 annual report lists shares in 113 corporations, from Agnico-Eagle Mines to Teck Corporation, and including banks, beer (both Labatt and Molson), oil (Nova, an Alberta Corporation), tobacco, liquor, groceries, and even publishing (Maclean-Hunter). It is a major holder in Alcan Aluminium (7.8 per cent), Bell Canada Enterprises (5.0 per cent), Domtar (14.8 per cent), Provigo (18.2 per cent), Canadian Pacific (8.3 per cent) and Sceptre Resources (26.8 per cent).

With $25 billion in assets to invest, the Caisse makes a lot of people nervous. It made them more nervous when it was, frankly, an instrument of political as well as economic influence in the hands of the Parti Quebecois. Although it is not so blatantly political today, the Caisse still wields enormous clout, and it is still a government body. Which means, among other things, that it doesn't have to disclose as much as private firms, even when it is competing directly with them. The Caisse was barred from the Toronto Stock Exchange in 1982, when it refused to file insider reports during its purchase of 15 per cent of Domtar, the forest giant. (Incidentally, it also owns shares in Donohue, another forest giant.) The Caisse went to court, saw its right to refuse to file the reports upheld, because of its Crown status, and then filed them voluntarily. This was good public relations, and the company is trying to make itself more open—its annual reports are much more detailed and clearer than formerly—but it remains an aggressive, secretive, tough-minded, profit-driven investment giant, which quite properly tries to exercise all the muscle it can inside the companies whose shares it owns.

It will be interesting to see if, over the next decade or so, the Quebec government can privatize corporations faster than the Caisse is de-privatizing them. On the record so far, I put my money on the Caisse, which has $2 billion in profits annually to sink into the chase.

What has become clear by now, I hope, is that privatization is a very tricky business indeed. Any time you read that something has been privatized, read the small print. It is also clear that, if governments allow themselves to be ruled by ideology, and sell at any price, the public purse is going to take a trimming. If, on the other hand, they simply get greedy, and use privatization for a quick cash fix for leaky budgets, they may wind up selling things we will all later regret. Finally, it is clear that, at the present rate of progress, and with the present chaotic conditions prevailing at the planning levels, we will all be with the choirs of angels long before privatization does much about restoring order to Canada's Crowns.

Time to look at other ways to sort out the mess.

13
Sorting Out The Mess

"There's no wonder our Crown corporations lose money when they are run by a bunch of political hacks."

Nelson Riis, MP,
House of Commons, March 20, 1985

If you ever take up writing magazine articles for a living—I wouldn't, it's hard work—you will discover that, at the end of a long tough article in which you have Viewed With Alarm, you are expected to come up with the answer to everything in 200 words or less. I don't mean those articles on Brian Mulroney's chin, or how to make wall decorations from discarded bottle caps. I mean the serious stuff; "Whither the UN?" or "What Is Wrong With Modern Marriage?" Magazine editors, a strange bunch who are wont to eat rusty nails and sacrifice their young to pagan gods, will hound you mercilessly for what is known as "The Seven Steps to God" at the end of each article. Their reasoning is that it is no good stirring the reader up with nameless dread and then wishing him or her the best of British luck and walking away. No, you have to take the poor fish up to the mountain top and point over to the far horizon where—can't you see it?—a new day is about to dawn. All will be well if only we keep our heads, you are to say, and here are the head-keeping rules. You give the rules, seven in all, if you can make it come out right, and *then* you can depart and leave the reader to ascend to heaven, jump, or work his way back down.

In many cases, the dilemma for the writer is that there

are usually more problems to be discovered than solutions to be proffered, which is why so many magazine writers wear that glassy look, and start at sudden sounds. They are trying to come up with solutions for all the problems they have dug up, and are not having any luck. We, on the other hand, are in much better shape, because in the course of this book we have learned so much about Crown corporations and how they work, and what is wrong with them, that the holy Seven Steps pretty well look after themselves. Just for the hell of it, though, we will write them down and call them—why not?—The Seven Steps to God (Crown Corporations Division):

Step 1: Let There Be Light

Time after time, in the course of our rambles, we have come across the need to open the Crowns to greater public access. In practical terms, "direction, control, accountability"—the catch words used in the federal government's 1977 study of the Crowns, are really one and the same thing. Every time someone dreams up a new way to curb the Crowns, they duck around it. Make them submit operating budgets to Parliament if they want funds from the Consolidated Revenue Fund—as the 1977 study suggested—and they will find other ways to raise the money. Quite often it's the government itself that is up to dark and dirty deeds—as with the uranium cartel, as with the Atomic Energy sales, covered by Letters of Comfort. But no Crown can long survive a concerted parliamentary attack based on solid information. When the facts start to come out, managers dive for cover, swear seven oaths that it was all a ghastly mistake, and scurry to make amends.

Shouldn't that tell us something? For one thing, it tells us to appoint the Auditor-General of Canada as auditor for every federal Crown and the provincial Auditors-General as auditors of the provincial Crowns. The Auditor-General is not responsible to the government, but to Parliament; he has a big, shiny whistle, and he loves to blow it. Always has; it is the tradition of the office since it was first established in 1878. History has shown that you can't buy the Auditor-General off, turn him away, tone him down, or shut him up. Once he has the information, he goes blatting it out, shamelessly, in his annual report, a document that causes more chewed knuckles and churned ulcers than any other in Ottawa.

Why should Petro-Can be using two private auditors? They are no doubt fine fellows, but they are not *our* fine fellows. They are only required to certify that, in the classic phrase, "these consolidated financial statements present fairly the financial position of the corporation" and that there has been no violation of the legislation governing the Crown. The Auditor-General has quite a different task. From the very beginning, his job has been to "report to the House of Commons any expenditures or transactions which, in his opinion, ran counter to the wishes of Parliament," to quote from Sonja Sinclair's history of the office. He is also to withhold his approval if he thought the price charged for work or materials was not "fair or just"—something which is, frankly, none of an ordinary auditor's business. In addition, there is a catch-all clause allowing the Auditor-General to comment on "unusual transactions" (unusual? some of them are unbelievable), and that gives him plenty of scope. The Auditor-General's working rule is, "When in doubt, shout," and even the hint that he is concerned about some contemplated action is often enough to cause deep second thoughts.

If the Auditor-General had been looking over the books during the Petrofina acquisition by Petro-Can, he would have known—and we would have known—exactly what was paid, and when, and how. If anything was wrong—and years later, we still don't know the answer to that—we would all have known while there was still time to do something about it.

There's nothing like a squealer on the premises to promote virtue, and the Auditor-General is a squealer par excellence. He is the auditor of the agency and departmental crowns and some of the proprietary ones; but many of the largest, most robust and fastest-proliferating ones are privately audited, including Petro-Can, Canadian National, Telesat Canada, Air Canada, the CDIC, the Cape Breton Development Corporation, the Canadian Wheat Board, and Via Rail. Since these represent about half the assets and many of the really big problems associated with Crowns, it is small comfort to know that the Auditor-General has his beady eye on the Canadian Saltfish Corporation, the Great Lakes Pilotage Authority, and the Royal Canadian Mint. Neither Canadair nor de Havilland, incidentally, were under his scrutiny.

Increase the Auditor-General's staff and put all the Crowns under his audit, and a good many of our wayward corporations will become susceptible of control in one fell swoop.

Step 2: Sort and Prune

Almost every legislative jurisdiction in the country either now has, or shortly will have, a minister responsible for privatization, and he or she ought to make it part of his or her business to re-catalogue all the Crowns. It would be nice to have a central register somewhere, with a complete listing. At both federal and provincial levels, we also need a reworking of the rules governing the formation of Crowns, and a common definition of what is a Crown. When one Crown can quietly whistle up five subsidiaries without leaking a word to Parliament, as the Canada Lands Company did, there is something wrong. It ought not to be beyond the mind of man to come up with a set of standard rules to define what constitutes a Crown; I can't help feeling that much of the confusion is deliberate, just another way of escaping legitimate control.

There will always be categories of Crowns. The main ones now are departmental, agency, and proprietary, reflecting different levels of independence, in theory at least. I can see no need for any departmental Crowns whatever. Corporations which are, by definition, responsible to a government department for financial control and funding ought not to be separate entities at all. God knows, the departments are secretive enough, but they have fewer places to hide than a Crown, which is supposed to be, somehow, at arm's length. There are currently fourteen departmental Crowns (the Agricultural Stabilization Board, Atomic Energy Control Board, Canada Employment and Immigration Commission, Director of Soldier Settlement, Director, The Veterans' Land Act, Economic Council of Canada, Fisheries Prices Support Board, Medical Research Council, National

Museums of Canada, National Research Council, Natural Sciences and Engineering Research Council, Science Council, and Social Sciences and Humanities Research Council. However, there is no rational reason why, for example, the Atomic Energy Control Board should be a corporation any more than, say, the health and safety sections of Consumer Affairs. The Economic Council of Canada may feel it needs some distance between itself and a ministry. If so, it should be made into an agency corporation, which is what it really is.

Agency Crowns, which are "quasi-commercial," and proprietary Crowns, which are supposed to be independent of Parliament, for money, anyway, represent a distinction without a difference, at least in practice. Air Canada is proprietary and makes money; so does the Royal Canadian Mint (in both senses), which is agency. Canada Post is quasi-commercial, but the Cape Breton Development Corporation and the CBC are, in the legislation, proprietary, that is, wholly commercial and self-supporting. It is to laugh. Then there are all the "other" Crowns, like the Bank of Canada, the Canadian Wheat Board, and CDIC.

The whole boiling of them needs to be re-catalogued. In the process, whoever does it will stop, quite often, and say, "Why have we got a whole separate Crown to sell fresh fish and another to sell saltfish, when all the money comes from the Department of Oceans and Fisheries?" Zap will go some Crowns, back into the departments where they belong.

This sorting and pruning process will cause some heavy decision making, for example, should Canada Post be a Crown, or would it be just as happy—or unhappy—back in a department? This one is beyond me; the postal system was in a mess when it was under direct political control, and it is still a mess as a Crown. I'm not sure the form matters, in which case, perhaps the more direct control that can be exerted, the better. That argues for a Post Office Department, once more. Oh, dear.

Step 3: Unmix the Crowns

The Americans have it right; government enterprises ought not to be able to own shares in private companies, and they ought not to be able to sell part of themselves to a private company. This new-fangled tom-foolery, which is certainly what my grandfather would have called it, is not merely confusing, but dangerous. In a recent report to Parliament, Auditor-General Kenneth Dye cited thirteen cases in which "financial and other information available to Parliament is fragmented and incomplete." When a government buys in—as the Ontario government did with Suncor—it becomes responsible without having control for the activities of a company operating in the commercial field. The results are usually horrendous. The commercial activities of the mixed corporation are frequently cited as a reason for concealing information from the public, while the Crown connection is used by the same corporation as a kind of guarantee that, whatever happens, it will not be allowed to fail. If it does, everyone knows the government will step in to pick up the pieces. What we have here is the worst of both worlds.

If governments want to operate in the commercial sector—and, in most cases, they ought not to—they should do so as governments. If they want to support private companies, they ought to do so by way of grants, subsidies, loans, or guarantees, which are all subject to the inspection and control of legislatures. If the loans crash and they wind up owning something they didn't intend to own, they ought to get rid of it as fast as possible. Sounds easier than it is, but the current situation cannot be described as either easy or tolerable.

Step 4: Don't Give Us Salvation, Just Understanding

Half of the problem with Crowns comes from a misunderstanding of their function. They are political animals. That is what they are for. Politics, like sex, represents primal shame in Canada, but that hasn't substantially interfered with either function—only with our understanding of them. It is a perfectly legitimate role of government to decide to invest money for political and social reasons; for example, to promote jobs in an area of high unemployment. A Crown corporation is one way to do this. Creating the Cape Breton Development Corporation made sense, given the alternatives, as did turning the Sydney Steel Corporation into a Crown. What does not make sense is, having taken these political steps, to try to pretend that what was involved was hard-headed economics, and that, therefore, everything can be hidden from the public on the grounds that this is, after all, a commercial operation.

If it is commercial, let it pay for itself; if it cannot pay for itself, then it must abide by the rules of the public sector, which means, first and foremost, full disclosure. Full disclosure, it is always argued, will hurt the firm competitively. Too bad; it is the necessary price of government support.

A word about partisan politics and the Crowns. Cosmologists speculate on the possibility of parallel universes; they flirt with the notion that somewhere in the Great Beyond, there exist worlds exactly like our own, but with small differences. The Vancouver Canucks win hockey games, say, or TV stations hire ugly women to read the news. It may be that in one of these parallel worlds they have Crown corporations free of the taint of politics; it will never be so in our own. One of the most misleading aspects of the Crowns—whether it is Ontario Hydro, under that canny wire-puller Adam Beck, or CN, doffing chairmen as fast as elections make it necessary—is the argument that they are independent of political control. Since the only justification for a Crown is political, in the real meaning of that word, this attitude is not merely futile, but silly. Ontario Hydro pretending to be a non-political public service has always reminded me of Groucho Marx dressed up to play Shirley Temple; bold rather than convincing. The arrival of large and aggressive unions has insulated the Crowns from the worst abuses of politics, where merit is discarded for a party card. With that settled, we ought to expect governments to appoint to senior Crown posts people who will cheerfully carry out government policy, and we ought not to be surprised if a change of government changes these appointments.

Step 5: Establish the Presumption of Guilt

You don't have to be a cynic to form the assumption that, left to themselves, the Crowns will be up to every kind of deviltry, with the aid of government funds. History has also shown us that, because they are Crowns, they are often in a difficult position when it comes to bargaining over wages. If a tough strike can be mounted against a Crown, the pit is pretty well bottomless. It will always be easier to settle at whatever price than to face the flak in Parliament because the country has been brought to a standstill. Thus workers on the St. Lawrence Seaway in 1965 were able to grab a 30 per cent raise in one pass, with repercussions that affected every segment of the economy.

These things being so, it ought to be very difficult for anyone to create or maintain a Crown. We have enough, too many, far, far too many. Anybody who wants to form another one ought to have to comply with the most rigorous rules, under the Financial Administration Act or a provincial equivalent, and in the teeth of a strong presumption that there is likely to be waste and wickedness afoot.

Step 6: Privatization if Necessary, but not etc.

There are a large number of Crowns now operating in the public sector which properly belong in the private sector. But—and it is a large but—the movement in that direction ought to be taken with care. The kind of schmozzles outlined earlier will multiply a hundredfold if we begin selling them off on the basis of ideology.

For example, there is no cogent argument for Petro-Can, as it presently exists, to be a Crown. We ought to sell it for many dollars, and let it do what it wants to do, which is to sell gas and oil through service stations. However, some of the reasons for creating the company (forgotten, mostly, in Red Square) remain; that is, to promote research and exploration, to explore other energy sources, and to work as Canada's national oil company with other national oil companies. What is required is to re-cast the company, separating the commercial sectors from the others, and to sell the commercial sectors.

We no longer need a government airline to fly the routes from Toronto and Ottawa to Montreal, or from Calgary and Edmonton to Vancouver. But we do need, and will always need, an airline to fly from, say Moose Jaw to

Thompson, Manitoba. Again, what we want to do is to privatize—at a big fat profit—the part that will support itself commercially, and keep the rest in a Crown.

We own dozens of Crowns, with hundreds and hundreds of subsidiaries, which either never had, or have lost, the need to be Crowns, but it doesn't follow that we ought to privatize them all, even if we could get a market to absorb them all. Many should simply be written off, or gradually allowed to atrophy. Many should be absorbed back into government departments (frankly, I don't see why the Mint shouldn't run out of the Department of Finance), and some should remain as they are, with stricter accountability and control.

It is foolish, in my mind, to talk of selling off the Canadian Broadcasting Corporation, although God knows it could be re-drawn without any harm done. The Canadian Wheat Board has run well for decades, and ought to be governed by the if-it-ain't-broke-don't-fix-it rule. Privatization may provide fast funds for beleaguered governments, but it is at best, only a partial solution for some of our Crowns.

Step 7: A Sunset Law

The history of government enterprises—not only our own, but all over the world—shows that they all tend to follow the same pattern. A Crown created for sound policy and social reasons becomes, over time, nothing more than an entrenched bureaucratic corporation defending itself against all comers with guile, evasion, and secrecy. I am reminded of those biological treatises about animals striving to re-produce themselves as often as possible to spread their own genes, the driving engine of evolution. If you want to see urgent genes, stroll through the offices of Petro-Can some day. What we need, then, is a periodic review of each Crown, before a parliamentary committee. Most would not need to be looked at more than once a decade, and they would only need to respond to two questions:

- Why were you incorporated? and
- What the hell have you been up to?

Comparing the original legislation, or regulations, with the current performance would allow us to dispense with many of them, reform others, and keep a salutary eye on the rest.

Ontario has a sunset review process, covering all government agencies and Crowns (they tend to be lumped together in Ontario). All agencies and Crowns established after March 12, 1980, are automatically subject to periodic review, unless the cabinet specifies otherwise. (It frequently does; of thirty new bodies established after March 12, 1980, eight have exemptions. Why?) When the time-clock strikes midnight (different dates apply to different kinds of bodies), a review is undertaken by the responsible ministry with, as the legislation says, "other ministries, individuals and groups as appropriate." What with its built-in exemptions, it is not a very rigorous system. But even so, it succeeded in lopping eight agencies off during the latest fiscal year—1984–85—for which the Provincial-Auditor has reported. That's the good news. The bad news is that, during the same time, fourteen new agencies were established, so that the province finished the year with six more than it started with. Oh, well, I don't say a sunset law is perfect; but that a rigorously applied one will, in the long run, curb growth.

And so We Bid Farewell, as the Sun Sinks in the West

All seven of my points are really one, that is, an argument that in any nation there will always be social, political, and mixed social-political-and-economic goals that can best be achieved through government enterprise. In a limited number of cases, a separate corporation is a more effective tool than, say, a departmental organization, or simply slipping subsidies to a private firm. Like the poor, Crowns will be always with us. At the same time, cruel experience has taught us that there is a constant danger that self-perpetuating, self-aggrandizing, self-promoting Crowns will always try to shake off the shackles of control, and go forth to be fruitful and multiply. That is an argument to control Crowns, not an argument to reject the concept of government enterprises.

We want to use these enterprises intelligently to perform the tasks we set them, and we want to make sure they are as efficient as possible. If they make money, because they control some natural monopoly, we will probably be best served by ploughing the funds back into the service. Because Crowns ought to be for service, not profit. If they are performing a service that makes a profit, chances are that private enterprise can and will do it better. "Profit," "efficiency," and "cost effectiveness," the great touchstones of modern accounting, are useful concepts, but only if we understand what they mean. It is not efficient to curb the postal deficit by wrecking the service; it is not cost-effective to run "The Dukes of Hazzard" on the CBC. We don't want Sysco to make a profit at the expense of polluting Cape Breton. That way madness lies.

At the same time, it is essential to bring the Crowns back under control, back to a sense of accountability—now more than ever. The two overwhelming economic problems that confront Canadians today are budget deficits and unemployment. The Crowns are at the heart of both. God knows they do their bit to promote budget deficits, and they will have to be at the heart of any programme to deal with unemployment.

There is in this, as in all matters political, a balance to be reached, and it is never an easy one. I am not of the school that believes that budget deficits will cause hair to grow on the palms of our hands and make us all insane. Most of the money represented by such shortfalls consists of funds Canadians owe other Canadians. One way we meet the need for the required funds is through Canada Savings Bonds, which are not, most of us would agree, instruments of the devil. Just the same, it is clear to the simplest economic mind—my own—that constant deficits will, as the cliche has it, mortgage the present to the future, and sharply curtail the options of coming generations—or else, by requiring ever-higher taxes and ever-higher interest rates to attract the necessary funds, promote unacceptable inflation. In this regard, money spent foolishly by governments is a threat to this generation and the generations to come. While Crowns have no monopoly on foolish spending, they are in there churning away with the worst government departments and without—I repeat one last time—the same degree of accountability we have with funds that flow openly through Parliament.

As to jobs, the Crowns can obviously be effective generators of employment, and, especially in disadvantaged areas of the country, that is a proper role for them to fill. But poorly run corporations, public or private, will not long survive in a competitive world, and no economy can long sustain the constant drain on resources that such firms represent. Whatever the benefits in jobs, the cost will be seen to be too high, and the portcullis will come down. This is the threat that faces Sysco, a mainstay of Nova Scotia, as I write this. Everyone agrees that Sysco is needed, but there is no agreement that it is needed at any price. Because of its monumental inefficiency, the balance is tipping away from Sysco, even though its closing would represent a body blow to the region.

So we are back to the basic problem of dealing with the Crowns, of deciding in our own minds, what role we want them to play in the economy, and how we want them to play it. We are, I hope, better positioned to make these decisions now that we know something more about the Crowns. Despite their enormous size, variety, and complexity, it is not that hard to deal with the Crowns if we remember what they ought to be. They ought to be public service corporations carrying out some of the social, political, and economic goals our society requires and which are not now being looked after by private enterprises. They exist as corporations only when and if they can operate more effectively, from the point of view of the public, not themselves, as incorporated bodies rather than as arms of government departments. They do not have any automatic right to exist, any more than any other corporation does. They ought to be open, responsible, and responsive, and the moment they cease to be any of these things, we ought to drown them in a bucket, before they can grow up and do us harm.

BIBLIOGRAPHY

I have not included chapter notes in this book, for two reasons.
The first is that such notes might give the book the appearance
of a definitive academic study, which, as the reader will have
realized by now, is neither either intended nor achieved. The
second is that, in ten previous books, I have included such notes,
and have never once had any indication from a reader that they
provided the slightest aid or insight. Just the same, there may
be readers who would like a list of some of the original source
material used. For their benefit, I have prepared the following
bibliography of major sources.

1. Annual and Periodical Reports

Annual Reports

All of the major companies mentioned here (but only a handful
of subsidiaries) issue annual reports. These are obtainable either
by writing to the company or, in most cities, at the reference
library. These reports must be read with caution; often what is
concealed is as important as what is revealed; but the raw numbers on matters such as annual sales, profits and, to some extent,
capital investment, do appear.

Report of the Auditor-General of Canada: Ottawa; Minister of Supply
  and Services. (Various years.)
Report of the Provincial-Auditor of Ontario. Toronto: (Various years.)
The National Finances. Toronto: Canadian Tax Foundation, Publi-
  cations Department. (Produced annually.)
Provincial and Municipal Finances. Toronto: Canadian Tax Foun-
  dation, Publications Department. (Produced annually.)
How Ottawa Spends Your Tax Dollars. Ottawa: School of Public
  Administration, Carleton University. (Produced annually.)
Public Accounts of Canada. Ottawa: Minister of Supply and Ser-
  vices, Ottawa. (See especially Vol. III each year, "Financial
  Statements of Crown Corporations.")
Inter-Corporate Ownership. Ottawa: Statistics Canada, Minister of
  Supply and Services. (Invaluable. Well, almost. The govern-
  ment is now charging $250.00 a copy.)

Periodical Reports.

The following periodicals all have special reports on Crown corporations. All are good, the best is the *Report on Business Magazine*.

"Canada's Top 500 Companies." *Canadian Business Magazine*.
"The Financial Post 500." *The Financial Post*.
"Banking Corporate Performance in Canada." *Report on Business Magazine*.

2. Major Canadian Books Consulted

Bricklin. H. A. Fredericks, with A. Chambers. Fredericton: New Brunswick, 1977.

Broadcasting in Canada. E. S. Hallman, with H. Hindley. Toronto: General, 1977.

Business and Social Reform in the Thirties. Alvin Finkel. Toronto: James Lorimer, 1979.

Canada, 1896–1921: A Nation Transformed. Robert Craig Brown and Ramsay Cook. Toronto: McClelland and Stewart, 1974.

Canada: An Economic History. William L. Marr and Donald G. Paterson. Toronto: Macmillan of Canada, 1980.

Canada's Nuclear Story. Wilfrid Eggleston, Toronto: Clarke, Irwin, 1965.

Canada's Oil and the American Empire. Ed Shaffer. Edmonton: Hurtig, 1983.

Canadians in the Making. Arthur R. M. Lower. Toronto: Longmans, 1958.

The Cape Breton Coal Problem. J. R. Donald. Ottawa: Queen's Printer, 1966.

The Choice of Governing Instrument. Michael J. Trebilcock, Douglas G. Hartle, J. Robert S. Prichard, and Donald N. Dewees. Ottawa: Economic Council of Canada, Minister of Supply and Services, 1982.

Cordial But Not Cosy: A History of the Office of the Auditor-General. Sonja Sinclair. Toronto: McClelland and Stewart, 1979.

The Creation of Regional Dependency. Ralph Matthews. Toronto: University of Toronto Press, 1983.

Crown Corporations in Canada: The Calculus of Instrument Choice. Edited by Michael J. Trebilcock and J. Robert S. Prichard. Toronto: Butterworth, 1983.

Crown Corporations as Instruments of Public Policy. Elaine Kirsch. Ottawa: Economic Council of Canada, 1985.

Crown Corporations: Direction, Control, Accountability. Ottawa: Privy Council Office, 1977.

Crown Corporations and Other Canadian Government Corporate Interests. Ottawa: Treasury Board of Canada, 1984.

Electric Empire. Paul McKay. Toronto: Between the Lines, 1983.

Energy Shock. Lawrence Solomon. Toronto: Doubleday Canada, 1980.

Forced Growth. Philip Mathias. Toronto: Lorimer, 1971.

From Coast to Coast: A Personal History of Radio in Canada. Sandy Stewart. Toronto: CBC Enterprises, 1985.

Fuelling Canada's Future. Wade Rowland. Toronto: Macmillan of Canada, 1974.

Government in Business. Marsha Gordon. Montreal: C.D. Howe Institute, 1981.

The Great Uranium Cartel. Earle Gray. Toronto: McClelland and Stewart, 1982.

A History of Canadian Wealth. Gustavus Myers. Toronto: Lorimer, 1972.

The History of Canadian Business, 1867–1914. Two volumes. Tom Naylor. Toronto: James Lorimer, 1975.

Investments in Failure. Sanford Borins, with Lee Brown. Toronto: Methuen, 1986.

Let Us Prey. Edited by Robert Chodos and Rae Murphy. Toronto: James Lorimer, 1974.

The Life and Times of Industrial Estates Limited. Roy E. George. Halifax: Dalhousie University, Institute of Public Affairs, 1974.

Ordeal by Fire. Ralph Allan. Toronto: Doubleday, 1961.

A Nation Unaware: The Canadian Economic Culture. Herschel Hardin. Vancouver: J. J. Douglas, 1974.

Other People's Money. Peter Foster. Toronto: Collins, 1983.

Plain Talk! Memoirs of an Auditor-General. Maxwell Henderson. Toronto: McClelland and Stewart, 1984.

The People's Power. Merril Denison. Toronto: McClelland and Stewart, 1960.

Political Corruption in Canada: Cases, Causes and Cures. Edited by Kenneth M. Gibbons and Donald C. Rowat. Toronto: Institute of Canadian Studies McClelland and Stewart, 1976.

The Politics of Canadian Broadcasting, 1920–1951. Frank W. Peers. Toronto: University of Toronto Press, 1969.

The Politics of Development. H. V. Nelles. Toronto: Macmillan, 1974.

The Politics of Food. Don Mitchell. Toronto: Lorimer, 1975.

Public Corporations and Public Policy in Canada. Edited by Allan Tupper and G. Bruce Doern. Montreal: The Institute for Research on Public Policy, 1981.

The Rise and Fall of a Business Empire: Clairtone. Garth Hopkins. Toronto: McClelland and Stewart, 1978.

Stanfield. Geoffrey Stevens. Toronto: McClelland and Stewart, 1973.

The Search for Identity, Canada: Postwar to Present. Blair Fraser. Toronto: Doubleday, 1967.

The Sorcerer's Apprentices. Peter Foster. Toronto: Collins, 1982.

Times of Trouble: Labour Unrest and Industrial Conflict in Canada, 1900–66. Stuart M. Jamieson. Ottawa: Information Canada, 1971.

Years of Hard Labour. Morden Lazurus. Don Mills, Ont.: Ontario Federation of Labour, 1974.

3. Major Foreign Books Consulted

The Arms Bazaar. Anthony Sampson. London: Hodder and Stoughton, 1977.

The Changing Anatomy of Britain. Anthony Sampson. London: Hodder and Stoughton, 1982.

The Coming of the New Deal. Arthur M. Schlesinger, Jr. Boston: Houghton Mifflin, 1959.

Dirty Business. Ovid Demaris. New York: Avon, 1975.

Dismantling America. Susan J. Tolchin and Martin Tolchin. Boston: Houghton Mifflin, 1983.

Economics and the Public Purpose. John Kenneth Galbraith. New York: Houghton Mifflin, 1972.

Energy Future: Report of the Energy Project at the Harvard Business School. New York: Random House, 1979.

The Founding Finaglers. Nathan Miller. New York: David McKay, 1976.

Foreign State Enterprises: A Threat to American Business. Douglas F. Lamont, New York: Basic Books, 1979.

National Oil Companies. Leslie E. Grayson. New York: John Wiley and Sons, 1981.

Petro-Canada: A National Oil Company in the Canadian Context. Ghislaine Cestre. Washington: Committee on Energy and Natural Resources, 1977.

Privatization: Principles, Problems and Priorities. Michael Beesley and Stephen Littlechild. London: Lloyd's Bank, 1983.

The Public's Business: The Politics and Practices of Government Corporations. Annmarie Hauck Walsh. (A Twentieth Century Fund Study.) Cambridge: The MIT Press, 1980.

Louis Renault: A Biography. Anthony Rhodes. New York: Harcourt Brace, 1969.

State-Owned Enterprises in the Western Economies. Edited by Raymond Vernon and Yair Aharoni. New York: St. Martin's Press, 1981.

The Sovereign State of ITT. Anthony Sampson. Greenwich, Ct.: Fawcett, 1973.

TVA, Fifty Years of Grass-roots Bureaucracy. Edited by Erwin C. Hargrove and Paul K. Conkin. Urbana, Ill.: University of Illinois Press, 1983.

TVA, The First Twenty Years. Edited by Roscoe C. Martin. Knoxville: University of Tennessee Press, 1956.

The Tennessee Valley Authority—A Study in Public Administration. C. Herman Pritchett. New York: Russell and Russell, 1943.

Trading with the Enemy. Charles Higham. New York: Delacorte Press, 1983.

The United States Government Manual, 1985–86. Washington: U. S. Government Printing Office, 1986.

Vodka-Cola. Charles Levinson. London: Gordon and Cremonesi, 1978.

The Volkswagen Story. K. B. Hopfinger. Henley-on-Thames: G. T. Foulis, 1971.

APPENDICES

Appendix I

Fifteen Biggest Federal Crowns
(Ranked by Performance)

Crown	Revenue Latest Year $000	Profit (Loss) Latest Year $000	Return on Capital (%)
1. Teleglobe Canada	700,530	53,229	25.69
2. Federal Business Development Bank	217,817	932	9.55
3. Export Development Corporation	685,512	4,511	9.48
4. Farm Credit Corp.	528,168	(30,178)	9.16
5. Canada Mortgage and Housing	957,529	39,251	9.12
6. Northern Canada Power	90,390	5,875	8.27
7. Atomic Energy	340,119	9,763	8.21
8. Canadian National	4,994,951	60,280	7.11
9. Air Canada	2,775,782	(21,895)	2.87
10. Eldorado Nuclear	220,784	(57,204)	1.92
11. CN Marine	193,660	1,668	1.20
12. Via Rail	729,302	923	0.70
13. St. Lawrence Seaway	70,962	(3,236)	−0.75
14. CBC	228,443	(15,699)	−3.62
15. Petro-Canada	5,380,931	(691,021)	−7.15

N.B. In many cases, "Revenue" includes substantial parliamentary appropriations—the CBC, Atomic Energy, and Via Rail, for example, are given money that appears as earnings. In addition, some Crown corporations make payments to the owner—the government—even when the year's operations result in a loss. Thus there may be a return on equity even when there was no profit.

Appendix II

Canada's Fifteen Largest Non-Financial Corporations (Ranked by Assets)

Corporation	Assets Most Recent Year $000	Profit (Loss) Most Recent Year $000	Return on Capital (%)
1. Ontario Hydro*	29,320,000	252,000	6.15
2. Hydro-Quebec*	29,183,000	209,000	8.68
3. Genstar**	25,370,085	171,227	13.30
4. Caisse de Dépôt et Placement*	22,543,379	2,659,822	12.92
5. Canadian Pacific**	21,445,926	246,720	5.5
6. Bell Canada Enterprises**	20,583,400	1,050,800	16.6
7. B.C. Hydro*	10,579,000	3,000	8.97
8. Canada Mortgage & Housing*	10,051,090	39,251	9.12
9. Alcan Aluminium**	9,951,000	246,000	6.40
10. Imperial Oil**	9,202,000	684,000	14.90
11. Petro-Canada*	9,045,282	251,532	13.92
12. Seagram**	8,934,176	438,727	10.80
13. Dome Petroleum	8,179,000	(15,000)	—
14. Canadian National*	8,138,781	60,280	7.11
15. Export Development Corp.*	7,296,138	4,511	9.48

*Crown Corporation
**Shares in this private corporation are held by Caisse de Dépôt

N.B. Eight of Canada's largest non-financial corporations are Crowns, and four of these are provincial. Three of our largest four corporations are provincial Crowns:

> Caisse de Dépôt et Placement holdings, by number of shares; Genstar—2,686,219; Canadian Pacific—28,970,655; Bell Canada Enterprises—10,795,413; Alcan—8,472,256; Imperial Oil—814,250; Seagram—3,485,924. The Caisse does not own shares in Dome Petroleum, but does have holdings in two associated companies, Dome Canada and Dome Mines (*Source*: Annual reports).

Appendix III: Federal Crown Corporations

Sources: The Financial Administration Act; Crown Corporations and Other Canadian Corporate Interests (Annual), The Treasury Board of Canada; Report of the Auditor General (Annual); Inter-Corporate Ownership, Statistics Canada (Annual); Canada Gazette; newspaper articles and advertisements.

Note: In attempting to make this list as complete as possible, by including subsidiaries which are not wholly owned by the mentioned Crowns, I have created some anomalies. For example, you will see Air Jamaica listed in the holdings of Air Canada. In point of fact, Air Canada has never had control of Air Jamaica. But it seemed to me important to indicate the wide reach of the Crowns, even if it leads to the apparent claim that a foreign airline is somehow a Canadian Crown. Similarly, in the Alberta listings, the Alberta Energy Company Limited, is, in fact, only 44.8 per cent held by the government, in partnership with private owners. In turn, Alberta Energy owns 56.0 per cent of Chieftan Development, which holds a number of subsidiaries. I have listed them to show that, while Alberta doesn't control the entire gaggle, it is a major player with all of them. In the Quebec listings, Donohue is 55.7 per cent held by the province through Dofor, which is in turn 90 per cent held by another Crown, the Société Général de Financement du Quebec. At the same time, the Caisse de Dépôt et Placement holds another substantial portion of Donohue. The government is currently trying to sell the Donohue shares it owns through Dofor, but not those held by the Caisse. Indeed, the Caisse owns substantial portions in both of the major bidders for the Donohue shares, and may buy more on its own account. So I have shown Donohue and its subsidiaries.

In some cases, where ownership is clearly shown in such documents as annual reports, I have sub-grouped the holdings to indicate, for example, subsidiaries held 50–99 per cent. In other cases, where the Inter-Corporate List details holdings, I have placed an asterisk beside any holdings of less than 50 per cent—and I have probably missed some of these cases.

Once I started into this task, I discovered how complex it is, and understood why no one else has been foolish enough to try to compile such a listing. But it seemed to me that if we are ever to know where we are, we have to start somewhere and this listing—which is certainly out-of-date in some parts already—is at least a beginning.

1. Abenaki Motel Ltd.
2. Agricultural Stabilization Board
3. Air Canada
   4. Air Canada Services Inc.
   5. Airline Maintenance Buildings Limited
   6. Airtransit Canada
   7. Guiness Peat Aviation Ltd.*
   8. Innotech Aviation Ltd.*
   9. Matach Cargo Ltd.
   10. Touram Inc.
      11. Touram Group Service Inc.
   12. Air Cargo Facilities
   13. Air Jamaica Ltd.*
   14. Airline Tariff Publishing Co.
   15. GPA Group Limited*
16. Air Maple Limited
17. Air Tara Limited
18. Aviation Consultants Limited
19. GPA Insurance Brokers Limited
20. GPA (UK) Limited
21. GPM (Cayman) Limited
22. Guillemot Limited
23. Irish Aerospace Limited
24. Transportation Analysis International Limited
25. Transportation Analysis International Inc.
26. Cross Canada Flights Ltd.
27. Innotech Aviation Nfld. Ltd.

28. Intertech Remote Sensing Ltd.
29. International Aeradio (Caribbean) Ltd.
30. Société intérnationale de télécommunications aeronautiques
31. Atlantic Pilotage Authority
32. Atomic Energy of Canada Ltd.
33. Atomic Energy Control Board
34. Bank of Canada
35. Canada Council
36. Canada Deposit Insurance Corporation
37. Canadian Development Investment Corporation
38. Canadair Financial Corp. Inc.
39. Eldorado Nuclear Limited
40. 119371 Canada Ltd.
41. Eldor Resources Ltd.
42. Key Lake Mining Corp.
43. Eldor Mines Ltd.
44. Eldorado Aviation Limited
45. Teleglobe Canada
46. Teleglobe Canada Ltd.
47. Canada Employment and Immigration Commission
48. Canada Lands Company Limited
49. Canada Harbour Place Corporation
50. Canada Lands Company (Mirabel) Limited
51. Canada Lands Company (Le Vieux-Port de Montreal) Limited
52. Canada Lands Company (Vieux-Port de Quebec) Inc.
53. Canada Museums Construction Corporation Inc.
54. Canada Mortgage and Housing Corporation
55. Canada Ports Corporation
56. Ridley Terminals Inc.
57. Canada Post Corporation
58. Canadian Broadcasting Corporation
59. Master FM Limited*
60. Visnews Limited
61. News Film Services Ltd.
62. British Commonwealth International Newsfilm Agency Ltd.
63. Viscom International (USA) Ltd.
64. Canadian Centre for Occupational Health and Safety
65. Canadian Commercial Corporation
66. Canadian Dairy Commission
67. Canadian Film Development Corporation
68. Canadian International Grains Institute
69. Canadian Livestock Feed Board
70. Canadian National Railways System
71. Canadian National Railway Company
72. Autoport Limited
73. CN Tower Ltd.
74. The Canadian and Gulf Terminal Railway Company
75. Canadian National Express Company
76. Canadian National Railways Securities Trust
77. Canadian National Steamship Co. Ltd.
78. Canadian National Telegraph Company
79. Great North Western Telegraph Company of Canada
80. Canadian National Transfer Company Ltd.
81. Canadian National Transportation, Ltd.
82. Chapman Transport Ltd.
83. Eastern Transport Ltd.
84. Provincial Tankers Ltd.
85. Royal Transportation Ltd.
86. Transport Route Canada Inc.
87. Chalut Transport (1974) Inc.
88. Entreprises Bussieres Ltee.

89. Canat Limited
90. CN (France) S.A.
91. CNM Inc.
92. Compagnie de Gestion de Matane Inc.*
93. CN Marine Inc.
94. CN Tower Restaurants Ltd.
95. CN Transactions Inc.
96. Autoport Ltd.
97. Canac Consultants Limited
98. Canadian National Hotels (Moncton) Ltd.
99. Canaprev. Inc.
100. Canaven Ltd.
101. CN Exploration Inc.
102. CNM Inc.
103. Coastal Transport Ltd.
104. Halifax Industries (Holdings) Ltd.
105. EID Systems Ltd.
106. Halterm Ltd.*
107. Northern Consolidated Holding Co. Ltd.
108. Northwestel Inc.
109. Grand Trunk Corporation
110. Central Vermont Railway Inc.
111. Domestic Four Leasing Corporation
112. Domestic Three Leasing Corporation
113. Domestic Two Leasing Corporation
114. Duluth, Winnipeg and Pacific Railway Company
115. Grand Trunk Land Development Corporation
116. Grand Trunk Radio Communications, Inc.
117. Grand Trunk Western Railroad Company
118. Belt Railway Co. of Chicago
119. Chicago and Western Indiana Railroad Company
120. Trailer Train Company
121. The Minnesota and Manitoba Railroad Company
122. The Minnesota and Ontario Bridge Company
123. Mount Royal Tunnel and Terminal Company, Limited
124. NorthwesTel Inc.
125. Terra Nova Telecommunications Inc.

Subsidiaries of CN held at 50–99 per cent:
126. The Canadian Northern Quebec Railway Company
127. EID Electronic Identification Systems Ltd.
128. Northern Consolidated Holding Company Ltd.
129. OCRA Communications Inc.
130. Public Markets Limited
131. Quebec and St. John Railway Company
132. Shawinigan Terminal Railway Company

Associates in which less than 50 per cent held:
133. Compagnie de Gestion de Matane Inc.
134. Computer Sciences Canada, Ltd.
135. Eurocanadian Shipholdings Limited
136. Fort Point Holdings Ltd.
137. Intercast S.A.
138. Canadian National (West Indies) Steamships Ltd.
139. Canadian Patents and Development Corp.
140. Canadian Producers' Arctic Co-operative Ltd.
141. Canadian Saltfish Corporation
142. Canadian Sports Pool Corporation
143. Canadian Wheat Board
144. Cape Breton Development Corporation
145. Cape Breton Marine Farming Ltd.
146. Darr (Cape Breton) Limited

147. Dundee Estates Limited
148. International Limestone Industries Ltd.*
149. Reeves Modular Homes Ltd.*
150. Whale Cove Summer Village Inc.
151. Cape Breton Woolen Mills Limited

Associates held at less than 50 per cent:

152. Bay Lumber Limited
153. Cape Breton Offshore Fabricators Limited
154. Eastern Carbide Tools Limited
155. Frank Elms Screw Products Limited
156. Haak Conveyor & Manufacturing Limited
157. Margaree Window and Doorframe Limited
158. Newco Mining Limited
159. Sun Mountain Development (Cape Breton Ski Club)
160. 4 M Panga Hotel Co. Limited
161. Co-operative Energy Corp.
162. Crane Cove Oyster Farm Ltd.
163. Crown Assets Disposal Corp.
164. Defence Construction (1951) Ltd.
165. Director of Soldier Settlement
166. Director, Veterans' Land Act
167. Economic Council of Canada
168. Export Development Corporation
169. Farm Credit Corporation
170. Federal Business Development Bank
171. Birla Industries Ltd.*
172. BTL Inc.*
173. Canada West Shoe Manufacturing Inc.
174. Digital Dynamics Ltd.*
175. Encast Inc.*
176. Flamingo Woven Fabrics Ltd.
177. Fortress Mountain Resorts Ltd.
178. Graham Products Ltd.*
179. Granpac Ltd.
180. J. Kobelt Manufacturing Co. Ltd.*
181. Kakabeka Timber Ltd.
182. Monarch Industries Ltd.*
183. Northeast Pine Products Ltd.*
184. Omnicron Data Systems Ltd.*
185. Plastics Holdings Ltd.*
186. Powerbel Raceways Ltd.*
187. Sekine Canada Ltd.*
188. Thompson Machine Works Ltd.*
189. Westbay Instruments Ltd.*
190. Westerham Leasing Ltd.*
191. Winpack Ltd.*
192. Fisheries Price Support Board
193. Federal Mortgage Exchange Corp.
194. Freshwater Fish Marketing Corporation
195. Great Lakes Pilotage Authority Ltd.
196. Harbourfront Corporation
197. Art Gallery at Harbourfront
198. School-by-the-Water
199. International Centre for Ocean Development
200. International Research Centre
201. Laurentian Pilotage Authority
202. Loto Canada Inc.
203. Medical Research Council
204. Mingan Associates Ltd.
205. Mohawk St. Regis Lacrosse Ltd.
206. Montreal Port Corporation
207. National Arts Centre Corporation
208. National Battlefields Commission
209. National Capital Commission
210. National Museums of Canada
211. National Research Council of Canada
212. Canada-France-Hawaii Telescope Corporation*
213. Natural Sciences and

Engineering Research
Council
214. Northern Canada Power
Commission
215. Northern Transportation
Company Limited
   216. Grimshaw Trucking and
   Distribution Ltd.
   217. Nortran Offshore Limited
218. Pacific Pilotage Authority
219. Petro-Canada
   220. Arctic Pilot Project Inc.
   221. Canertech Inc.
      222. Canertech Conservation
      Inc.
      223. Pacific Enercon Ltd.
      224. Mechron Energy Ltd.
      225. 107744 Canada Inc.
         226. Omnifuel Gasification
         System*
   227. Petro-Canada Consulting
   Corporation
   228. Petro-Canada Inc.
      229. Asher American, Inc.
      230. Big Eagle Oil and Gas
      Ltd.
         231. Aquilla Holdings Ltd.
      232. Fifth Pacific Stations
      Ltd.
      233. GMI Co. (Bahamas)
      Limited
      234. Opal Oils Limited
         235. Commodore Oils
         Limited
            236. First Pacific Stations
            Ltd.
            237. Second Pacific
            Stations Ltd.
            238. Third Pacific
            Stations Ltd.
            239. Fourth Pacific
            Stations Ltd.
      240. Pacific Petrochemicals
      Ltd.*
      241. Pacific Pipelines, Inc.
      242. Pacific Petroleums
      (Overseas) Limited
      243. Petro-Canada Drilling
      Inc.
      244. Petro-Canada
      Enterprises Inc.
         245. 103912 Canada Inc.
         246. 106617 Canada Inc.
         247. 106618 Canada Inc.

248. 106619 Canada Inc.
249. 106620 Canada Inc.
250. 106621 Canada Inc.
251. Independent Fuels &
Lumber Ltd.
252. Joseph Elie Limitee
253. Marc Dufresne (1979)
Inc.
254. Petro-Canada
Chemicals Inc.
255. Petro-Canada Petroleum
Inc.
   256. Arctic Islands
   Resources Ltd.
257. Petro-Canada Ventures
   258. Prairie Leaseholds
   Ltd.
   259. Prairie Minerals Ltd.
260. Xychem Inc.
261. Petro-Canada Espagnola
S.A.
262. Petro-Canada Norway A/
S
263. Petro-Canada Oil & Gas
Inc.
264. Petro-Canada Products
Inc.
265. Petro-Canada Resources
Inc.
266. Petro-Canada (U.K.)
Limited
267. Petroleum Transmission
Company
268. Petron Petroleum Ltd.
269. Rocair Limited
270. Tri-Mountain
Petroleums Ltd.
271. Value Service Stations
Ltd.
272. Venezuelan Canada Oils,
C.A. (under confiscation)
273. Venezuelan Pacific
Petroleums, C.A. (under
confiscation)
274. 103912 Canada Inc.
275. Petro-Canada
International Assistance
Corporation
276. Petro-Canada Oil & Gas/
Petrole et Gaz Petro-
Canada In.
277. Petro-Canada Products
Inc.
   278. 106616 Canada Inc.

279. B. P. Home Comfort Ltd.
280. B. P. Marketing Canada Ltd.
281. Chatelaine Restaurants Ltd.
282. Depanneurs Le Frigo Ltée.
283. L.M. Petroleum Inc.
284. Montreal Pipe Line Ltd.
285. Petro-Canada Chemicals Inc.
286. St. Laurent Petroleum Inc.

Subsidiaries held at 50–99 per cent:
287. CAL-JET Holdings Ltd.
288. CANSTAR Oil Sands Ltd.
289. Keyanaw Oil Sands Ltd.
290. Wapisoo Oil Sands Ltd.
291. Petro-Canada Centre Inc.
292. Panarctic Oils Ltd.
293. Sedpex Inc.
294. Viatec Resource Systems, Inc.

Associates held at less than 50 per cent:
295. Syncrude Canada Ltd.
296. Northward Developments Ltd.
297. Westcoast Transmission Company Limited
298. Foothills Pipe Lines (Yukon) Ltd.
299. Pacific Northern Gas Ltd.
300. Saratoga Processing Co. Ltd.
301. Vancal Properties Ltd.
302. Westcoast Petroleum Ltd.
303. Westcoast Transmission Company (Alberta) Ltd.
304. Royal Canadian Mint
305. Science Council of Canada
306. Shong-Way-Shi Corp.
307. Social Sciences and Humanities Research Council
308. Standards Council of Canada

309. St. Lawrence Seaway Authority
310. The Jacques Cartier and Champlain Bridges Incorporated
311. The Seaway International Bridge Corporation, Ltd.
312. Vancouver Port Corporation
313. VIA Rail Canada Inc.

Mixed Enterprises
In addition to corporations owned outright by the federal government, there are many significant federal Crowns owned in conjunction with other governments, such as the International Bank for Reconstruction and Development, (less formally known as the World Bank), which is jointly owned by a number of governments, or in which ownership is shared with private stockholders. Some, although not all, of these appear in the Treasury Board of Canada document "Crown Corporations and Other Canadian Government Corporate Interests," issued in March, 1984. This document shows many subsidiaries that do not appear elsewhere, but for reasons best known to itself, leaves out many others.

314. African Development Bank
315. Africaire
316. African Development Fund
317. National Development Banks
318. Shelter Afrique
319. SIFIDA
320. Asian Development Bank
321. Asian Development Fund
322. Canarctic Shipping Company Limited
323. Canada Development Corporation
324. Canterra Energy Ltd.
325. 110693 Canada Ltd.
326. 116596 Canada Ltd.
327. Canshore Exploration Ltd.

328. Cansulex Ltd.
329. CDC Petroleum Inc.
330. Chieftan Mac Gas Ltd.
331. Rainbow Pipe Line Co. Ltd.
332. Sultran Ltd.
333. Capvest Enterprises Inc.
334. CDC Data Systems Ltd.
  335. AES Data Inc.
    336. AES Data International Inc.
  337. Savin Corporation
    338. Savin Canada Inc.
339. CDC Life Sciences Inc.
  340. Bio-Research Laboratories Ltd.
    341. Bio-Research Laboratories of Canada Ltd.
    342. Steele Chemical Co. Ltd.
343. Connaught Laboratories Ltd.
  344. Conbio Ltd.
  345. Connaught Biologics Ltd.
    346. K-Vet Ltd.
  347. Connaught Laboratories Inc.
  348. Dominion Biologicals Ltd.
349. Laboratoires Nordic Inc.
350. CDC Nederland B.V.
351. CDC Ventures Ltd.
  352. Atlantis Corp. Ltd.
  353. HSA Systems Inc.
  354. The Vase Fund Inc.
355. CDC Wordplex Ltd.
  356. Wordplex International Inc.
357. Fishery Products International Ltd.
358. Petrosar Ltd.
359. Polysar Ltd.
  360. Com-Share Ltd.
  361. Polysar Holdings Ltd.
362. Sentrol Systems Ltd.
363. Technology Development Corp.
364. Caribbean Development Bank
365. Cooperative Energy Corp.
  366. Co-operative Energy Development Corp.
367. Inter American Development Bank
368. International Bank for Reconstruction and Development
  369. International Development Association
  370. International Finance Corporation
371. Lower Churchill Development Corporation Limited
372. Nanisivik Mines Limited
373. Newfoundland and Labrador Development Corporation Ltd.
374. Oo-Za-We-Kun Centre Inc.
375. Saint John Harbour Bridge Authority
376. Societe Inter-port de Quebec
377. Telesat Canada (50 per cent)

Other Entities

The federal government either owns or operates a number of entities which are not, formally, corporations, because they have no share capital. I have listed them because this legal distinction is confusing without being illuminating. The commissions that operate most of our harbours, for example, are indistinguishable from corporations such as the New York and New Jersey State Port Authority in terms of the powers they wield. In each case, the federal government has the power to appoint members to the boards of Directors of these entities.

378. Army Benevolent Fund
379. Association for the Export of Canadian Books
380. Blue Water Bridge Authority
381. Board of Trustees of the Queen Elizabeth II Canadian Fund to Aid in Research on the Diseases of Children
382. Canada Grains Council
383. Commonwealth War Graves Commission
384. Footwear and Leather Institute of Canada

Appendix IV: Twenty Provincial Giants

Twenty Largest Provincial Crowns
(Ranked by Revenue)

Crown	Province	Revenue Latest Year $000	Profit (Loss) Latest Year $000	Return on Capital (%)
1. Ontario Hydro	Ontario	3,863,153	471,651	6.25
2. Hydro-Québec	Quebec	3,736,000	707,000	8.36
3. Caisse de Dépôt	Quebec	2,078,807	2,033,120	10.76
4. B.C. Hydro	B.C.	1,702,000	51,000	8.11
5. Alberta Govt. Telephones	Alta.	933,471	− 30,959	10.54
6. Insurance Corp. of B.C.	B.C.	876,600	4,768	13.77
7. Le Groupe SGF	Quebec	871,746	5,209	7.58
8. N.B. Electric	N.B.	791,588	1,952	10.57
9. Sask. Power	Sask	730,985	− 19,724	7.97
10. Régie de l'assurance automobile	Que.	564,069	46,294	24.24
11. Manitoba Hydro	Man.	494,795	− 3,674	9.32
12. Nova Scotia Power	N.S.	494,432	27,904	11.52
13. Treasury Branches	Alta.	355,294	3,513	10.25
14. SaskTel	Sask.	341,800	11,974	10.86
15. Manitoba Telephones	Man.	308,335	2,127	8.92
16. Sask. Govt. Insurance	Sask.	300,613	—	—
17. Urban Transport	Ont.	262,702	12,312	20.63
18. Nfld. & Labrador Hydro	Nfld.	252,505	16,447	8.10
19. Man. Public Insurance	Man.	231,688	9,737	22.89
20. B.C. Rail	B.C.	223,072	39,967	10.60

Appendix V: Provincial & Territorial Crowns
Note: Asterisk denotes less than 50% ownership.

Alberta Crowns
1. 259431 Alberta Ltd.
2. 474243 Ontario Ltd.
3. Alberta Agricultural Development Corp.
4. AIL-Alberta Investments Ltd.
5. Alberta Educational Communications Corp.
6. Alberta Energy Company Ltd.*
  7. 116583 Canada Ltd.
    8. 70705 Alberta Ltd.
  9. AEC Coal Company Ltd.
10. AEC Heavy Oils Ltd.
11. AEC Power Ltd.
12. Alberta Industrial Gas Suppliers Ltd.
13. Alberta Oil Sands Pipeline Ltd.
14. Chieftan Development Co. Ltd.
  15. Cabri Pipe Lines Ltd.
  16. Chiefco Enterprises Ltd.
    17. Chieftan Minerals Ltd.
    18. Hartfield Chieftan Leasing Ltd.
      19. Hartfield Easy-Park Ltd.
  20. Chieftan Columbian Explorations Ltd.
  21. Chieftan Management Ltd.
  22. Chieftan Petrochemicals Ltd.
  23. Engineering Specialties Ltd.
  24. Trans Central Pipelines Ltd.
  25. Tri-City Drilling 1968 Ltd.
26. Northward Developments Ltd.*
27. Pan-Alberta Gas Ltd.
28. Pan-Alberta Resources Inc.
29. Steel Alberta Ltd.
30. Alberta Government Telephone System
  31. 288922 Alberta Ltd.
    32. 288951 Alberta Ltd.
      33. Novatel Communications Ltd.
34. Alta-Can Telecom Inc.
35. Alberta Telecommunications International Ltd.
36. Elinca Communications Ltd.
37. Alberta Hail and Crop Insurance Corporation
38. Alberta Home Mortgage Corporation
39. Alberta Housing Corporation
40. Alberta Investment Fund
41. Alberta Liquor Control Board
42. Alberta Opportunity Co.
43. Alberta Terminals Ltd.
44. Treasury Branches Deposits Fund
45. Western Canada Lottery Foundation*

British Columbia Crowns
1. British Columbia Building Corporation
2. British Columbia Cellulose Company
3. British Columbia Development Corporation
  4. Duke Point Developments Ltd.
  5. Duke Point Terminals Ltd.
  6. First Capital City Development Co. Ltd.
  7. Lonsdale Key Development Co. Ltd.
8. British Columbia Ferry Corporation
9. British Columbia Harbours Board
10. British Columbia Housing Management Commission
11. British Columbia Hydro and Power Authority
  12. Columbia Hydro Constructors Ltd.
  13. Peace Power Constructors Ltd.
14. British Columbia Liquor Administration
15. British Columbia Petroleum Corporation

16. British Columbia Gas Corp.
17. British Columbia Railway
    Company
18. British Columbia Regional
    Hospital District Financing
    Authority
19. British Columbia Schools
    Districts Capital Financing
    Authority
20. British Columbia Steamship
    Company 1975 Ltd.
  21. British Columbia Steamship
      Co. Inc.
22. Canada Harbour Place Corp.
23. Expo 86 Corporation
24. Housing Corporation of
    British Columbia
  25. Dunhill Development Corp.
  26. HCBC Construction Ltd.
  27. W.K.P. Construction
28. Insurance Corporation of
    British Columbia
29. Ocean Falls Corporation
30. Provincial Capital Commission
31. Provincial Rental Housing
    Corporation
32. Surrey Farm Products
    Investments Ltd.
  33. Surrey Farm Products
      Hatchery Ltd.
  34. Western Feed Co. Ltd.
35. Urban Transit Authority of
    British Columbia
36. W.L.C. Developments Ltd.
  37. Whistler Village Land Co.
      Ltd.
38. Western Canada Lottery
    Foundation*

Manitoba
1. A.E. McKenzie Co. Ltd.
  2. McFaydon Seed Co. Ltd.
  3. Steele Briggs Ltd.
4. Canada Seeds Ltd.
5. Dawn Plastics Ltd.
6. Leaf Rapids Town Properties
   Ltd.
7. Liquor Control Commission of
   Manitoba
8. Manfor Ltd.
9. Manitoba Data Services
10. Manitoba Development
    Corporation

11. Evergreen Peat and
    Fertilizer Inc.
  12. Perron Investments Ltd.
  13. Seedhouse Holdings Ltd.
14. Flyer Industries Ltd.
15. Saunders Aircraft Corp.
    Ltd.
16. Tantalum Mining Corp.*
17. William Clare (Manitoba)
    Ltd.
  18. William Clare Ltd.
19. Manitoba Forestry Resources
    Ltd.
20. Manitoba Housing and
    Renewal Corp.
21. Manitoba Hydro Electric
    Board
22. Manitoba Mineral Resources
    Ltd.
23. Manitoba Potash Corp.
24. Manitoba Telephone System
  25. MTX Telecon Services Inc.
    26. Saudi Arabian Datacom
        Co. Ltd.
27. Manitoba Water Services
    Board
28. Manitoba Waste Management
    Corp.
29. Venture Manitoba Tours Ltd.
30. Western Canada Lottery
    Foundation*

New Brunswick
1. Algonquin Properties Ltd.
2. Forest Protection Ltd.
3. Fredericton Hotel Company
   Ltd.
4. Galleon Ware Inc.
5. Innovent Limited
6. N.B. Coal Ltd.
  7. Grand Lake Resources Ltd.
8. New Brunswick Electric Power
   Commission
9. New Brunswick Forest
   Authority
  10. Bathurst Woodland
      Holdings Ltd.
11. New Brunswick Housing
    Corporation
  12. Cirtex Knitting Ltd.
13. Passamaquoddy Properties
    Ltd.
14. Provincial Holdings Ltd.

15. Burchill Laminating and Groovefold Ltd.*
16. Chan Food Products Ltd.
17. Geo. Burchill and Sons Plywood Ltd.
18. Juniper Lumber Co. Ltd.*
19. Maritime Fabricators Ltd.
20. Regie des Alcools du Nouveau-Brunswick
21. Westmorland Fertilizer

Newfoundland Crowns

1. B.L.C. Building Corporation
2. Bell Island Hospital Building Corporation
3. Burgeo Fish Industries Ltd.
4. Burgeo Leasing Ltd.
5. Coastal Realties Ltd.
6. Corner Brook Hospital Building Corp. Ltd.
7. Fisheries Development Corporation
8. Gander Hospital Corporation Ltd.
9. Grace Hospital Extension Corporation Ltd.
10. Grand Falls Hospital Corporation Ltd.
11. Harmon Corporation
12. Hotel Buildings Ltd.
13. Marystown Shipyard Ltd.
14. Memorial University of Newfoundland Building Corp. Ltd.
15. Mooring Cove Building Co. Ltd.
16. Newfoundland Farm Products Corporation
17. Newfoundland Hardwoods Ltd.
18. Newfoundland Computer Services Ltd.
19. Newfoundland and Labrador Housing Corporation
20. Newfoundland and Labrador Hydro
21. Churchill Falls Labrador Corporation Ltd.*
22. Twin Falls Power Corporation Ltd.
23. Gull Island Power Company Ltd.
24. Lower Churchill Development Corp.

25. Newfoundland and Labrador Petroleum Corporation
26. Newfoundland Liquor Corp.
27. Newfoundland Municipal Financing Corporation
28. Nordco Ltd.
29. Geonautics Limited
30. Northern Hospitals Building Corporation Ltd.
31. Nurses Training School Building Corporation Ltd.
32. Pepperell Hospital Reconstruction Corporation Ltd.
33. Power Distribution District of Newfoundland and Labrador
34. St. John's Infirmary Building Corporation Ltd.
35. Technical College Building Corporation Ltd.
36. Vocational Schools (Western) Building Corporation Ltd.

Nova Scotia Crowns

1. Atlantic Lottery Corp.
2. Canso Superport Ltd.
3. Cansteel Corp.
4. Check Inns Ltd.
5. Clairtone Holdings Ltd.
6. Dartmouth Recreation Ltd.
7. Deuterium of Canada Ltd.
8. Cape Breton Heavy Water Ltd.
9. Halifax-Dartmouth Bridge Commission
10. Halifax International Containers
11. Halterm Limited*
12. Industrial Estates Ltd.
13. Atlantic Bridge Company Ltd.
14. Forceten Enterprises Inc.*
15. Le Gay Fibreglass Ltd.*
16. Maitland Investment Ltd.
17. Mercator Enterprises Ltd.*
18. Nova Scotia Liquor Commission
19. Nova Scotia Municipal Finance Corporation
20. Nova Scotia Place Ltd.
21. Nova Scotia Power Corporation
22. Eastern Light & Power Co. Ltd.

23. Nova Scotia Light & Power Co. Ltd.
24. Nova Scotia Rehabilitation Centre Corporation
25. Nova Scotia Resources Limited
26. Nova Scotia Resources (Ventures) Ltd.
27. Novaco Limited
28. Nova Scotia Research Foundation Corporation
29. Port Development Authority Inc.
30. Richmond Fisheries Ltd.
31. Small Business Development Corporation
32. Sydney Steel Corporation
33. Scotia Limestone Ltd.
34. International Limestone Industries Inc.
35. Tidal Power Corporation
36. Trade Centre Ltd.
37. Waterfront Development Corporation

Ontario

1. Algonquin Forest Authority
2. Allelix Inc.*
3. Beechgrove Regional Children's Centre
4. Clarke Institute of Psychiatry
5. Board of Governor's of the Ontario Institute for Studies in Education
6. Canada's Capital Congress Centre Corp.
7. Centennial Centre of Science and Technology
8. Eastern Ontario Development Corp.
9. Farm Income Stabilization Commission
10. George R. Gardiner Museum of Ceramic Art
11. Liquor Control Board of Ontario
12. Livestock Financial Protection Board
13. McMichael Canadian Collection
14. Metropolitan Toronto Convention Centre Corp.
15. Minaki Lodge (*sold 1986*)
16. Minaki Development Company Limited

17. Niagara Parks Commission
18. Northern Ontario Development Corporation
19. North Pickering Development Corporation
20. Ontario Agricultural Museum
21. Ontario Centre for Advanced Manufacturing
22. Ontario Centre for Automotive Parts Technology
23. Ontario Centre for Farm Technology
24. Ontario Centre for Microelectronics
25. Ontario Centre for Resource Machinery
26. Ontario Cream Producers' Marketing Board
27. Ontario Development Corporation
28. HSA Systems Inc.*
29. Ontario Education Capital Aid Corporation
30. Ontario Educational Services Corporation
31. Ontario Educational Communications Authority
32. Ontario Energy Corporation
33. Omnifuel Gasification Systems Ltd.
34. Onexco Oil & Gas Ltd.
35. Trillium Exploration Corp.
36. Ontario Energy Resources Ltd.
37. Suncor Inc.*
38. Ontario Energy Ventures Ltd.
39. Selachii International Ltd.*
40. Ontario Food Terminal Board
41. Ontario Historical Studies Series
42. Ontario Housing Corp.
43. Ontario Hydro
44. Ontario International Corporation
45. Ontario Junior Farm Establishment Corporation
46. Ontario Land Corporation
47. Ontario Lottery Corp.
48. Ontario Milk Marketing Board
49. Ontario Mortgage Corporation

50. Ontario Municipal Employees Retirement Board
51. Ontario Municipal Improvement Corp.
52. Ontario Northland Transportation Commission
53. Nipissing Central Railway
54. Norontair
55. Owen Sound Transportation Co. Ltd.
56. Nipissing Marine Ltd.
57. Star Transfer Ltd.
58. Ontario Place Corp.
59. Ontario Share and Deposit Insurance Corp.
60. Ontario Stadium Corp.
61. Ontario Research Foundation
62. Ontario Racing Commission
63. Ontario Stock Yards Board
64. 416879 Ontario Ltd.
65. Ontario Telephone Development Corp.
66. Ontario Transportation Development Corp.
67. Ontario Trillium Foundation
68. Ontario Universities Capital Aid Corp.
69. Ontario Van Pool Organization Ltd.
70. Ontario Waste Management Corp.
71. Province of Ontario Savings Office
72. Royal Ontario Museum
73. Thunder Bay Ski Jumps Inc.
74. Toronto Area Transit Operating Authority
75. York Regional School of Nursing

Prince Edward Island Crowns
1. Charlottetown Area Development Corporation
2. Crown Building Corporation
3. Housing Corporation
4. Georgetown Shipyards, Inc.
5. Land Development Corp.
6. Liquor Control Commission
7. Prince Edward Island Energy Corp.
8. Prince Edward Island Grain Elevators Corp.
9. Summerside Waterfront Development Corp.

Quebec Crowns
1. Bio-mega Inc.
2. Institut de Bio-Endocrinologie Inc.
3. Laboratories Omega Ltée.
4. La Caisse de Dépôt et Placement du Québec
Holdings (in most cases less than 25 per cent):
Agnico-Eagle Mines Ltd.
Alberta Energy Co. Ltd.
Alcan Aluminium Ltd.
AMCA International Ltd.
American Express Company
Amsterdam-Rotherdam Bank NV
Artopex International Inc.
Asamera Inc.
Bank of Montreal
Bank of Montreal, Realty Inc.
Bank of Nova Scotia
Bell Canada Enterprises Inc.
Bow Valley Industries Ltd.
Brascade Holdings Inc.
Brascade Resources Inc.
Brascan Ltd.
Bristol-Myers Co.
Brunswick Mining and Smelting Corp.
CAE Industries
C-I-L Inc.
Caisse Centrale Desjardins du Quebec
Campbell Red Lake Mines Ltd.
Campbell Resources Inc.
Campeau Corp.
Canada Northwest Energy Ltd.
Canadian Imperial Bank of Commerce
Canadian Marconi Co.
Canadian Occidental Petroleum Ltd.
Canadian Pacific Ltd.
Canadian Tire Corp. Ltd.
Canam Manac Inc., Groupe
Canron Inc.
Celanese Canada inct.
Cominco Ltd.
Comterm Inc.
Consolidated-Bathurst Inc.
Coopérative Féderée du Québec
Crédit Industriel Desjardins Inc.
Denison Mines Ltd.
Dofasco Inc.
Domco Industries Ltd.

Dome Canada Ltd.
Dome Mines Ltd.
Dominion Textile Inc.
Domtar Inc.
Donohue Inc.
Dylex Ltd.
Echo Bay Mines Ltd.
Falconbridge Ltd.
Fédération des Caisses
populaires Desjardins du
Québec
Fiat
Fujitsu Ltd.
Gaz Metropolitain Inc.
General Electric Co.
Genstar Corp.
Gulf Canada Ltd.
Imasco Ltd.
Imperial Oil Ltd.
Inco Ltd.
Innopac Inc.
International Business Machines
Corp.
Interprovincial Pipeline Ltd.
Ipsco Inc.
Ivaco Inc.
Karstadt AG
Kuraray Co. Ltd.
Labatt Limited, John
Lac Minerals Ltd.
Lafarge Corp.
Logistec Corp.
Lonvest Corp.
Maclean Hunter Ltd.
MacMillan Bloedel Ltd.
Marine Industrie Ltee.
Molson Companies Ltd.
Moore Corp. Ltd.
National Bank of Canada
National Bank Leasing
Nationale-Nederlanden NV
National Victoria and Grey
Trust Ltd.
Noranda Inc.
Norcen Energy Resources Ltd.
Northern and Central Gas
Corp. Ltd.
Northern Telecom Ltd.
Nova, an Alberta Corporation
Oshawa Group Ltd.
PanCana Minerals Inc.
PanCanadian Petroleum Ltd.
Peerless Rug Ltd.
Philip Morris Inc.
Place Desjardins Inc.

Placer Development Ltd.
Power Financial Corp.
Prenor Group Ltd.
Provigo Inc.
Québec-Telephone
Ranger Oil Ltd.
Reitman's (Canada) Ltd.
Rio Algom Ltd.
Royal Bank of Canada
Royal Trustco Ltd.
Sceptre Resources Ltd.
Seagram Co. Ltd.
Sears Canada Inc.
Shell Canada Ltd.
Siemens AG
Société d'investissement
Desjardins
Sony Corp.
Southam Inc.
Steinberg Inc.
Stelco Inc.
Swiss Bank Corp.
Teck Corp.
Télé-Métropole Inc.
Texaco Canada Inc.
Thomson Newspapers Ltd.
Tokyo Electric Power Corp.
Toronto-Dominion Bank
TransAlta Utilities Corp.
TransCanada Pipelines Ltd.
Trizec Corp. Ltd.
Trust Général du Canada
Union Bank of Switzerland
Vidéotron Ltee, Le Groupe
Volkswageverk, AG
Walker Resources Ltd., Hiram
Westburne International
Industries Ltd.
Weston Limited, George
Winterthur
5. Cooperative Forestière du
   Temiscamique
   6. Cedre Fabre Inc.
7. Ethylec Inc.
   8. Commercial Alcohols Ltd.
9. Foranco Ltee.
10. Hydro-Québec
    11. Churchill Falls Labrador
        Corporation Ltd.
    12. La Compagnie d'Energie de
        la Vallée de l'Outouais
    13. Hydro-Québec
        International
    14. Nouveler Inc.
       15. Econoler Inc.

16. Societe de Energie de la Baie James
17. Loto-Québec
18. Madelipeche Inc.*
19. Office des Autoroutes du Québec
20. Raffineries de Sucre du Québec
21. Regie des Installations Olympiques
22. Rexfor
23. Enerbois Inc.
24. Gestion 1195 inc.
25. Nouveler Inc.*
26. Papier Cascades Cabano Inc.
27. Les Produits Forestiers Bellerive-Ka'N'Enda Inc.
28. Lignarex Inc.*
29. Proforet
30. Sciérie Bearn Inc.
31. Cedre Fabre Inc.
32. Temfor Inc.*
33. Tembec Inc.
34. Science Le Grand Inc.
35. Sciences Chic-Chocs Inc.
36. Sidbec
37. Dosco (Quebec) Limited
38. Sidbec-Dosco Inc.
39. Acadia Coal Co. Ltd.
40. Nova Scotia Steel & Coal Co. Ltd.
41. Truscon Steel of Canada Inc.
42. Sidbec-Feruni Inc.
43. Ferauto Inc.
44. Sidbec International Inc.
45. Sidbec-Normines Inc.
46. Société des Alcools du Québec
47. Societe de Developpement des Industries Culturelles
48. Librarie Dussault Limitée
49. Libraries Garneau Ltée.
50. Société de Developpement de la Baie James
51. Albanal Minerals Ltd.
52. Société de Telecommunications de la Baie James
53. Sotel Inc.
54. Société Géneral de Financement du Québec
55. Artopex Canada Ltee.
56. Artopex Inc.

57. Cegelec Enterprises Inc.
58. Cegelec Industrie Inc.
59. 1167-4025 Québec Inc.
60. Logging Development Corp.*
61. Dofor Inc.
62. Domtar Inc.
63. Donohue Inc.
64. Bois Chibougamau (1977) Ltee.
65. Donohue Charlevoix Inc.
66. Donohue Malbaie Inc.
67. Donohur Normick Inc.
68. Donohue St. Felicien Inc.
69. Produits Forestiers M.P. (1977) Ltée.
70. J.E. Therrien Inc.
71. Marketing Donohue Inc.
72. Industries Tanguay Inc.
73. John Meunier Inc.
74. Marine Industrie Ltée.
75. Milthom Ltd.
76. Nouveler Inc.*
77. Petromont & Co. Ltd.
78. Société de Montage Automobile-Soma Inc.
79. Volcano Inc.
80. Societe National de L'Amiante
81. Ceram-SNA Inc.
82. Chrysophosphate-SNA Inc.
83. Descon-SNA Inc.
84. Filac SNA Inc.
85. Lupel SNA-Inc.
86. Atlas-Turner Inc.
87. Metemag-SNA Inc.
88. Les Mines d'Amiante Bell Ltée.
89. Les Mines Seliene Inc.
90. Asbestos Corporation Ltd.
91. Ontario Atlas Sales Inc.
92. Panfab-SNA Inc.
93. Sodac-SNA Inc.
94. Turners Building Products Ltd.
95. Société Québecoise d'Exploration Minière (Soquem)
96. Explo-Zinc Inc.*
97. Niobec Inc.
98. Les Sociétés Minières Louvem
99. Soquemines Inc.
100. Les Tourbières de Sept-Isles Ltée.

101. Sullivan Mines Inc.
102. Société Quebécoise
     d'Initiatives Petrolières
     (Soquip)
103. Exploration Soquip
     Alberta Inc.
104. Exploration Soquip Inc.
 105. Soquip Atlantique Inc.
106. Gaz Initiatives Ventures
     Ltd.
107. Gaz Inter-Cité Québec
     Inc.*
108. Soquip Alberta Inc.
109. Société Québecoise des
     Transports
 110. 1848-7199 Québec Inc.
111. Société de Tourisme de la
     Baie James
112. Société des Traversiers du
     Québec
113. Société Québecoise
     d'Initiatives Agro-
     Alimentaires (Soquia)
 114. Les Abbatoirs R. Roy Inc.*
 115. Centre d'Insemination
     Artificielle du Québec
     (CIAQ)*
 116. Culinar Inc.*
 117. Desidratec Inc.*
 118. Nutribec Ltee.*
 119. Secobec Ltee.
 120. Semico Inc.*
 121. Snyder & Fils Inc.*
 122. Sodispro Technologie
     Ltee.*

Saskatchewan Crowns
1. Cablecom Ltd.*
 2. 438046 Ontario Ltd.
 3. Jarmain Cable Holdings Ltd.
  4. Canada Cablesystems Ltd.
 5. Canadian Teleconference
    Network Inc.
 6. Jarmain Holdings Ltd.
   7. 436440 Ontario Ltd.
   8. Jarmain Capital
      Corporation
     9. Jarmain Industries Inc.
     10. Jarmain Investment
        Corp.
      11. Omnibus Video Inc.
    12. Jarmain Communications
       Inc.

 13. Jarmain Ventures Inc.
 14. Kelly Jarmain Inc.
15. Crown Investments
    Corporation of Saskatchewan
 16. Agricultural Development
     Corporation
 17. CIC Industrial Interests
     Inc.
   18. Interprovincial Steel and
       Pipe Corp.*
   19. Ipsco Inc.*
   20. Prairie Malt Ltd.*
   21. SED Systems Inc.*
 22. Municipal Financing
     Corporation of
     Saskatchewan
 23. Potash Corporation of
     Saskatchewan
   24. Canpotex Bulk Terminals
       Ltd.
 25. Prince Albert Pulp
     Company Limited
   26. Prince Albert Pulp
       (International) Corp.
   27. Prince Albert Pulp Sales
       Corp.
   28. Woodlands Enterprises
       Ltd.
 29. Saskatchewan Computer
     Utility Corp.
 30. Saskatchewan Development
     Fund Corp.
 31. Saskatchewan Economic
     Development Corp.
   32. Damont Electrical
       Industries Ltd.*
   33. Fibre Form Industries Ltd.*
   34. Green Circle
       Manufacturing Ltd.*
   35. Meadow Lake Wood
       Industries Ltd.
   36. Plains Poultry Ltd.*
   37. Westank Industries Ltd.*
 38. Saskatchewan Forest
     Products Corp.
 39. Saskatchewan Fur
     Marketing Service
 40. Saskatchewan Government
     Insurance
 41. Saskatchewan Government
     Printing Co.
 42. Saskatchewan Minerals
 43. Saskatchewan Mining
     Development Corp.

44. Kay Lake Mining Corp.
45. SMD Mining Co. Ltd.
46. Saskatchewan Oil and Gas Corp.
47. Key Pipe Line Co. Ltd.*
48. Nottingham Gas Ltd.*
49. Saskoil Resources Inc.
50. Saskatchewan Power Corporation
51. Many Islands Pipe Lines Ltd.
52. Many Islands Pipe Lines (Canada) Ltd.
53. Consumers Oil Ltd.
54. NorthSask Electric Ltd.
55. Saskatchewan Telecommunications
56. Saskatchewan Transportation Co.
57. Liquor Board Saskatchewan
58. Potash Corporation of Saskatchewan
59. Potash Corporation of Saskatchewan Sales Ltd.*
60. Canpotex Ltd.*
61. Potash Corporation of Saskatchewan Mining Ltd.
62. Saskatchewan Housing Corporation
63. Prairie Housing Development
64. Saskatchewan Liquor Licensing Commission
65. Western Canada Lottery Foundation*

Northwest Territories

1. Arctic Co-operatives Limited*
2. West Baffin Eskimo Co-op Ltd.
3. Northwest Territories Housing Corporation
4. Northwest Territories Liquor Control System

Yukon Territory

1. Yukon Housing Corp.
2. Yukon Liquor Corp.

Appendix VI: Federal Crowns Established
Before 1939

1. Bank of Canada—1934
2. Canadian Broadcasting Corp.—as Canadian Radio Broadcasting Commission—1932
3. Canadian Farm Loan Board—1929
4. Canadian National Railways—1919
5. Canadian National (West Indies) Steamships—1929
6. Canadian Wheat Board—1935
7. Director of Soldier Settlement—1919
8. Federal District Commission—1927
9. Halifax Relief Commission—1918
10. National Battlefields Commission—1908
11. National Gallery of Canada—1913
12. National Harbours Board—1936
13. National Research Council—1917
14. Trans-Canada Air Lines, later Air Canada—1937

(*Source*: Privy Council Office)

Appendix VII: Federal Crowns Established During World War II

1. Aero Timber Products Ltd.
2. Allies War Supplies Corp.
3. Atlas Plant Extension Ltd.
4. Canadian Wool Board
5. Commodity Prices Stabilization Corp.
6. Citadel Merchandising Co.
7. Cutting Tools and Gauges Ltd.
8. Defence Communications Ltd.
9. Eldorado Mining and Refining (now Eldorado Nuclear Ltd.)
10. Fairmount Co. Ltd.
11. Federal Aircraft Ltd.
12. Machinery Service Ltd.
13. Melbourne Merchandising Ltd.
14. National Railway Munitions Ltd.
15. Northwest Purchasing Ltd.
16. Polymer Corp. (now Polysar Ltd.)
17. Park Steamship Co. Ltd.
18. Plateau Co. Ltd.
19. Quebec Shipyards Ltd.
20. Research Enterprises Ltd.
21. Small Arms Ltd.
22. Toronto Shipbuilding Co. Ltd.
23. Turbo Research Ltd.
24. Veneer Log Supply Ltd.
25. Victory Aircraft Ltd.
26. War Supplies Ltd.
27. Wartime Food Corp.
28. Wartime Housing Ltd.
29. Wartime Merchant Shipping Ltd.
30. Wartime Metals Corp.
31. Wartime Oils Ltd.
32. Wartime Salvage Ltd.

Appendix VIII: Federal Government Enterprises in the United States

1. ACTION
2. Administrative Conference of the United States
3. Appalachian Regional Commission
4. Board for International Broadcasting
5. Central Intelligence Agency
6. Civil Aeronautics Board
7. Commission on Civil Rights
8. Commission of Fine Arts
9. Commodity Futures Trading Commission
10. Export-Import Bank of the United States
11. Farm Credit Administration
12. Federal Communications Commission
13. Federal Deposit Insurance Corporation
14. Federal Election Commission
15. Federal Emergency Management Agency
16. Federal Home Loan Bank Board
17. Federal Labor Relations Authority
18. Federal Maritime Commission
19. Federal Mediation and Conciliation Service
20. Federal Reserve System
21. General Services Administration
22. Inter-American Foundation
23. Interstate Commerce Commission
24. Merit Systems Protection Board
25. National Aeronautics and Space Administration
26. National Capital Planning Commission
27. National Credit Union Administration
28. National Foundation on the Arts and the Humanities
29. National Labor Relations Board
30. National Mediation Board
31. National Science Foundation
32. National Transportation Safety Board
33. Nuclear Regulatory Commission
34. Occupational Safety and Health Review Commission
35. Office of Personnel Management
36. Panama Canal Commission
37. Peace Corps
38. Pennsylvania Avenue Development Corporation
39. Pension Benefit Guaranty Corporation
40. Postal Rate Commission
41. Railroad Retirement Board
42. Securities and Exchange Commission
43. Selective Service System
44. Small Business Administration
45. Tennessee Valley Authority
46. United States Arms Control and Disarmament Agency
47. United States Information Agency
48. United States International Development Cooperation Agency
49. United States International Trade Commission
50. United States Postal Service
51. Veterans Administration

Quasi-Official Agencies

52. Legal Services Corporation
53. National Consumer Cooperative Bank
54. National Railroad Passenger Corporation (Amtrak)
55. Smithsonian Institution
56. United States Railway Association
57. United States Synthetic Fuels Corporation

These are bodies which are not agencies—the usual U.S. term for what we would call Crowns—under American law, but which are run by directors entirely or partly appointed by the federal government. In most cases, these agencies were originally funded by government, although they may have since become voluntary groups. The Canadian equivalents would be the Army Benevolent Fund, Hockey Canada, and the various harbour commissions.

Finally, there are fifty-eight federal boards, centres, commissions, councils, panels, and study groups, which operate independently of any parent department or agency, but which are not "government entities" in the sense of having shares owned by the government, like the Postal Service, or being dependent on government funding, like the United States Information Agency. They are usually advisory, like the Arthritis Interagency Coordinating Committee, the California Debris Commission, or the Veterans Day National Committee. I have not listed them because they are not strictly comparable to Canadian Crowns. An argument could be made that, say, the Mississippi River Commission is as much a government entity as a Canadian Harbour Board, but in fact the River Commission is much more independent, so it seemed safest merely to point to the existence of such entities without claiming them as near-Crowns.

(*Source*: The United States Government Manual, 1986–87)

INDEX